Palgrave Studies in Languages at War

Series Editors: **Hilary Footitt**, University of Reading, UK and **Michael Kelly**, University of Southampton, UK.

Languages play a crucial role in war, conflict and peacemaking: in intelligence gathering and evaluation, pre-deployment preparations, operations on the ground, regime-change, and supporting refugees and displaced persons. In the politics of war, languages have a dual impact: a public policy dimension, setting frameworks and expectations; and the lived experience of those 'on the ground', working with and meeting speakers of other languages. This series intends to bring together books which deal with the role of languages in situations of conflict, including war, civil war, occupation, peace-keeping, peace-enforcement and humanitarian action in war zones. It will offer an interdisciplinary approach, drawing on applied linguistics, sociolinguistics, translation studies, intercultural communication, history, politics, international relations and cultural studies. Books in the series will explore specific conflict situations across a range of times and places, and specific language-related roles and activities, examining three contexts: languages and the military, meeting the other in war and peace-making, and interpreting/translating in war.

Titles include:

Hilary Footitt and Michael Kelly (*editors*)
LANGUAGES AT WAR
Policies and Practices of Language Contacts in Conflict

Hilary Footitt and Michael Kelly (*editors*)
LANGUAGES AND THE MILITARY
Alliances, Occupation and Peace Building

Michael Kelly and Catherine Baker
INTERPRETING THE PEACE
Peace Operation, Conflict and Language in Bosnia-Herzegovina

Forthcoming titles:

Hilary Footitt and Simona Tobia
'WARTALK'
Foreign Languages and the British War Effort in Europe 1940–46

Amit Aviv
REGIONAL LANGUAGE POLICIES IN FRANCE DURING WWII

Ian Jones and Louise Askew
LANGUAGES AT WAR AND PEACE
NATO Language Policy and Practice in Operations since 1994

Palgrave Studies in Languages at War
Series Standing Order ISBN 978-0-230-35516-3 Hardback
978-0-230-35517-0 Paperback
(outside North America only)

You can receive future titles in this series as they are published by placing a standing order. Please contact your bookseller or, in case of difficulty, write to us at the address below with your name and address, the title of the series and one of the ISBNs quoted above.

Customer Services Department, Macmillan Distribution Ltd, Houndmills, Basingstoke, Hampshire RG21 6XS, England

Interpreting the Peace

Peace Operations, Conflict and Language in Bosnia-Herzegovina

Michael Kelly
University of Southampton, UK

and

Catherine Baker
University of Hull, UK

palgrave
macmillan

First published 2013 by
PALGRAVE MACMILLAN

Palgrave Macmillan in the UK is an imprint of Macmillan Publishers Limited, registered in England, company number 785998, of Houndmills, Basingstoke, Hampshire RG21 6XS.

Palgrave Macmillan in the US is a division of St Martin's Press LLC, 175 Fifth Avenue, New York, NY 10010.

Palgrave Macmillan is the global academic imprint of the above companies and has companies and representatives throughout the world.

Palgrave® and Macmillan® are registered trademarks in the United States, the United Kingdom, Europe and other countries

ISBN: 978–1–137–02983–6

This book is printed on paper suitable for recycling and made from fully managed and sustained forest sources. Logging, pulping and manufacturing processes are expected to conform to the environmental regulations of the country of origin.

A catalogue record for this book is available from the British Library.

A catalogue record for this book is available from the Library of Congress.

10 9 8 7 6 5 4 3 2 1
22 21 20 19 18 17 16 15 14 13

Printed and bound in Great Britain by
CPI Antony Rowe, Chippenham and Eastbourne

Contents

Preface and Acknowledgements

The authors worked on this book as part of a collaborative project, entitled Languages at War, which was funded by the Arts and Humanities Research Council. We gratefully acknowledge their support and that of the partner institutions in the project: the University of Southampton, where both the authors were working, the University of Reading, which led the overall project, and the Imperial War Museum, London, which provided invaluable support and facilities. The study of operations in Bosnia-Herzegovina was conducted in parallel with the study of languages in the Allied occupation of Europe in 1945, and the themes and issues arising from both case studies have been discussed and developed by all the members of the group. A comparative study of the two cases was published as the first volume in the 'Languages at War' series (Footitt and Kelly (ed.) 2012b). Its findings have informed our thinking and suggested new approaches which the present book has developed in different ways.

We are particularly grateful to Professor Hilary Footitt, who led the overall project with enormous skill, patience and imagination and enabled us to develop insights and make connections which made the research so intellectually and culturally stimulating. We would like to thank Dr Simona Tobia, who brought fresh perspectives to the European context, and Dr Louise Askew, who generously shared her experience of leading the Linguistic Services Branch in Sarajevo and contributed to our understanding of the cultural and institutional context. We were fortunate to have the support of our colleagues in the Imperial War Museum, especially Samantha Heywood and James Taylor, who gave generously of their precious time and vast knowledge. And we were very grateful to have the advice and support of colleagues in the Ministry of Defence with responsibility for language issues, in particular Christine Adamson, Lt Col Andrew Parrott and Lt Col Justin Lewis, who helped us to understand the institutional contexts and recent developments.

We were very pleased to be able to draw on the guidance and support of a distinguished advisory group of academics and practitioners. In addition to the colleagues already mentioned, we should like to thank Dr Robin Aizlewood, Professor Mark Cornwall, Professor Anne Curry, Professor Christopher Duggan, Professor Debra Kelly, Dr Charles Kirke,

Professor Andrew Knapp and Dr Frank Tallett, who offered their advice and help in this way. We benefited greatly from the discussions in workshops held at the Imperial War Museum in 2009 and 2010, where academics and practitioners shared their expertise, and we were fortunate also to have the participation of Ian Jones and Nick Stansfield, who gave detailed help and advice from their knowledge of the operations in Bosnia-Herzegovina.

We owe a particular debt of gratitude to more than 50 men and women who agreed to be interviewed by Catherine, and shared with us their experiences of languages in the Bosnian operation. Through their memories, reflections and vivid insights, we were able to recapture a feeling of the events and the people involved in them. In most cases, they have agreed to allow the record of their interviews to be lodged in the archives of the Imperial War Museum, where they will be available to future generations of researchers and inquirers. Three of them have given permission for their names to be used in this book: Louise Askew, Ian Jones and Nick Stansfield. All other interviewees are identified here by appropriate pseudonyms which they have agreed with us.

And finally, we should like to express our deepest gratitude to our friends and families who have supported us through the preparation of this book.

Catherine says: While helping to write this book I have benefited, as ever, from the insights and warmth of friends inside and outside academia, and my contributions to the book are the better for my discussions with them. Thanks are also due to my family for their understanding and patience while I researched this project. I am grateful also to the intellectual community at Southampton, and it was fitting that the final preparation of this manuscript should have been one of my last acts there before my move to Hull.

Mike says: I received great personal and institutional support from colleagues at Southampton who saw the interest of the project and helped me find the time to pursue it. I am grateful to the many friends who listened to tales of the unexpected, curious incidents from an unfamiliar country not very far away. I would like to thank my sons Tom and Paul for their constant encouragement and some sharp questions, and above all my wife, Jo Doyle, for her unfailing love, support and understanding, without which I would not have completed my part of the book.

Michael Kelly
Catherine Baker
June 2012

About the Authors

Michael Kelly is Professor of French at the University of Southampton, and a specialist in modern French culture and in language policy. He edited *Languages at War: Policies and Practices of Language Contacts in Conflict* and *Languages and the Military: Alliances, Occupation and Peace Building* with Hilary Footitt (2012). He is Director of LLAS Centre for Languages, Linguistics and Area Studies. He is the author of Chapters 1, 2, 4 and 7.

Catherine Baker is Lecturer in Twentieth Century History at the University of Hull. She has previously worked as a researcher for the Languages at War project at the University of Southampton and as a Teaching Fellow at UCL SSEES. In parallel with her interests in international intervention, she is the author of *Sounds of the Borderland: Popular Music, War and Nationalism in Croatia since 1991* (2010). She is the author of Chapters 3, 5 and 6.

Abbreviations

1 COLDSTREAM	1st Battalion, the Coldstream Guards
1 DWR	1st Battalion, the Duke of Wellington's Regiment
1 PWO	1st Battalion, Prince of Wales's Own Regiment of Yorkshire
AAP	Allied Administrative Publication
ABiH	Armija Republike Bosne i Hercegovine (Army of the Republic of Bosnia-Herzegovina)
AIIC	Association internationale des interprètes de conference (International Association of Conference Interpreters)
ANOLIR	Association Nationale des Officiers de Liaison et des Interprètes de Réserve (National Association of Reservist Liaison Officers and Interpreters)
BiH	Bosna i Hercegovina (Bosnia-Herzegovina)
BILC/BCLI	Bureau for International Language Coordination
BRITBAT	British Battalion
CEFR	Common European Framework of Reference
CIMIC	Civil–Military Co-Operation
DG SCIC	Directorate-General for Interpretation
DOCEX	Document Exploitation
DOLSU	Defence Operational Language Support Unit
DSL	Defence School of Languages
DSO	Director of Staff Operations
EUFOR	European Union Force
FIT-IFT	Fédération Internationale des Traducteurs-International Federation of Translators
HDZ	Hrvatska Demokratska Zajednica (Croat Democratic Union)
HIS	Hrvatska Izvještajna Služba (Croatian Intelligence Service)
HQ SFOR	Headquarters, Stabilization Force
HVO	Hrvatsko Vijeće Obrane (Croat Defence Council)
ICTY	International Criminal Tribunal for the Former Yugoslavia
IFOR	Implementation Force
IPTF	International Police Task Force

JNA	Jugoslavenska Narodna Armija (Yugoslav National Army)
JSLEB	Joint Services Language Examination Board
LSB	Linguistic Services Branch
MND (N)	Multi-National Division (North)
MND (SE)	Multi-National Division (South-East)
MND (SW)	Multi-National Division (South-West)
NATO	North Atlantic Treaty Organization
NCO	Non-Commissioned Officer
NORDPOL	Nordic–Polish (Brigade)
OHR	Office of the High Representative
OS BiH	Oružane Snage Bosne i Hercegovine (Armed Forces of Bosnia and Herzegovina)
OSCE	Organization for Security and Cooperation in Europe
RAEC	Royal Army Educational Corps
REME	Royal Electrical and Mechanical Engineers
RPG	Rocket-Propelled Grenade
RS	Republika Srpska
SDA	Stranka Demokratske Akcije (Party of Democratic Action)
SDS	Srpska Demokratska Stranka (Serb Democratic Party)
SFOR	Stabilization Force
SHAPE	Supreme Headquarters Allied Powers Europe
SOE	Special Operations Executive
STANAG	Standardization Agreement
TEFL	Teaching English as a Foreign Language
UKLF	United Kingdom Land Forces
UN	United Nations
UNHCR	United Nations High Commission for Refugees
UNICEF	United Nations Children's Fund
UNPROFOR	United Nations Protection Force
VRS	Vojska Republike Srpske (Army of Republika Srpska)

Introduction

In 1954, the then British Prime Minister Winston Churchill made a widely quoted remark that it is 'better to jaw-jaw than to war-war.'[1] While this is usually interpreted as a metaphorical declaration that negotiations are preferable to war, it does highlight the point that peacemaking is a matter of talking and therefore of language. However, the importance of language in peacemaking is rarely examined in detail. It has been particularly neglected where, as is most often the case, different languages are in play between the protagonists.[2] The authors were participants in a research programme, Languages at War, which set out to rectify this neglect by examining the policies and practices relating to languages in situations of conflict.[3] This book presents our findings on the complex issues of language confronting the international forces that sought to bring peace to Bosnia-Herzegovina in the 1990s. It examines how the issues were approached by the military and the key role of people from the area in helping to resolve them.

The collapse of Yugoslavia into a melee of warring states, entities and ethnicities was the most serious hot war in Europe since the Second World War. Unlike the conflicts in Cyprus or in Northern Ireland, it tested the ability of the European and international communities to contain a conflict comparable to that which 80 years before had plunged the continent into the Great War of 1914–18. The situation in Bosnia-Herzegovina was particularly complex, both on the side of the local elites, who represented three main ethnic groups, and on the side of the peace operations forces, who came from forces of many nationalities, first under the United Nations and then under NATO command. Differences of language and culture were an integral part of the conflicts and posed many challenges in establishing peace and rebuilding the country.

Interpreting the peace

The mission of the forces was to build peace in the region. In order to achieve it, they had to communicate effectively with the local people and with each other. In this sense, an important part of their task was to 'interpret the peace', understanding what was said or written in whatever language it was expressed, and conveying their own intentions with clarity in the languages that would be understood. The processes involved were complex and interleaved, extremely varied, and changed significantly over time. The aim of this book is to understand how the multinational forces in Bosnia-Herzegovina sought to overcome the language barriers confronting them and how this affected the people mainly concerned, especially the military linguists and the civilian interpreters and translators they employed from among the local population.

The political and military context of Bosnia-Herzegovina is notoriously complex, and we sketch in some of the key events later in this Introduction. This may help the reader to locate the people and language issues they describe during the difficult years of conflict and its aftermath. We also offer a short discussion of the complexities that attend the naming of the language or languages of Bosnia-Herzegovina.

In elucidating the language issues in the conflict and in the uneasy peace which followed it, we have focused on two interrelated aspects: the practices that emerged and the people whose job it was to make them work. To do this, we have drawn on conceptual tools from two relatively new disciplinary areas. Language policy studies, within the broad discipline of applied linguistics, provided tools for understanding the patterns and structures behind the language practices. Oral history studies, within the broader area of cultural history, provided a framework for analysing the memories and narratives of participants and picking out the subtexts and the broader meanings that are woven through their accounts. As the final part of this Introduction suggests, documents and written accounts proved sparse, and the main means of access to the practices were through the people. This approach was implemented by a series of some 50 interviews with participants, carried out in 2009 and 2010 by Catherine Baker. The process of constructing this oral archive is described in detail below.

In subsequent chapters, we draw extensively on the insights and experiences of our informants to reconstruct the policies and processes in which they were engaged. We have also sought to let their voices be heard in the text, to convey the experience of living with languages in conflict and peacemaking. The discussion focuses on the main patterns that have emerged through their narratives, structured by the changing conditions in which language contacts took place.

Chapter 1 confirms that very few military personnel had enough previous language knowledge to be useful while serving in the foreign field of Bosnia-Herzegovina. The forces responded by deploying personnel who were heritage speakers of the local language. They met with mixed success. The military planners also put in place instruction for general language purposes during the early months of the campaign but rapidly encountered the difficulty of achieving useful proficiency within a short period of training. Longer courses achieved a 'colloquial' level of language proficiency. But commanders in the field generally expected a much higher level of expertise than was actually achievable.

Chapter 2 looks at the specialist military interpreters and linguists that were trained from within the armed forces. The intensive courses they followed were designed to equip them with high-level language skills. However, their role was more than purely linguistic. Over time, locally employed civilian linguists tended to replace them in the technical language roles of formal interpreting and translating as well as the routine work of accompanying patrols. Military linguists typically assumed a wider range of military roles, which were more likely to bring them recognition and promotion than their specifically linguistic expertise.

Chapter 3 examines the steps that were taken by UN forces to recruit local staff to provide language support on the ground. The arrangements were initially pragmatic and ad hoc, but very quickly commanders were obliged to put more sustainable structures in place and address the social and human issues that resulted from their actions. The interpreters also had many adjustments to make in order to meet the requirements of the forces they worked with.

Chapter 4 shows how the language support services that had been established in haste began to show their limitations. The patchwork of improvised services failed to meet almost every criterion of quality management. The result was a great diversity of provision. As a result of complaints and reorganization, NATO command ordered a review of headquarters provision by their senior linguist, who found that it was not fit for its purpose. He proposed that the scattered arrangements should be brought together in a single unified service centred in Sarajevo. This resulted in the establishment of an effective Linguistic Services Branch (LSB), which provided a model of good practice for international organizations in the region.

Chapter 5 examines the roles and experiences of locally employed interpreters. In some respects they were highly privileged economically and culturally, in comparison to the rest of the local population, though they were aware of their inequalities in comparison with the forces they served. There was often an unspoken social contract between them and the forces, though it did not prevent them from taking the brunt of local resentments that might build up. Their anomalous position in the local economy could prove difficult after bases closed, although some did use their posts as a doorway into a longer-term career as professional interpreters and translators.

Chapter 6 explores the sensitive ethnic identities of the region, which affected the ways in which language contacts could be carried out. Processes of ethnic identification were central to the conflict, and success in carrying out important tasks was sometimes dependent on the ethnic identity of the participants as much as on their linguistic capability. Ethnic identity and nationality were also important in determining how far individuals could be trusted: a concern which affected the deployment of interpreters but which could also affect attitudes to military personnel.

Chapter 7 demonstrates that the forces engaged in peace operations were conspicuously multilingual. Their members instinctively used multiple language strategies to communicate, but problems were encountered in the formal command structure between units of different nationalities. NATO forces largely adopted English as the language of military communication, although French and Russian remained *linguas francas* among several contingents. The use of English increased the effectiveness of military cooperation, however language differences often concealed differences in military culture between countries. Native English speakers sometimes struggled with English as a language of general communication, particularly where they spoke strong local or regional varieties.

Reviewing the patterns that have emerged from these analyses, Chapter 8 identifies lessons that may be drawn. These may inform the future research of scholars studying similar issues and inform the future practice of those who have responsibilities in respect of languages in conflict and peacemaking.

Bosnia-Herzegovina during the 1990s

Before beginning to analyse the language issues, we hope it will be helpful to outline the political and military context of the period in some detail. This will not only set the language issues in their historical circumstances but will also help the reader to locate the people and events which appear in the course of later discussions.

The war, which flared up in Bosnia-Herzegovina in 1992, lasted until the end of 1995.[4] It was a complex conflict which is commonly depicted as a triangular conflict between three armed forces: the Army of the Republic of Bosnia-Herzegovina (ABiH), representing the government of Alija Izetbegović and his Party for Democratic Action (SDA) in Sarajevo, the Croat Defence Council (HVO), and the Army of Republika Srpska (VRS). Each was primarily associated with one ethnic group, the HVO with Bosnian Croats, the VRS with Bosnian Serbs and the ABiH with Bosnian Muslims or (an alternative term that came into use during the war) Bosniaks. The states of Croatia and Serbia rendered financial, logistical and military assistance to the HVO and VRS respectively, whereas ABiH depended entirely on whatever arms and material it could smuggle past international sanctions or capture from other forces. The ABiH and HVO sometimes fought in alliance against the VRS and sometimes competed for territory against each other. Besides these main actors, the war contained dozens of smaller military and paramilitary formations supporting particular private interests: the parallel Bosniak army of the businessman Fikret Abdić in the far northwest of the country; paramilitary units under the command of such infamous figures as Željko Ražnatović-Arkan, Vojislav Šešelj and Mladen Naletilić; foreign volunteers such as the Greeks and Russians who fought alongside the VRS or the mujahedin who offered their services to the ABiH in support of imported hard-line versions of Islam. The tactic of ethnic cleansing, the brutalization and murder of those who belonged to different ethnic groups in order to intimidate their co-nationals to flee, accounted for the bloodiness of the conflict, which caused the loss of 102,622 lives, including 55,261 civilians, according to figures compiled by the International Criminal Tribunal for the Former Yugoslavia (ICTY) (Tabeau and Bijak 2005), and the temporary or permanent displacement of approximately 1.5 million of the country's 4.4 million total population.

Although all sides in the conflict used the discourse of ethnicity to justify their extreme violence, to characterize the war as an 'ethnic war' would obscure the part played by elites and the importance of their material goals. Sometimes more than one armed force claimed to represent an ethnic group and sometimes certain forces fell into paradoxical local alliances. The war, as one dimension of the post-Yugoslav conflicts, represented a struggle between elite power centres – remnants of the old political regime and army, politicians who had been marginalized under the old system, businessmen-patrons and career criminals – who took advantage of ethnicity, understood through a set of practices that corresponded to religious denomination, as the most widely available resource for mobilizing populations and producing fear. Their goals were to claim, secure and legitimize control over territory on the principle that international arbitration procedures were likely to award land to the entity whose ethnic group was in the majority there; establish a monopoly over internal politico-military power backed up by paramilitary and criminal terror campaigns; and turn the presence of foreign media, peacekeeping forces, agencies and donors to their own groups' advantage. As Mary Kaldor's concept of 'new wars' implies (Kaldor 1999), such is the likely shape of many future conflicts in which coalition forces will become involved.

In socialist Yugoslavia, Bosnia-Herzegovina had been one of six increasingly autonomous republics that each supplied a representative to the rotating presidency established after Josip Broz Tito's death in 1980.[5] The situation of the republic became untenable after the rise to power of the centralist Slobodan Milošević in Serbia, the parallel rise of a president in Slovenia (Milan Kučan) who looked towards the democratization movements of central Europe and the collapse of the Yugoslav League of Communists in January 1990, which enabled both Slovenia and Croatia to move towards independence. With Slovenia and Croatia preparing to leave the federation, Bosnia-Herzegovina faced systemic marginalization if not exploitation, since it could always be outvoted by the remaining presidency members and Milošević now controlled the votes of Serbia, Montenegro, Vojvodina and Kosovo. Meanwhile, Croatian Serb militias with the covert support of Milošević in Belgrade began to resist the Croatian police in Krajina (on Croatia's border with Bosnia-Herzegovina) and eastern Slavonia. The militias and police grew into opposing armies and the Yugoslav National Army (JNA) in alliance with Milošević intervened in an attempt to prevent Slovenia and Croatia seceding in June 1991. While the situation in Croatia was escalating into open armed conflict, Radovan Karadžić's Serb Democratic Party (SDS) in Bosnia was obstructing the Bosnian assembly and organizing Serb militias of its own. SDS followed the strategy of the Krajina Serbs and declared a Serb republic in Bosnia in January 1992, while behind the scenes the JNA attempted to disarm territorial defence units in Bosniak- and Croat-majority areas of the country. The campaign to convince the public that it was no longer safe to live in the same state as members of different ethnic groups was now entrenched in the country.

Bosnia-Herzegovina declared independence on 3 March 1992, after more than 99 per cent of respondents to a referendum – boycotted by SDS – voted in favour. While an underground SDA organization known as the Patriotic League established the nucleus of the future ABiH in cooperation with functional territorial defence units loyal to Sarajevo, Izetbegović publicly remained more conciliatory until full-scale war broke out; the HVO had already formed in response to events across the Croatian border.[6] Confrontations between Serb and Croat forces broke out in Herzegovina and Bosanska Posavina throughout March 1992, and, at the beginning of April, Arkan's paramilitary unit entered the eastern Bosnian town of Zvornik to commit the first massacre of Bosniaks. The VRS, now officially spun off from the JNA but still receiving orders from Belgrade, began to take over eastern Bosnia and besiege Sarajevo in the first days of April, immediately after Bosnia-Herzegovina's independence had been recognized by the European Community and the United States. During the spring and summer, Serb forces proceeded to murder, imprison and deport non-Serbs.

The United Nations Security Council had already agreed that a peacekeeping force (UNPROFOR: United Nations Protection Force) should enter Croatia in February 1992 to demilitarize four Serb-majority Protected Areas. In Bosnia-Herzegovina, the international community's first practical response to the war was humanitarian, delivered through aid airlifts into Sarajevo airport. UNPROFOR was extended into Bosnia-Herzegovina as a peace support operation – a different role from its function in Croatia – where its mission was to back up the UN High Commission for Refugees (UNHCR) in delivering aid. Every local force in the country (but particularly the VRS) regularly obstructed convoys or skimmed supplies off for itself (Gow 1997; Andreas 2007). UNPROFOR's mandate was extended in May 1993 to include the protection of six 'UN Safe Areas', cities such as Sarajevo, Goražde and Srebrenica where the VRS had besieged towns with largely Bosniak authorities.

In January 1993, the alliance between the HVO and ABiH broke down over the unsuccessful Vance–Owen Peace Plan, a settlement that would have divided Bosnia-Herzegovina into 10 cantons based on ethnic distribution and therefore on military gains. As the Croatian state ordered the Bosnian branch of the Croat Democratic Union (HDZ) party to leave the Sarajevo government and the SDA began to propagate an ideology of Bosnia-Herzegovina as a Bosniak nation-state rather than a multi-ethnic democracy, both forces fought to ethnically homogenize the land they had expected to be offered; HDZ BiH now used the same methods to deny the concept of a multi-ethnic Bosnian community that SDS had used at the start of the war (Lovrenović 2001). The destruction of the Old Bridge at Mostar, the massacre of Bosniaks at Ahmići and the murder of two Catholic friars at the monastery in Fojnica belonged to this phase of the conflict. The alliance was restored in February 1994 after US diplomatic intervention, yet its shape would have been unrecognizable in 1992: an uncomfortable combination of a Bosniak nationalist government and a HDZ BiH parastate implementing Croatian state policy in western Bosnia, Herzegovina and Posavina. The ABiH's initial multi-ethnic composition had degenerated, dealing a severe blow to the chances of non-nationalists being included in the post-war settlement.

For NATO, guaranteeing the United Nations no-fly zone over Bosnia-Herzegovina became 'the first real-world operation in its history' (Gow 1997: 133) and a test of its post-Cold War resolve. NATO was also enabled to provide UNPROFOR with close air support, yet UNPROFOR commanders found in practice that clearance from the UN Secretary-General took so long to arrive that it was often impossible for them to use the desired and permitted force. Air strikes were threatened after the shelling of the Markale marketplace in Sarajevo in February 1994 and first took place in April 1994 during the VRS attack on Goražde. The fall of Srebrenica in July 1995, when 8000 Bosniak men and boys were murdered by VRS troops and paramilitaries who had overrun the Safe Area, humiliated UNPROFOR and NATO but persuaded the US Congress to lift the arms embargo on the Sarajevo government. In August, soon after the Croatian Army had pushed the Serb forces – and civilians – out of Krajina and a HVO–ABiH operation liberated Bihać, a British–French–Dutch Rapid Reaction Force deployed to Bosnia-Herzegovina and joined NATO aircraft in attacking Serbian artillery positions around Sarajevo. Diplomatic pressure from the United States brought Izetbegović, Milošević and the president of Croatia, Franjo Tuđman, to a month of talks in Dayton, Ohio, which resulted in the Dayton Peace Agreement of December 1995.

Despite the military advances of the HVO and ABiH in late 1995, the settlement agreed at Dayton employed the Contact Group Peace Plan ratio of July 1994, allotting Republika Srpska (RS) 49 per cent of territory and the Federation (the ABiH–HVO alliance) 51 per cent. The Federation would be subdivided into ten cantons of which five had Bosniak majorities, three had Croat majorities and two were mixed. Arms control limits were imposed on all three forces and the strategically located town of Brčko remained under international administration. Dayton provided for a NATO-led force, IFOR (Implementation Force), to oversee the military aspects of the peace, and for elections to take place as soon as the Organization for Security and Cooperation in Europe (OSCE) certified they were feasible. IFOR observed the tense process of returning captured and devastated areas to new administrations and began confiscating proscribed weapons. Its year-long mandate was extended in December 1996 into an ongoing but gradually drawn down peace enforcement role under the new name of SFOR (Stabilization Force).

SFOR became the lead agency in the process of defence reform which ultimately, to make Bosnia-Herzegovina an acceptable candidate for NATO membership, would need to make one federal Bosnian army out of the three so-called 'former warring factions'. Military liaison at many levels, which had already been a significant activity of UNPROFOR, thus assumed growing importance in SFOR's work alongside capacity-building of local forces and assistance in the arrest of indicted war criminals. ABiH and HVO combined into one Federation army in 1998 and this eventually amalgamated with the VRS in 2005 to form the Armed Forces of Bosnia and Herzegovina (OS BiH).

Defence reform was in many ways the most successful of the post-Dayton processes. The tension between Bosnia-Herzegovina's main international political organizations, the Office of the High Representative (OHR) and OSCE, and the nationalist politicians who had won democratic mandates in the 1996 elections continued even after Biljana Plavšić, Karadžić's nominee as president of the RS, was voted out of office in 1998, and the Croatian state distanced itself from Bosnian Croat politics in 2000 after Tuđman's death. High Representatives were able to dismiss political office holders and make other interventions such as the selection of a non-ethnic state flag in 1998. The most serious challenge faced by the international community when SFOR handed over to an EU-led force, EUFOR ALTHEA, was nationalist parties' continued brinkmanship over whether the RS should be abolished. The people of Bosnia-Herzegovina – those who had remained in the country and those few who had chosen to return from abroad after the war – faced the existential challenges of seeking economic security and finding their place in a post-war society still structured around parallel ethnic institutions.

Naming the language(s)

The complexity of the military and political situation in Bosnia-Herzegovina is mirrored by the difficulty of numbering or naming the language or languages in the country. It testifies to the inseparability of politics and language planning in states where ethnonational identity is routinely contested. The legacy of the disintegration of 'Serbo-Croatian' or 'Croato-Serbian' during and after the break-up of Yugoslavia is nowhere more complicated than in Bosnia-Herzegovina. Here, the Titoist concept of a 'unified (*jedinstven*) language' with so-called 'western' and 'eastern' standards (which roughly correspond to today's 'Croatian' and 'Serbian' languages, respectively) has been replaced by an entire field of discourses and language planning attempts, including many that enter Bosnian linguistic life from the states of Croatia and Serbia. The three official languages of today's Bosnian state – Bosnian, Croatian and Serbian – represent the symbolic assertion of national identity over the pragmatism of mutual intelligibility. They confronted the international forces with sensitivities which they understood but generally viewed as a political rather than a linguistic matter, and therefore as an operational inconvenience. A more detailed discussion of the language variants is provided in the Appendix.

As a result, the authors have confronted the recurrent question of how to refer to the language or languages of Bosnia-Herzegovina. The issue was frequently alluded to in the interviews carried out in 2009–10. At the outbreak of hostilities, it was generally understood that there was a single language, usually referred to in English as Serbo-Croat, but also called Serbo-Croatian or Croato-Serbian. Twenty years later, it could plausibly be thought of as one, two, or three languages, or even as four, since Montenegro gained independence. Linguists from English-speaking countries commonly take the view that, for practical purposes, one language still exists. Ronelle Alexander's sociolinguistic grammar of 'Bosnian, Croatian, Serbian', for instance, views them as a pluricentric language containing three symbolic 'language[s] of cultural and national representation' ('S-languages') and one 'language of everyday interaction' and communication (a 'C-language') with which speakers belonging to the communities of all three symbolic languages can communicate (Alexander 2006: 425). Yet speakers need to adapt their speech only slightly to switch from one symbolic language to another.

The disputed number of languages is ultimately a political, not a linguistic, question, making the naming of the language perhaps the most important act of all (Askew 2011). Vanessa Pupavac (2006: 124) puts the political element even more starkly when she argues that the language variants within former Yugoslavia are less diverse than American and British English. Since the term 'Serbo-Croatian' has become unacceptable among many who speak the symbolic languages derived from it, naming the contemporary communicative language is fraught. Alexander's grammar prefers the neologism 'BCS', which has also been adopted by the International Criminal Tribunal for former Yugoslavia, though it has a somewhat forensic resonance. The solution commonly used in the language itself, 'naš jezik' ('our language'), is not feasible for a non-native speaker; informal communication among scholars sometimes adopts strategies such as 'vaš jezik' ('your language', from a non-native to a native speaker), 'the language' or, with a nod to popular culture, 'the language formerly known as Serbo-Croat'.[7] The pragmatic solution of the English-speaking military in Bosnia-Herzegovina appeared to be 'local language', so that one might speak of 'translation between English and local'. The people quoted in this book employ many terms, from 'Serbo-Croat' in the account of an expatriate to 'Serbian' in the account of a foreign officer posted to a predominantly Serb town in the RS. Each name reflects understandings of the language grounded in a particular personal positionality, place and time. Rather than attempting to impose a single consistent terminology, we have sought to respect the positionality that our informants have expressed and have generally mirrored it in our own comments. Naming languages is always a political gesture, and we have taken the view that recognizing the multiplicity of names better reflects the complexity of the context.

Constructing an oral archive

Relatively little official documentation is available about the peace operations in Bosnia-Herzegovina. That which does remain, such as British parliamentary papers, tends to concentrate on the more newsworthy topics of foreign policy, strategy and defence procurement. They scarcely mention the operational experiences of the soldiers and their local civilian employees. This may not be surprising, since by comparison the much graver dangers subsequently faced by locally employed interpreters in Iraq and Afghanistan (see Fitchett 2012) did not enter the headline news for almost a decade after the events concerned. Some soldiers published their own memoirs. In particular, Milos Stankovic (2000) wrote a dramatic narrative which throws a lot of light on the linguistic and cultural context of the conflict.[8] Other memoirs such as those by military commanders Bob Stewart (1993) or Ben Barry (2008) give vivid accounts of their military experience but throw little light on language issues and how they were handled.

There were periodicals aimed at or produced by the forces, such as the British Army magazine *Soldier*,[9] the UK and US brigades' own newsletters, or the weekly bulletin produced for the civil population by SFOR's information operations personnel with the minimalist title of *SFOR Informer*.[10] These gave fragmentary insights into everyday life on the multinational force's bases and, from time to time, introduced the names of individuals who would become important in the project's own narrative of people and practice. More detailed knowledge was not to be found in print but belonged to the people whose actions and values had constituted the practices of language support.

The source material on which we have mainly worked consists of 52 interviews with people who participated in the UN and NATO activities as military personnel, as language professionals or as civilian translators and interpreters. These oral history interviews are the main means of reconstructing how the practices of interpretation, translation and communication emerged. It was, at first, a necessity. We were working in parallel with colleagues who had set out to research how language support was organized by the Allies who liberated and occupied Western Europe during and after the Second World War. They had the benefit of detailed and declassified documents available to consult at the National Archives and in the Imperial War Museum. The potentially equivalent documents for the peace operations in Bosnia-Herzegovina, on the other hand, were less accessible. Many were likely to have been subject to the 30-year rule that restricts access to sensitive UK documents, because languages in the British forces had become the domain of the Intelligence Corps during the 1990s. Many documents were not retained after their immediate use or were discarded as irrelevant once the originating organization was no longer involved in the intervention. Many other documents were unavailable for reasons of technology: they were composed using obsolete word processing software or archived on obsolete hardware.

The earliest interview participants were recruited through the contacts of team members and staff of the institutions involved in *Languages at War*, including the Imperial War Museum. These were supplemented by an advertisement in *Soldier* in April 2009 which explained the project to a British military audience and an announcement posted to the Internet mailing list *Balkan Academic News* and two online reunion groups in September 2009 which targeted former local interpreters. A preliminary consultation of published sources (memoirs and forces periodicals) had brought key actors in the early stages of UK operational language support in Bosnia-Herzegovina to our attention: of those we interviewed, some were approached using existing contacts as intermediaries and some responded to open invitations to participate. Using a further round of 'snowball sampling', interviewees were invited to recommend others, such as former comrades or workmates, who might be interested in taking part. Snowball sampling was particularly effective in Denmark, where one approach produced three interviews and two informal meetings, and in recruiting former local interpreters. Many interviewees responded to the announcement as soon as they saw the email or online post; ex-soldiers and civilian professionals from other countries forwarded the announcement to interpreters with whom they had worked; the invitation circulated around close-knit friendship networks; interpreters still working in some language services told other team members about the project.

In the meantime, early dissemination work, such as the annual *Languages at War* workshops at the Imperial War Museum, brought the project to the attention of further interviewees: one man, for instance, contacted the authors to suggest himself as a participant after reading about the project in a book of abstracts passed on to him by a relative who had attended one of our conference presentations. The oral histories at the core of this project represent 51 participants and 52 interviews (in one case the interviewer returned to do a second interview with a military linguist about her experiences in the same role in Rwanda). They include 13 British soldiers, two British professional linguists, three Danes (two soldiers and a civilian), 29 local civilian interpreters who worked in Bosnia-Herzegovina, two civilian interpreters who worked in Croatia, and two Bosnian civilians involved with Ministry of Defence language training in the United Kingdom.

In arranging an interview, potential interviewees were asked to choose a convenient date and location, offered the option to contribute the recording to the Imperial War Museum Sound Archive if they so wished, and sent an information pack containing release forms from the University and the Museum. Inviting interviewees to select the interview location was intended to put them at their ease by ensuring they would be speaking in the setting they considered most comfortable. Many interviewees who were still in work chose to meet the interviewer at their workplace, which might be a civilian office or a military base. Others, especially those who had retired, kindly invited the interviewer to their home. Some who lived in the Southampton area asked us to arrange a meeting room at the University instead. Most interviews with British military personnel, and some with former local interpreters, took place in the United Kingdom; two British soldier interviews took place in Germany and one in Kosovo. The senior linguist at SHAPE was interviewed there and one ex-interpreter was interviewed at her current workplace in the Netherlands. More than twenty interviews with current and former interpreters were carried out over two visits to Bosnia-Herzegovina in October 2009 and May 2010. These visits took in major cities in both the Federation and Republika Srpska (Sarajevo, Banja Luka, Tuzla, Doboj and Bihać), which also served as convenient locations for meeting interviewees from smaller towns, and settlements in all three of the 'Multi-National Divisions' into which IFOR/SFOR had been organized. Some interviews in Bosnia-Herzegovina took place in homes and offices, though the majority of the participants chose to meet in cafés in their neighbourhood or city centres.

Interviews with local civilian interpreters added a further dimension to negotiating the interview arrangements: language choice. Although the written announcement targeting local interpreters had offered the chance to do interviews in Bosnian-Croatian-Serbian or English, all respondents to it opted for English, into which they had been interpreting their own language for some or all of their linguistic career. The one interview conducted in Serbian was the result of a personal approach through a language tutor in the United Kingdom. The decision to speak directly into English, structured by the power and significance of English in a global context, had several effects: it avoided an intermediary having to translate the narrative for anticipated English-language audiences; it allowed narrators to position their speech a certain way by including everyday military slang acquired while working alongside English-speaking troops; it made the encounter an opportunity to practice speaking skills with a native speaker of British English (an opportunity several former employees of UK forces remarked that they had missed); to interviewees positioning themselves as hosts, it sustained a norm of hospitality in sparing the interviewer–guest the extra trouble of the further stages in processing a transcript.

Conducting every interview threw up a tension between the purpose of gathering data about little-known language support arrangements and the goal of an interviewee structuring the narrative in their own terms. Sometimes the interviewer was already aware that the interviewee had been involved in significant moments such as the reform of a language service or the establishment of an interpreters' cell; sometimes the course of an interview would introduce a previously unconsidered location, force or activity. At the suggestion of Richard McDonough of the Imperial War Museum, most interviews, except a handful focused entirely on an advisory role held by the interviewee, began with the question, 'Please could you tell me when and where you were born?' This invited the interviewee to introduce whatever elements of their personal background they considered an important context for the interviewer's understanding of the narrative to come; as the project went on, she increasingly used a follow-up question to ask about the speaker's language learning experiences if these were not mentioned. Following a semi-structured format explained before the interview, the interviewer's questions aimed at 'keeping things chronological' and asking for more detail about incidents or events which had already been mentioned.

Within this format, the course of the interviews varied widely according to the narrative style of the speaker and the level of 'composure' associated with the content of the narrative.[11] Some interviewees answered questions with long anecdotes, often as accounts of the most colourful or telling scenario among many typical incidents; others replied with two or three sentences at a time, placing a much greater onus on the interviewer to sustain the conversation. The most composed narratives, where the speaker was most confident in narrating his or her identity and the choices he or she had made in exercising agency, usually seemed to take the form of a chronological life-story narrative guided by the interviewee, then the interviewer returning to the beginning to ask more detailed questions related to translation/interpreting, language teaching and learning, and language contact. Interviews typically lasted 90 minutes to two hours; only two or three lasted less than an hour. The two longest each lasted more than three hours with breaks, and several more lasted two and a half. The 52 interviews consist of a total of 86 hours of audio material.

The interviewer's first stage in processing the interviews was to make a raw transcript herself as soon as reasonably possible and email it back to the interviewee for checking. A CD copy of the audio file was also offered and approximately a fifth of interviewees chose to ask for one. The planned procedure for interviews that required translation into English was for the interviewer to transcribe the original, return it for checking, translate the checked text and then send the translation to be checked: a more laborious procedure for both the interviewer and interviewee. In the event, only one interview required translation. The interviewer then used the qualitative data analysis package NVivo to mark significant information in the agreed transcripts. This allowed important topics and themes to be highlighted and referred to by both authors.

The first round of interviews in early 2009 astonished the team with the richness of their material. Since the planning stages of the project, we had borne in mind Mona Baker's observation (2006: 30–1) that the people who translate and interpret in conflict situations strive to relate their personal ontological narratives to the collective narratives that surround them. These include the moral narratives of a local community, the historical and political narratives of ethnopolitical elites, the institutional and professional narratives of the military force, or the Western narratives of democracy and management. We expected to hear about how trained users of language had found their professional ethics and neutrality thrown into crisis, as articles by Mila Dragović-Drouet (2007) and Zrinka Stahuljak (2000) had explained. And we expected to see where linguistic difference had forced members of the forces to confront familiarity and foreignness. A wealth of historical detail emerged when soldiers and civilians talked about the conditions in which they lived and worked or the local political situations in Bosnia's new garrison towns. It became clear that our findings would go far further.

Our participants' readiness to share their experiences was just as striking. Again and again, stories of dedication, achievement, frustration, disappointment and danger came tumbling out. Many of our participants emphasized that language knowledge, a set of skills they considered part of their identity, were undervalued by the military career structure. There were numerous reasons why our participants decided to share their experience with us. It was certainly part of the motivation for some of them that this gave them the chance to affirm their contribution and reflections to researchers who had recognized languages in the military as a worthy field of study. We hope they will feel that their memories and reflections have helped to shed light on a vital but neglected dimension of the peace operations to which they contributed.

1
Serving in a Foreign Field

When they were ordered to intervene in Bosnia-Herzegovina, UN and NATO commanders recognized the need for their forces to develop some level of expertise in language and culture. It was a routine requirement for troops to be prepared for the conditions they would meet on being deployed. But the conditions in Bosnia-Herzegovina were quite unlike other situations they had experienced. It was NATO's first 'out of area' engagement and therefore situated outside the environments which they normally encountered. In particular, they did not have significant expertise in the language or the culture of the area, and it proved difficult to acquire it. From an early stage the military employed local people to provide language services, but it still remained a problem that so few of the military themselves were able to function independently in the field. This chapter will seek to understand how this arose, and how it was addressed, and why it proved difficult to resolve.

Existing linguistic capital

To examine the linguistic resources at the disposal of the military and to assess how they were developed, it is useful to adopt the concept of 'field' developed by the French sociologist, Pierre Bourdieu (1991). Bourdieu used the term 'field' to designate a particular social arena which has its own structures, logic and rules that govern the activity of people involved in it. The concept of the field is a flexible one, which can be applied to many different settings and certainly to the different metaphorical 'fields' used in military terminology. In Bourdieu's own work, a field was often identified with a particular profession, social group or region, but he also recognized the existence of a 'linguistic field', as a social context in which the use of a particular kind of language is valued (Bourdieu 1991: 52–7). Ultimately this field operates as a market in which individuals compete and gain benefits ('distinction') by possessing language skills that are valued, because they are useful but not widely distributed. Bourdieu mainly considers the language skills of people in their native French, but he notes that it also applies to classical or foreign languages, and argues:

> One cannot save the *value* of a competence unless one saves the market, in other words, the whole set of political and social conditions of production of the producers/consumers. (Bourdieu 1991: 57; emphasis original)

Hence, the value of a particular language depends on the existence of an entire social context in which competence in the language is seen as valuable. Where this occurs, Bourdieu argues, the ability to speak a particular language becomes a form of capital, which can be traded by the individual for other things of value, such as employment or social recognition. Linguistic capital is part of an individual's broader 'cultural capital', which is made up of forms of knowledge, skills, education, cultural possessions and formal qualifications. It is a characteristic of language that it exists in an 'embodied' state, as a set of 'long-lasting dispositions of the mind and body' (Bourdieu 1986: 244), and is therefore relatively difficult to acquire, through personal experience, education or training.

Applying this to the situation in 1992, it is clear that language skills had some value in the field of the armed services. Within NATO, English had operational value as a language of military communication. Proficiency was highly valued and recognized as a factor in being able to progress to more senior roles, particularly in forces where English was not a native language. To a lesser extent, these considerations also applied to French, which was spoken by officers in many forces. Throughout the Cold War period, Russian was also valued as an asset, which could contribute to understanding the activities of the Warsaw Pact and negotiating with its representatives. As a result, the languages that were valued were the subject of significant investment, and large numbers of personnel received training programmes. Individuals who developed their proficiency could expect this cultural capital to be traded for benefits such as interesting postings or promotions. The market for other languages was less certain, though for British troops based in Germany there could be advantages in picking up German, which many did. The demand for other languages was relatively limited, and take up of training was largely confined to specialists in diplomatic or intelligence roles.

With entry into the Bosnian operation, the market for languages shifted. The language of the region, then known as Serbo-Croat, had not been required to any great extent. In Britain, for example, a small course had been offered by the Defence School of Languages (DSL), to support dealings with Yugoslavia, but had recently been withdrawn. In consequence, there was an acute scarcity of service personnel with competence in the language of the new field of operations. And, since the acquisition of linguistic capital is a lengthy process, it was not an easy task to build it up to the point at which it became operationally valuable. One of the first responses was therefore to identify existing military personnel who already had a knowledge of Serbo-Croat. For the most part, they were people who had acquired the language in their family background, but for whom it had not been regarded as having value as cultural capital. In fact, in the first instance, it appears to have had negative value. This was the case for Milos Stankovic, a captain in the Parachute Regiment with Serbian links through his father, who had emigrated from Yugoslavia to Britain in 1947. He reported that his Serbian background was initially regarded as an obstacle to assigning him to the Bosnian mission, since, as one officer told him, 'They'd no more send you to Yugoslavia than they would a Greek or Turkish officer to sit on the Green Line in Cyprus' (Stankovic 2000: 46). Despite this obstacle, he was eventually deployed, though concern over his safety was also echoed by his father, when he informed him of his deployment:

> Exactly as my aunt had predicted, breaking the news to my father was not easy.
>
> 'You don't know what you're doing, what you're letting yourself in for.' There was a horrible pause. The phone felt like a brick in my hand. 'Son, please, you're making a terrible mistake...a huge mistake.' (Stankovic 2000: 49)

Stankovic's memoir of this period, *Trusted Mole* (2000), describes his experience as an interpreter and liaison officer in the dark and complex operations of the conflict. From 1992, he served in the area for more than two years, longer than any other British officer, but was later arrested on suspicion of spying for the Serbs. He was acquitted of the charges, but his readers cannot help but sympathize with his father's view that he was inadequately prepared for the dangers. Stankovic was not the only officer deployed who had language expertise through family connections with the area. Fred Whitaker, who was a military language instructor, recalled:

> *Fred Whitaker*: And there were a number of people who were actually native Serb or Croat or Serbo-Croat speakers. The Army was trawled to find those people, and I think that they all went out to Bosnia. Some of whom had very difficult times and worked in very difficult circumstances. I knew four of them.[1]

It is a measure of the urgent need for language expertise in the early stages of the operation that the Army was willing to override its normal reluctance to deploy individuals to areas where they might run extra risks by virtue of their personal background. In recognition of the dangers, the British Army took the precaution of allocating them an alias to conceal their real name. Stankovic was initially given the name Captain Laurel, and discovered that a corporal and a lieutenant of similar backgrounds had been deployed under the names of Nick Abbott and Nick Costello. He was eventually renamed Mike Stanley. A conversation reported in his memoir reveals his indignation:

> 'D'you know what names they gave the three of us? The first two they called Abbott and Costello. Can you believe it? And then I flew out as Laurel and then they changed my name to Stanley... Abbott, Costello, Laurel and Stanley. Big joke, Ian. Very funny if it wasn't so serious. It's our lives they're playing with!' I'm breathless, furious, almost shouting.
>
> And then quietly, 'Ian, Abbott was blown after only three months there. The Croats found out who he was, threatened to kill him, just because he was a Serb. He was removed from theatre within twenty-four hours. He never came back.' (Stankovic 2000: 32–3)

Naming the three officers after film comedy actors no doubt amused those who devised the names, and they must have imagined that no one would notice. But the dangers were serious, as the example of Abbott confirms. This is also expressed in the subtitle to Stankovic's memoir, *A Soldier's Journey into Bosnia's Heart of Darkness*. The reference to Joseph Conrad's novel suggests not only that the circumstances of war were horrifying but that the identity and values of the narrator were deeply challenged by the experience. Whitaker, with some understatement, pointed to the 'very difficult circumstances' these soldiers encountered, and it is perhaps surprising that some of them survived the experience and continued to pursue successful military careers. Certainly, the fact that the Army was prepared to put these young officers in danger suggests that their linguistic and cultural background was considered vital. In Bourdieu's terms, the linguistic market had changed, and proficiency in Serbian-Croatian language was highly sought after and in extremely short supply. The linguistic capital of the native speakers therefore acquired a high value, which outweighed the risks attached to their deployment.

At a later stage in the operation, the language issues were less pressing, mainly because the language mediation work had largely been allocated to locally employed interpreters and translators. The risks were also much less once the armed conflict subsided. So Nikola Andrijašević, a young reservist officer in the Royal Engineers with Yugoslav and Italian parents, was deployed to Sarajevo as a bomb disposal officer in 1999, without any reference to his language skills or his family background. He agreed that he knew of a few other British officers who had a family background from the area, but that he had never met any of them. In the event, his language skills proved very useful and he was assigned to escort a group of Bosnians to the UK:

> *Nikola Andrijašević*: In addition, there was the ambition to send thirty Bosnians, ten from each of the former warring factions, back to the UK to attend a bomb disposal course, three weeks in length. And as very few of the personnel selected in Bosnia would speak English, there would be a requirement to provide interpreters, translators, and it was deemed I would probably be the best escort to bring them back to the United Kingdom and to supervise the training and to ensure that the correct level of training was achieved, and iron out any difficulties, either during transit back to the United Kingdom or any friction that might arise during the course.[2]

The fact that Andrijašević was of Serbian and Slovenian extraction did not pose any obstacle to his selection for the task, and from his account it appears that the programme passed off in a good-humoured way. He gives no indication that he experienced any challenges based on his background. His work was to supervise the process. It is clear that his language skills were frequently called upon to solve problems:

> *Nikola Andrijašević*: We then had to recover back to Bosnia, which involved a trip back to Split, and then moving from Split back to Sarajevo where all the students would disperse. One of the Bosnian

Serb officers couldn't fly on the same flight because he was flying on an old Yugoslav passport, so the Croats wouldn't allow him entry into the country, so we had to reroute him on another flight through, I believe Austria, then into, into Sarajevo from there. So there were a few diplomatic issues that had to be overcome, one related to crossing borders.

Catherine Baker: So he'd been allowed out but he wasn't allowed back in?

Nikola Andrijašević: He was allowed out after a long argument between myself and one of the Croatian border control posts at the airport, as he'd travelled on an SFOR bus, and he was boarding an SFOR plane, which were all outside of the remit of the Croatian jurisdiction. But it did take some convincing and some finger-pointing to eventually get him on to the flight.[3]

In the complex arrangements that prevailed, it is evident that solving problems required linguistic and cultural competence, as well as a good deal of ingenuity and determination. Andrijašević was not specifically employed as a linguist but used his linguistic skills to carry out his duties. Deployed when the market for his language skills had subsided, he was able to use his linguistic capital to secure an interesting posting. The value of these skills was recognized, and his later duties drew more heavily on them. After the end of this deployment, he attended a six-month-long Bosnian language course and returned to Bosnia-Herzegovina as a military interpreter.

The experience of Stankovic and Andrijašević reveals the strengths and limitations of serving personnel with a family background in the area. The main strength is that they are native or near native speakers of the local language, and therefore able to communicate readily. However, their fluency is principally in the spoken language, speaking and listening, used in the context of the family. As Andrijašević explained:

Nikola Andrijašević: I also learnt Serbo-Croat at home, and as the family language, and I was also exposed to Slovenian as my grandmother that was living with us at the time, spoke it only, and often spoke it with my mother, but I never had any formal training or understood it to a great extent.[4]

He was bilingual in English and Italian, and educated in England, so that his knowledge of Serbo-Croat was entirely informal, as was also the case for Stankovic. This knowledge is valuable for everyday relationships but does not extend to the language of professional or technical spheres. And it does not extend to the written language, where they typically have had little experience of reading and writing in the language. For these reasons, Andrijašević underwent a six-month training programme in the language before being deployed as a military interpreter, which demanded the written skills. Informal knowledge does not usually include a reflective awareness of language and how it works, which is normally part of formal language education, and would certainly be required to teach the language to other people. Moreover, informal knowledge does not equip the speaker to distinguish between different varieties of the language. Abbott had to warn Stankovic of this issue:

> 'Well, people ask you where you've learnt the language, and you have to trot out the same old lie about university and coming here on holiday before the war. Throw in a few deliberate errors, struggle a bit and you might get away with it ...' He paused for a moment's thought and then added, '... if I were you I'd keep your mouth shut here in Croatia. Save it for Bosnia.'
>
> I was slightly alarmed. 'Why?'
>
> 'Simple. You speak with an *ekavski* accent...obvious you're from Serbia, whereas here they speak with an *ijekavski* Dalmatian accent. And the words are different too. What's bread?'
>
> '*Hleb*,' I replied.
>
> 'No, it isn't. Here it's *kruh* and in Bosnia it's *hljeb* or occasionally *kruh*.' (Stankovic 2000: 59)

The ability to understand language differences was particularly important in Bosnia-Herzegovina, where the Serbo-Croat spoken was diverging into Serbian, Croatian and other variants. Abbott had clearly learned these on the job, and he was able to alert Stankovic to them. However, his main tactic was to meet the difficulties by concealing his native-speaker status and pretending to have less fluency than he in fact possessed. This points to the main operational limitation of native speakers, that they are associated with a particular strand within the community, which places them in one group rather than another in a divided society. Abbott's Serbian links created a conflict with the Croats with whom he worked. His attempt to conceal his background was made more difficult by his physical appearance. His family were Krajina Serbs, and Stankovic (2000: 59) thought that '[h]e looked every bit a Dalmatian – swarthy, with black hair and dark eyes.' This danger was also the logic behind the Army's initial reluctance to deploy

Stankovic. However, in the event, his links created suspicion of a conflict of loyalties between the British Army and the Serb forces. This was a possible logic behind the change of names, as the Coldstream Guards commander speculated: 'I think it was just in order to make him seem less foreign to his own sort, rather than to, to the other side.'[5] The 'foreignness' of the native speaker is a significant issue in establishing trust and therefore in enabling the officer concerned to secure the cooperation of his colleagues, and contribute effectively to the operation.

Apart from the handful of heritage speakers, a small number of individuals brought exceptional language expertise to the operation as a result of their personal itinerary. In the British Army, there were one or two officers who had encountered the language at university. For example, Nick Stansfield, the first military interpreter deployed to Croatia and Bosnia-Herzegovina, had learned Serbo-Croat while studying for a degree in Slavonic Studies before joining the Army.[6] A female lieutenant in the British Intelligence Corps, who had previously studied at the University of Sarajevo, assisted the commanding officer of 1st Battalion, The Coldstream Guards, when that unit deployed to Bosnia-Herzegovina.[7] In another exceptional case, a British commander made personal arrangements, as George Dixson, a platoon commander with SFOR in 1999, described:

> *George Dixson*: He knew he was going over to take over as company commander, he knew he was going to Bosnia, so he went to the University of West Virginia, and found one of the few Serbo-Croat speakers there, and decided, more sort of night school, but by private arrangement, to actually learn Serbo-Croat.[8]

The commander concealed his knowledge from the company, and used it to monitor the work of the local interpreters. After observing these locally employed staff, he eventually called them all together and addressed them 'in fluent Serbo-Croat'.

> *George Dixson*: And it was very clever what he did, because actually it set down the gauntlet, that all the interpreters knew that basically they'd been kind of embellishing, lying, you know, not interpreting things in the right manner. And most of them were absolutely gobsmacked. If I remember rightly, I think one of them actually probably left a few days afterwards, because he was probably one of the worst offenders for not, you know, doing what was asked of him.[9]

Few officers could match the linguistic expertise of this commander, and most did the best they could with a more limited grasp of the language. The acute lack of capacity in Serbo-Croat was partly attenuated by a certain level of proficiency in Russian among NATO officers. This was the experience, for example, of Fred Whitaker, a British liaison officer with UNPROFOR and IFOR; Eric Wilson, a member of the Defence Debriefing Team; Thomas Nielsen, commanding officer of the Nordic-Polish brigade; and a group of Danish officers encountered by Frederick Laursen, an enlisted soldier in the Danish peacekeeping battalion that served with UNPROFOR.[10] The value of Russian in practice was explained by the Coldstream Guards commander:

> *Coldstreamer*: Russian was very useful, of course, because when I later moved to Yugoslavia, although I can't in any sense speak or write Serbo-Croat, there was enough commonality between the two languages for me to be able to work out what was being said to me, before the interpreter interpreted it, and for me to be clear on whether or not the interpreter was translating what I was trying to say or was using his or her own interpretation or just literally cutting things out, which sometimes they had a tendency for doing, particularly if they thought one was being political, or boring, they would shorten it, and then you'd have to grab them by the scruff of the neck and say no, that's not what I said.[11]

Knowledge of Russian gave him a passive knowledge of Serbo-Croat, which was a valuable asset in the field, especially in understanding what was said. It is likely that this extended to being able to understand the gist of a document, and would certainly make it possible to read documents written in Cyrillic script. Coldstreamer had studied Russian for 18 months earlier in his career, at a time when NATO troops regularly learned Russian as the language of the Warsaw Pact, and all NATO forces had well-established provision for Russian teaching.

As a result, at the beginning of the intervention in Bosnia-Herzegovina, the existing linguistic and cultural capital within UN and NATO troops was very limited. A minority of officers could use their knowledge of Russian to make some sense of what was going on in Serbo-Croat, but they did not have the active ability to speak or write the language. Beyond that, a bare handful of military personnel had inherited some fluency in spoken Serbo-Croat through their family background. But that background proved a double-edged sword, as we have observed. The overall level of expertise is difficult to quantify, but the scale of it can be estimated from the British contingent of around 3,400 troops that served in UNPROFOR,[12] of whom perhaps four or five had Serbo-Croat from their family background. If as many as 30 officers had acquired some proficiency in Russian, this still amounted to barely 1 per cent of the forces with relevant language skills. The scarcity of language skills in a buoyant language market for Serbo-Croat could then be remedied in two ways. One was to hire local people with knowledge of English to translate and interpret, as discussed in Chapter 3. This was in practice the solution adopted for the vast majority of purposes. The second remedy was to provide language training for troops, increasing the linguistic capital they could bring to bear. It was an expensive, arduous and uncertain solution, but one which was necessary for certain areas of work, especially where security and trust were at a premium.

Basic language training

Commanders began to recognize the need for basic language awareness as part of the detailed preparations for operations. Typically, they received advance notice of a planned deployment and took charge of arranging a programme of preparation and training. Much of the preparatory work focused on military strategy, conditions on the ground, the forces in place, logistics and equipment, but some of it dealt with the cultural context and the language requirements likely to be encountered. In the case of Bosnia-Herzegovina, the UN and NATO forces were mobilized to intervene at very short notice, and the first troops to be deployed received very limited preparation. As the operation continued, structures were set up to provide suitable courses, including training in language and culture. At the simplest level, all participants required a general familiarity with the situation on the ground, but as experience of the terrain developed, a growing number of troops were equipped with some working knowledge of the language. There were few who had any prior knowledge of the language and culture, but a basic level of training was put in place.

The military needed to arrange a significant amount of training in order to raise the linguistic capital of the forces to a level where they were adequate to the tasks they needed to carry out. In the first stages of the crisis, from late 1992, there was no provision for training, and arrangements had to be set in place very rapidly.[13] Since the operations came largely as a surprise to the participating forces, the new provision was established during the first months of the campaign and was strengthened as experience of conditions on the ground filtered back to training programmes. In the participating countries, training was mainly developed by the existing military education services. They had to meet three main areas of need, as Gregory Cook, a language instructor with the British Army, pointed out:

> *Gregory Cook*: And if you think of the type of operations that are currently going on, what we call out of area operations, it follows logically that languages will support the roles of intelligence gathering, and on the battlefield itself, or in the conflict zone, any form of contact that you might have with either the local inhabitants or the opposition if it happens to be a genuine conflict situation. There's the further role, which is the diplomatic role, of the military attachés and so on. So really we've got the three roles, which is intelligence, in support of operations, and the diplomatic one.[14]

In some countries, the different roles were served by different training facilities. Hence, in Britain the first course in Serbo-Croat was established by Military Intelligence at the Army Education Centre, Colchester, in November 1992. It also serviced some of the diplomatic requirements, although these were also met by the Diplomatic Language Centre in the Foreign and Commonwealth Office, in London. A little later, an operational language course was started at DSL, in Beaconsfield, under the auspices of the Russian Language Wing. In the United States, the main operational provision was offered at the Defense Language Institute Foreign Language Center in Monterey, California.[15] In France, the Ecole interarmées du renseignement et des études linguistiques in Strasbourg provided the same services, later reorganized as the Centre de formation interarmées au renseignement.[16] In Denmark, the Royal Danish Defence Academy in Copenhagen provided specialist language training.[17] In most cases, the teachers were initially civilian native speakers of Serbo-Croat who had teaching experience. As training developed, they were joined by military personnel who had learned the language and had used it in operations. However, resources were limited, and most countries contributing troops asked universities and other civilian education providers to deliver courses for military personnel. In Britain, the University of Westminster provided Serbo-Croat courses before the Beaconsfield programme was established, and it continued to provide a range of courses to supplement DSL.[18] The pattern of using both civilian and military courses was widespread through the NATO forces, and remains the case to the present day. The balance between the two has varied considerably over time, as policy has shifted to follow military and economic priorities.

Courses of different kinds were offered, aiming to produce personnel equipped for different purposes. In some cases, courses with a focus on particular content or tasks were offered to particular cohorts, such as the intelligence services or special forces. But the more general purpose courses were organized broadly to aim at the levels of proficiency developed by NATO Bureau for International Language Coordination (BILC/BCLI).[19] Non-members of NATO command, such as France or Russia, had their own systems of assessment, which served similar functions to the NATO system. Since re-entering the NATO command structure in 2009, the French military services have begun to adopt the NATO standards.[20]

Since 1976, the Bureau has developed a Standardization Agreement (STANAG), which defines language proficiency levels. This is set out in a document entitled STANAG 6001, which is updated periodically, and most recently in 2011. It provides a six-point scale for competence in Listening, Speaking, Reading and Writing, which in the latest version is mapped against the scale of the Common European Framework of Reference (CEFR) (Lewis 2012: 63). During the 1990s, the six levels were identified as:

Level 0 No Proficiency
Level 1 Elementary
Level 2 Limited Working
Level 3 Minimum Professional
Level 4 Full Professional
Level 5 Native/Bilingual (Vadász 2011: 288)

Each level was applied to the four traditional language skills of Listening, Speaking, Reading and Writing, and represented in a summary numerical form so that someone with native proficiency in all four skills would be graded as 5555. In practice, this top level was ignored for training purposes, since native-speaker competence was presumed to be the result of living and being well educated in a country where the language was spoken. It therefore lay beyond the scope of what could be achieved in a training course. The bottom level was also largely ignored, since it was usually understood literally to mean no knowledge at all of the language. Gregory Cook explained:

> *Gregory Cook*: Not everybody in the battalion would get language training, but you know, a selected few from each company or whatever it was within the ... I'm trying to think of the recent deployment packages. In the case of the Balkans, I think it was very much in its initial stages, because I don't think when the Balkans erupted that there was any training really for battalion personnel, except perhaps an awareness package. And they wouldn't get any STANAG qualification for that.[21]

For general personnel, the awareness package was an item in a general briefing programme, which would typically include information about the country, some cultural background and a limited amount of attention to language issues, with a few basic phrases. As the campaign progressed, the language component increased:

> *Gregory Cook*: and we're talking about low-grade linguists now, people who only do one or two weeks in a language, is really a short cultural awareness: how to address people, what not to do, how not to offend people. And that is often just blanket training, so you might get, in the case of the Balkans for example, you might get a whole battalion or regiment going out there, and most of the soldiers would get a week or two weeks of some form of language training.[22]

In some respects, the provision of up to two weeks of training seems quite substantial. It was not available in the early stages of the campaign, but as successive deployments had longer advance notice and more time to arrange training, the language content did increase. The outcomes at that stage might be sufficient to warrant a grade of STANAG level 1 for elementary speaking and listening (1100). But the outcomes were highly variable, and, as Alma Kovač pointed out, her experience as a language instructor in Britain did not confirm the value of these courses:

> *Alma Kovač*: To learn the language, it's very hard work, very very hard work, and you can't get it in 15 days. They would send us 15 people and say, train them, they should learn Bosnian. I said, 'I'm sorry, in 15 days?' I taught even in London, Wellington Barracks, there were lots of people, for two weeks, like are going to Bosnia, they need to speak the language. God! And they were ordinary soldiers, I don't want to say that they are less than officers, but still their language or linguistic abilities are very very low. And they just didn't want to

> learn it. They were forced to do it. And when you force someone to do it, it, the result is, there's no proper result at all (laughs).
>
> *Catherine Baker*: So what could they do after two weeks?
>
> *Alma Kovač*: They could say, 'Hello'. They could say, 'My name is ...' They can ask a few questions, and if they have a good memory (laughs). But that was. There was another one in, where was it, somewhere in Wales, we had to. I said, 'No way I'm going to do it once again'. It was, twice was more than ... Because when you put all your efforts, and your abilities, and everything, you wanted them to learn, and then after two weeks you don't see result, it was so frustrating and ... it's not worth. But, maybe it was worth for them, I don't know, we never had any replies from them.[23]

The value of a two-week language course in this instance was very questionable, particularly since the learners had no previous experience of learning languages and had no motivation to learn. The frustration of the tutor suggests that the 15-day course may well have been counterproductive in this instance, reinforcing the reluctance of the soldiers to engage with the language.

More recently, level 0 has been redefined to correspond with the lowest level of the Common European Framework, level A1. STANAG 0 now includes a higher level, which recognizes the ability to 'make short utterances and ask very simple questions using memorised material and set expressions', and to be able to deal with 'immediate needs such as greetings, personal details, numbers, time, common objects or commands' (Lewis 2012: 63). In practice, no strong distinction was drawn between the basic skills that might be acquired without STANAG recognition and the 'survival' level that could be achieved after a couple of weeks of training. In general terms, language skills at level 1 were still considered to be below the point at which they became an identifiable asset in operations.

Part of the basic training was concerned with advice on how to use the language cards that were increasingly issued. The United States invested substantially in them, as the *Chicago Tribune* reported in May 1993:

> The White House and Pentagon may be sending conflicting signals as President Clinton and his top advisers decide what to do about Bosnia, but Army Chief Warrant Officer Robert Higgins is taking no chances.
>
> Concluding it is better to be safe than sorry, Higgins has overseen the preparation of 25,000 laminated pocket cards for U.S. troops

> containing common, life-saving commands such as 'Stop!' 'Come here', 'Do not move' and 'Move slowly'. (de Lama 1993)

Several countries developed this approach, issuing cards which typically contained lists of words and phrases in two languages, such as might be found in a holiday phrase-book, but with content customized for military purposes. They were the main resource that troops could use to cope on their own with day-to-day contact with the local population. In a few cases, individuals might make the effort to memorize the words and phrases, but more often the cards were produced and read, either by the military themselves or by the local people with whom they were interacting. As the campaign developed, it became more common to include drawings or pictures on the cards, which could facilitate communication using signs and gestures. It appears that the linguistic skills of the troops may have been less important than their metalinguistic skills, that is, their ability to think about language and communicate using the language resources available. These resources included their own very limited knowledge, the language knowledge of those they met, body language, gestures, language cards and other materials. It may be concluded that, at the most basic level of language proficiency, STANAG level 0, understood to include CEFR level A1, the priority in language training should be metalinguistic.

Equipping troops with communication strategies that draw on the available language resources did not increase their linguistic capital to a level where it became a distinct asset. But it did contribute to developing the 'habitus' of personnel: the capabilities and dispositions which enable them to function in a particular field. At the same time, their own limited knowledge of the language is one of the resources on which they can draw. It does provide some cultural capital and confer limited benefits. As the Bosnian operation continued, there was more opportunity to increase the linguistic capital by developing more advanced language skills, particularly to the level of 'colloquial speakers'.

Colloquial speakers

Above the level of basic language awareness, the British forces recognized the need for all of its units to include someone who was sufficiently familiar with the local language to engage meaningfully with the population. At the time, this was the lowest recognized level of positive language proficiency. In Fred Whitaker's terms:

> *Fred Whitaker*: And I think that's one of the important things to remember about the level of language training in the British Army was that they use the term of, the levels of colloquial, linguist, interpreter, class two and class one, and alongside those use the NATO standard language profiles, which I'm sure you're familiar with, of level 2, roughly a colloquial level, level 3, linguist, and level 4 3, or 4 4, for interpreter level.[24]

The three terms of colloquial speaker, linguist and interpreter were inherited from the British Civil Service Commission, which used the three categories for staff in a wide range of jobs, especially in the diplomatic service. During the 1970s, they were mapped on to the STANAG levels, as Whitaker explains, but the earlier terms remained current and were widely used in Bosnia-Herzegovina in the 1990s, despite the ambiguities that caused.

In the first months of the conflict, there were few colloquial level speakers of Serbo-Croat in the British forces. This was inevitable in view of the length of time needed to achieve that level of proficiency, generally set at three months, as Whitaker explained:

> *Fred Whitaker*: The training development advice would be that three months was long enough to reach what was called a colloquial level. Well, yes. It's long enough to reach a level at which you could pass the test which would qualify you as a colloquial-level speaker. This is language profile 2222, I suppose, maybe 2221, because there was very little requirement to write in the foreign language.[25]

The first courses provided in Britain in fact did not last this length, mainly because of the pressure to deploy people urgently. Alma Kovač, who ran the first course for British Military Intelligence, recalls:

> *Alma Kovač*: I think the first course was only four, six weeks or something like that, so what can you learn in that period of time? But still they managed somehow, they had a colloquial exam at the end, and we enjoyed very much. Second course was a bit more serious.[26]

After the urgency of the beginning of the campaign, training settled into a more regular rhythm and later courses were extended to three months. In contrast to Kovač's experience at Wellington Barracks, two significant factors contributed to the successful outcome of the first Intelligence course. First, the students consisted of a dozen officers from the Regular and Territorial Army, who expected to be deployed to Bosnia or to gather intelligence from refugees who had arrived in the UK. They were urgently required and knew that they would be using the language for real after completing the course. This provided a high level of motivation, which is one of the key factors in successful language learning. Second, most of the students already had experience of learning another cognate language:

> *Alma Kovač*: I must say that at the beginning most of my students could speak Russian, so as you know Russian grammar is pretty similar as Serbo-Croat.[27]

The value of Russian was well recognized, and it seems that the first students to enrol were largely selected for their prior language knowledge. Thomas Nielsen notes that this was also the case in Denmark:

> *Thomas Nielsen*: And therefore we decided, I think it was in the middle of the 90s, that the young people who went through the army language school, just as myself, with Russian as the language, they were offered a contract afterwards where they were taught Serbo-Croat, for I think it was a couple of months.[28]

The rapid progress that Russian speakers could make in Serbo-Croat was a boon to the NATO forces, who took widespread advantage of it. In the United States, courses catering for learners with this background were referred to as 'Turbo-Serbo' (Quinn-Judge 1995). Conversely, learners who had no previous knowledge of a Slavonic language took a lot longer to reach the same level and struggled with language features that others had already come to grips with in learning Russian. Learning the language was even more difficult for those who had not learned any other language, and Nikola Andrijašević, who followed a colloquial course, commented:

> *Nikola Andrijašević*: I think one of the hardest concepts was the declensions. They just took a while to grasp the concept of declensions, and how the ending of a word might alter depending on the type of sentence construction, and the type of movement within a sentence, or the type of verb within a sentence. So that was totally alien to a lot of people, and caused a lot of confusion. Also having to learn the gender of words, which once again affects the ending of words, caused a lot of confusion and consternation.[29]

Basic grammatical features like nouns, verbs, declension, conjugation, genders and word agreements posed serious conceptual obstacles to those who had no language learning experience, Alma Kovač noted that this was a particular difficulty for 'ordinary soldiers' who had not learned languages at school, whereas most of the officers 'knew other languages' and had less difficulty learning Serbo-Croat as a result.[30]

The colloquial level courses were intended to achieve a limited working capability in the language, at STANAG level 2222 or 2221, equivalent to B1 level CEFR, roughly the level of a higher grade in the English GCSE examination at age 16. This is described as a 'Functional' level by STANAG 6001, and would aim to achieve the following outcomes:

> Can describe people, places and things; narrate current, past and future activities in full paragraphs; state facts; give instructions or directions; ask and answer questions in the workplace; deal with non-routine daily situations. (Lewis 2012: 63)

The colloquial speaker would be expected to be comfortable with 'concrete topics such as own background, family, interests, work travel and current events' (Lewis 2012: 63). Kovač outlined what this might mean in practice:

> *Alma Kovač*: The level was really colloquial. They did the grammar, first of all, you know, they couldn't speak without grammar. And then we had some listening exercises. And it was very low level, but still, the amount of knowledge of the language was enough to do the small chat or to break the ice, as you say, and the students were pretty happy with the knowledge they got after that level. And even after colloquial they could do a bit of learning on their own. You know, that was the basic of the language. Grammar, listening.... on that level they didn't write. They would read, and listen, and talk.[31]

The colloquial speakers could engage in small talk and break the ice in an encounter, but were not equipped to deal with complex professional situations. Once they had completed this training, they were ready to be deployed on active service. Their language skills were frequently valuable, and were certainly a personal asset. On rarer occasions, language training may have made the difference between life and death. Alma Kovač describes the experience of one of her first groups of students:

Alma Kovač: There is one officer, that was at the very beginning... that must be '94. He went on his own, in a Jeep, somewhere in... I don't know where exactly. In, deep in Bosnia, you know, not near the frontier or any kind. So he got lost. All of a sudden he was, he didn't know the road, which was all over the woods. And all of a sudden he found himself in the middle of a – lots of people with guns and not looking very friendly, with beards, and God, he was so... all of a sudden, he remembered, you know, our advice is don't go on your own, don't sniff around, you know... people – I don't know, maybe it would be here as well – are very suspicious if you are somewhere on your own, looking for something, and... they were very angry. They said, 'Who are you, with the guns?'. And... and we taught them, we had a student who was pretty good in the language. And he would collect the swear words. I wasn't happy to write down the swear words (laughs)... as you know, we have a very rich (laughs) vocab, swearing vocab. So he wrote down, I think two or three pages of swear words, with explanations, and translations. And students liked learning them, I don't know for what reason, but they liked that. So he remembered them. And he, like, kicked the Jeep, and said something very rude in Serbo-Croat, like, 'You... stupid car,' but, you know, in another way. And like something was broken. And these guys, there were like eight of them, they couldn't believe they heard from a foreigner such a word. And they started laughing. And after a while they were all drinking rakija, and like being friends, they showed him the way to wherever he was going, and... So he came back and said, 'Ah, thank God for these awful words,' but he was... that, I can't say that he would be killed, but still he got away with no problems, just because of knowing even the swear words. Rude, very rude words.[32]

The men with beards were almost certainly Serb militia, since long beards were an identifying characteristic of the Četniks, Serb paramilitaries implicated in the removal of non-Serbs through ethnic cleansing. An encounter with them was potentially dangerous in the period before the peace agreement of 1995. In this case, a repertoire of rude words in the local language, used with great presence of mind, proved to be almost literally a lifesaver. The incident reveals a number of ways in which embodied language knowledge can be a valuable asset, particularly in new fields. The swear words that were disapproved of in the field of the language classroom had high capital value in the military field of an encounter with paramilitaries.

However, the limited language knowledge of colloquial speakers was not always sufficient to achieve the tasks they were given. Very often, they would be the only colloquial speaker in their unit, and would be required to use their limited working knowledge in action. This typically led to a mismatch between the abilities of the colloquial speaker and the expectations of their commanders, as Fred Whitaker pointed out:

> *Fred Whitaker*: But then people were taken from that course and thrown into Bosnia, and people said 'Ah, we've got the linguists here'. Sometimes they would even say, 'We've got the interpreters here'. And sometimes people were asked to do, well, I think very often people were asked to do things which were way beyond their level. And I think that then meant that people who had the military colloquial speakers working with them sometimes were disappointed with the level of language ability that the individuals displayed. And though they may have been quite happy to sit and talk in very short pieces of language, to use a great deal of circumlocution and there was a little bit of imagination, get meaning across, then that was very different from what sometimes people expected of them. They expected them to be able to say anything (laughs) and understand anything, and it wasn't like that.[33]

This mismatch is perhaps inevitable where a limited resource is offered to meet a much larger need. This led to inexperienced language users attempting to carry out tasks far beyond their abilities. It also reflects misconceptions about the nature of language proficiency that were apparently widely held. Many commanders appear to see it as a low-level skill that can be acquired with ease, underestimating the difficulty of developing proficiency and overestimating the capability of staff who have taken language courses. The results were often dispiriting, as the Canadian-born British platoon commander George Dixson recounts:

> *George Dixson*: The first group of about 12 people who underwent this training went out to Bosnia, and I think in almost every case were unable to satisfy the needs of the people with whom they were working. And because of that, they were then moved into positions where they didn't actually use their language skills. They probably in some cases used their basic military skills. Because of course people came from all different corps and regiments, and so if they were from the Royal Electrical and Mechanical Engineers, then they may

> be sidelined into a role relating to that, or they may be sidelined into a role relating to their rank, where if they were a senior NCO, then they would take on some administrative role which would be in support of the effort of the unit, but not using the language, except occasionally here and there, for a few words to ask whether there was a good restaurant (laughs) in the area or not. And so consequently they arrived unable to do what people expected them to do, and were then not given the opportunity to improve in theatre so that they could actually do a better job. And I think that that was a disappointment for the receiving unit, and for the people who'd volunteered for the language training, spent three months' hard work doing their very best to learn the language, acquiring at least a good working knowledge of basic terms which they could have used, but then getting there and finding that there was no real opportunity for them to do that, and so the language faded away.[34]

The result was frequently disappointing for the staff with language skills and for their units. Arriving in the 'field' of operations, their linguistic capital was insufficient to be spent. Not only was their language proficiency too limited to be used in specialist contexts, but there were also more attractive alternatives available to commanders. From an early stage, the international forces recruited significant numbers of locally employed translators and interpreters, and as they developed strong relationships with the units employing them, commanders were increasingly inclined to entrust them with even the more sensitive language-related tasks. They had much more linguistic capital than the military colloquial speakers, who found it difficult to identify specific tasks that would require the limited working knowledge of language that they possessed. In response, colloquial speakers adopted different ways of internalizing the mismatch between their linguistic capital and the needs of the field. In some cases they responded by working to develop their grasp of the local language. Steve Morley, then a corporal and a military colloquial speaker with SFOR in Mrkonjić Grad in 1999, describes his experience:

> *Steve Morley*: But once we got into theatre, into Bosnia, it was like people were on speed, you know, how fast they were speaking. And I would say 'Polako, polako', you know, slow it down a bit. And once I got my head round getting them to slow down, and explaining, 'Speak like a child', it was fine, you know. But my depth of knowledge certainly improved by about, after I'd been out there three months, I

> was very, very confident in what I was doing. And by the end of the tour, you know, it was great. I used to speak to all the laundry people, round the camp, all the cleaners, and because I'd make an effort with their language, you know, I was quite popular with the locals.[35]

The contrast between the careful diction of his language tutors and the rapid delivery of local native speakers was a shock, but with a mixture of courage and ingenuity he was able to make significant improvement during his deployment. Other colloquial speakers distanced themselves from their status by minimizing their actual language achievements, echoing the repeated comments of instructors to the effect that not much could be expected after short courses of three months. Others responded by adopting a playful attitude, which in one extreme case proved dangerous, as Alma Kovač recalls:

> *Alma Kovač*: So I remember one guy, who was Polish by origin, well, a child when he came to the UK, probably small. He could speak Polish, he could speak Russian, perfect Russian, and Serbo-Croat wasn't difficult for him to learn. He was very good. And he was ... deployed to Gornji Vakuf, which is [in the] so-called Croatian part of ... of Bosnia. It's in central Bosnia. That was probably ninety ... three, four. And we told them that in the Croatian part of Bosnia they should use *kruh* for bread. In Bosnia we say *hljeb*, but in Serbia they say *hleb*. Slight difference. And he was like a joker most of the time. He ... I told him, 'Please don't use *hljeb* or *hleb* in Gornji Vakuf.' He said, 'Oh, what does it matter,' I said 'Please, that's my advice, so whatever you want.' And one day he was there, and he wanted, he went to a shop to buy bread. He deliberately said, *molim jedan hleb*, which is 'Please can I have a bread,' but using the Serbian version of the word. And the guy pulled out the machine-gun under the table. And that was a scandal really. They had – they put him in a jail, they arrested him, then the whole British (laughs), the environment, had ... that was really a mess, he made a mess, stayed a day and a half in the prison. He almost lost his life, you know, it was very – at that time, it was a very very serious thing. And I met him later, and I said, 'My God, why did you do that?' 'Oh, it's a – I just wanted to make a joke.' But for them, it's not a joke, you see, you see, it wasn't a joke.[36]

The sensitivity of the word for bread echoes the advice of 'Nick Abbott' to Milos Stankovic, quoted above. The joke in this case arose partly from the speaker's own ambiguous ethnic position. As a speaker of two

Slavonic languages, Polish and Russian, he was intrigued that another language in this group used a different word for bread. In fact it is in only two of the South Slavonic languages, Croatian and Slovenian, that the word 'kruh' is used. Other Slavonic languages (Russian, Polish, Serbian, Macedonian, Czech, Slovak) use a variant of the word 'hleb'. The joker's approach was to test how real this difference was, deliberately using the 'wrong' word for the context. He no doubt felt that his status as a member of the international forces would give him enough permission to do so, perhaps reinforced by his own background in two Western and Eastern Slavonic languages. The reaction of the baker suggests that he took the use as an indication that the soldier was aligned with the Serbs, with whom the Bosnian Croats were still at war at the time of the episode in 1993–4. This would be plausible if, as Kovač suggests, he spoke fluently, with a Polish or Russian accent. It is also likely that the baker took the language use as a deliberate slight, and may have detected a rejection of the Croatian identity as expressed in language. At all events, it is unlikely that the soldier concerned would have been invited to take on more specialist language duties, despite his obvious proficiency. That may in fact have been a satisfactory resolution of the underlying tension between the semi-specialist skills of the colloquial linguist and the specialist requirements that the colloquial speaker could not meet.

As Dixson pointed out, without a specialist role, colloquial speakers would typically find different roles, appropriate to their rank and their other expertise. In other words, they could draw on other parts of their cultural capital to secure an acceptable level of recognition within the local military field. In that case, there was no particular reason why they would be deployed to Bosnia-Herzegovina again after their first six-month tour of duty. There would also be no incentive to develop their linguistic capital. However, there were at least some colloquial speakers who did find that their capability was valued, and in a small number of cases they were able to take further language courses to become specialist linguists and interpreters.

Conclusion

Before 1992, very few military personnel had acquired enough language knowledge to be useful during the intervention in Bosnia-Herzegovina. This form of linguistic capital had not been in demand in the military language market. A handful of officers with family backgrounds in the region found that their heritage knowledge had suddenly acquired value, and they were deployed to the area. This arrangement met with mixed success since their personal connection gave them other forms of cultural capital, which might even have a negative value, offsetting their ability to communicate. There is a sharp contrast between Corporal 'Abbott', who was repatriated in haste under threat of death, and Captain 'Costello', who at the same period served with distinction in two tours of duty in the area. In any case, it was a limited solution since the number of heritage speakers was small. Apart from these few individuals, a small number of officers knew something of the local language, and rather more of them could use their knowledge of Russian to provide an entry into Serbo-Croat.

The forces put in place some instruction for general language purposes during the early months of the campaign, but they rapidly encountered the difficulty of achieving useful proficiency within a short period of training. At a later stage, awareness raising courses were introduced, lasting up to two weeks. They were able to provide a 'survival' level of knowledge, but their success was highly dependent on the troops being motivated to learn and having at least a rudimentary knowledge of language structure. Experience showed that while officers might meet these prerequisites, ordinary soldiers might often be discouraged and see the course as an unwelcome imposition. It seemed more effective at this level to focus on areas of metalanguage, encouraging soldiers to learn how to use tools such as language cards and how to recognize language resources that might assist them in communication.

The longer language courses of around three months, designed to achieve a functional level of language expertise, proved more effective, at least in maintaining the commitment of learners, who were often volunteers and could be highly motivated by the prospect of a forthcoming deployment to the area. Since the courses were mainly provided for officers, they could assume a previous level of education which equipped them to learn a further foreign language. While these courses achieved a 'colloquial' level of language proficiency, it was a common experience that commanders in the field expected a much higher level of expertise than was actually achievable in the time available, and were dissatisfied with the performance of colloquial speakers in an operational context. The mismatch between their linguistic capital and the requirements of the field frequently led to the trained officers choosing or being allocated to other duties that drew on other aspects of their cultural capital. It also reinforced the commitment of commanders to the locally-employed interpreters, whose higher linguistic capital could provide more sophisticated language services. The traditional dilemma of 'ars longa vita brevis' (the art is long but life is short) seems to apply, since language learning is an 'embodied' form of cultural capital, and it takes a relatively long time to achieve modest proficiency. The personnel planning of the forces does not easily accommodate a lengthy programme of language study, and nor does the career planning of individual officers, who are aware that the rewards may not be commensurate to the time they commit. They were obliged to judge whether the investment in their linguistic capital might be better used in developing other parts of their cultural capital. The problem was attenuated for individuals who had prior language learning experience, especially in a cognate language. However, the high expectations of commanders in the field remained an intractable aspiration, as even the more intensively trained military interpreters discovered.

2
The Multiple Roles of Military Interpreters

The role of interpreters and translators in civilian life stretches across a wide range of functions, including the voice from the conference booth and the hand behind the translated document, but also the supportive intermediary in public services and the critical annotator of a challenging text. Laurence Venuti (1995: 313) concludes his authoritative critique of the translator's invisibility by declaring that it 'raises such troubling questions about the geopolitical economy of culture that a greater suspicion toward translation is urgently needed to confront them', and believes that translators can contribute to 'the emergence of new cultural relations'. Kumiko Torikai (2009: 180) compares the interpreter's role to the *kurogo* in Japanese Kabuki theatre: the figure dressed in black who unobtrusively hands props to the actors while being conventionally ignored by the audience. She concludes that 'the interpreter is not simply an invisible linguistic conduit, but is an intercultural communication expert and coordinator, facilitating and mediating intercultural encounters'. Their shared view that the professional linguist has a wider social role applies with even greater force to military language specialists, who combine linguistic roles with military duties, which necessarily take precedence. Rather than being clothed in the unobtrusive black of the *kurogo,* they work in the uniform of their service, which places their linguistic role firmly in the context of a military profession.

The combination of military and linguistic roles provides the armed forces with the capability to work across languages and overcome issues of security and trust (see Chapter 6). There are many language tasks for which civilian specialists are not normally used, and where serving personnel are required. These tasks range from sensitive intelligence work behind the scenes to operations in action that may place individuals in imminent danger. For this reason, the forces invest considerable resources in developing the language expertise of some of their members. However, the combination of military and linguistic roles also brings complexities, arising from the much wider profile of tasks that these specialists can perform. Justin Lewis, a military specialist, explained:

> However, military linguists are called upon to interpret and translate within their competence, usually in less than ideal circumstances, and they are required to provide additional functions that are unlikely to be found in civil practitioners. Whilst they may be in similar roles, it might be best to consider military linguists and their civil counterparts as cousins, rather than siblings, with different outlooks, loyalties, strengths and weaknesses. (Lewis 2012: 61)

Operational priorities may require them to combine language duties with other roles, or take other roles entirely, and these other roles may be more valuable to the operation or to the future career of the individual. These complexities came to the fore during the intervention in Bosnia-Herzegovina, where the demand for expertise in the local language posed challenges to the training of military specialists, and where the improvement of conditions as the peace operations progressed enabled commanders to deploy civilian linguists over a greater range of duties.

The distinction between the terms 'interpreter' and 'translator' is a contested issue which generates communicative and symbolic tensions. English, like most Western European languages, contains different nouns for the two roles, which are readily distinguished when discussed together as mediation in spoken and written forms. This distinction is sharply emphasized by several professional bodies and public services. Hence, the European Commission, for example, has two quite distinct services: the Directorate-General for Translation is responsible for translating written texts and documents, while the Directorate-General for Interpretation (DG SCIC) provides conference interpreters and 'deals solely with oral communication'.[1] In less formal settings or smaller organizations, the roles are not so strictly segregated, but professional linguists generally observe the distinction.

In everyday speech, on the other hand, there is frequent confusion between the roles of translator and interpreter in native English on the part of non-professionals. This is compounded in the military context by the traditional use of 'interpreter' to designate an advanced level of language proficiency, and by the use of 'military interpreter' to include all the specialist language tasks. By contrast, the term 'military translator' is never used, and was not used in any of the interviews we recorded. The distinction between translation and interpreting is less readily marked in the Bosnian and Serbian languages, which incorporate both roles in the word *prevodilac*, as does the Croatian *prevoditelj*; the distinction is supplied in the adjective modifying the act itself, *usmeno/pismeno prevođenje* ('oral/written translation'). The same role may well undertake both tasks. English-language accounts by native speakers of Bosnian-Serbian-Croatian and everyday usage of native English speakers often use the word 'translator' even when the translator in question was mainly or entirely carrying out interpreting, and vice versa. Since all the narratives quoted in this book were produced in English, the authors have retained each speaker's terminology. We have been careful to clarify the distinction where it is significant to understanding an argument.

Training specialist linguists

At the outset, the different UN and NATO forces faced a serious dearth of trained linguists who could provide specialist language support for the forces deployed in Bosnia-Herzegovina so as to enable them to understand the situation as it developed and communicate effectively with the different armed forces then active in the country or with the local populations. The international forces had a range of specialist language requirements, which could not be fully satisfied by the use of the locally employed civilian translators and interpreters who carried out most everyday language tasks (see Chapter 3). It was a constant requirement that some military personnel should be able to act as intermediaries between their own forces and the local population. In some cases, the activities carried sensitive implications, for which a high level of security clearance was required. In other cases, the activities took place in dangerous circumstances, which required the participants to be trained military personnel. The NATO forces attempted to meet these needs by providing advanced language training, which would take personnel to the higher levels of proficiency, recognized under the NATO standards as STANAG levels 3 or 4. In the 1990s, these were generally referred to as linguists and interpreters, and they were considered to be able to work at minimum professional or fully professional levels, now distinguished as professional and expert levels (Lewis 2012: 63).

These trained specialists were used for a wide range of tasks, which included intelligence work on the ground, analysis of printed or broadcast media, liaising between their unit and other forces, liaising with the local population, specialist translation and interpreting, managing language services and providing language training. Many of those who achieved the higher levels of proficiency acted in several of these roles during the course of their career. The itinerary of Louise Robbins was characteristic of the professional linguist and military interpreter. A languages graduate in French and German, with some Russian, she joined the British Army for a short service commission of eight years. She learned some Danish and Swahili for different operations. After 18 months based in Germany, she became a language adviser and oversaw language training for the army in the Salisbury Plain area. In 1993, she undertook a five-month course in Serbo-Croat and was deployed to Bosnia-Herzegovina as a military interpreter. She completed her service after a further operation in Rwanda.[2] The experience of learning languages and also teaching them was not uncommon for military linguists. Nick Stansfield had a similar trajectory. Though he had studied some Serbo-Croat at university, he did a six-week course in the language before being deployed to Croatia and Bosnia in mid-1992, where he acted as interpreter to the British commander, Colonel Bob Stewart (see Chapter 3). After returning from the operation, he was placed in charge of Serbo-Croat training at the Defence School of Languages at Beaconsfield, the principal British military language training service.[3] An interpreter attached to the Danish army, Martin Lund Pedersen, provides the civilian equivalent, since he served with the Nordic-Polish brigade in SFOR, 1997–8 and was later employed as an instructor at the Danish army language school.[4] The notion of language specialists in the Bosnian operation is therefore a very broad one.

Very few specialist linguists were prepared and available for deployment at the beginning of the operations in Bosnia-Herzegovina. A handful of soldiers had acquired fluency in the local language from native speakers in their immediate family (Chapter 1), but with these few exceptions the specialists were drawn mainly from people who had a personal history of language expertise and who volunteered to develop a high level of competence in Serbo-Croat, as it was initially called. The training programmes were typically longer than the three months offered to 'colloquial' speakers, though there was not always a clear distinction between the colloquial training and the more specialist linguist or interpreter training. In Britain, the main provider of high-level language training was DSL. By chance, the small Serbo-Croat programme was closed in the aftermath of the ending of the Cold War, but was relaunched as the UN operations began in Bosnia-Herzegovina.

Placed under the aegis of the large Russian Language Wing, it was initially led by a Russian tutor who spoke Serbian because her father had been a Serbian pilot in the Yugoslav air force.[5] Louise Robbins described her training:

> *Louise Robbins*: So that was a five-month intensive course, I was thrown together with a hotch potch of people...lance corporals through to major. All different backgrounds, different arms and corps, but some of us were educators, some had more of a language background than others, and we were thrown together to sit in a classroom and learn Serbo-Croat from 8.30 to 4.30 five days a week, homework every night, homework every weekend, that was mid-May, and we deployed in mid-November. We were allowed some leave, and towards the end of that course we did the military training, the pre-operational training.[6]

A five-month intensive course represents a substantial training investment both for the individual and for the military, and the incentive for both was that those taking the course were expecting to serve in Bosnia-Herzegovina after completing it. Since this was early in the conflict, there was an urgent need to develop a cohort of linguists who could operate at a high level. Most of the courses offered by DSL were three months long and aimed to train colloquial speakers, but the school also taught 'refresher' and other higher-level courses. Similarly, the Military Intelligence school at North Luffenham offered initial courses of three months and then more advanced courses, typically to personnel who had completed a tour of duty in Bosnia. Alma Kovač remained sceptical about the level of expertise they achieved: 'You can't say that they knew language after, I don't know, six months, even. But they can manage.'[7] In practice, there was some ambiguity about how much people were expected to learn in the time allotted, as Robbins describes:

> *Louise Robbins*: So no, we weren't ready as interpreters, we could get by in certain scenarios, some of us were better than others. What an experience.
>
> *Catherine Baker*: Do you know what grade of language competency you were meant to have by the end of the five months?
>
> *Louise Robbins*: We all sat the colloquial test. It's difficult to equate it. It should really be sort of O-level standard, sorry, GCSE. Having gone through the Institute of Linguists and JSLEB, Joint Service Language Examination Board, I've gone through the exams, and I've helped

people prepare for the exams, and I've been a service colleague in the exams, so I've witnessed quite a bit of it. Colloquial is something that you do at the end of like a four- to six-week course. Then you need much further in-depth training to get to Linguist standard, they call it. That's supposed to be akin to A level. And Interpreter standard is supposed to be akin to a degree. But it doesn't equate. Because when you do a degree in languages, you study literature, you study culture. This interpreting is about very high-level technical, live interpretation, which you don't learn on an undergraduate degree. It's very hard to equate. But I felt, when we did our colloquial exam at Beaconsfield for Serbo-Croat, they built the exam around our abilities. They set something that was achievable for us. And having run the German colloquial courses, I said we're much much higher than colloquial. Not quite A-level. You know. The reading and the writing of it was difficult. We needed to do more listening. Because of the different dialects, because they as a nation they tend to mumble, they've all got rotten teeth because they're in a war (laughs), it affects their speech, you can't understand what they're saying.[8]

Her analysis highlights the difficulty in setting equivalences between what is learned in a course of this kind and a general educational qualification. The learning outcomes for this particular course were specified in terms of what the learners would need to be able to do in the military situations they were about to enter rather than in terms of an academic standard of attainment. The decision to examine the learners through an examination at 'colloquial' level possibly reflects the desire to ensure that the learners all achieved a transferable qualification. The course providers clearly wished to avoid the 'washback' effect of being compelled to shape the course to fit the examination specification of the higher level of qualification. Their priority was to prepare the learners for effective service.

The courses focused particularly on the spoken language, as it might be encountered on the ground. However, the teaching methods for the Serbo-Croat courses in most NATO countries were initially based on the traditional 'grammar-translation' approach (Richards and Rodgers 2001: 5–7). This required learners to understand the features of language structure, such as the declension of nouns in different genders and cases and the conjugation of verbs in different persons, tenses and aspects. In Britain, the only textbook available in 1992 was the Routledge guide to colloquial Serbo-Croat (Hawkesworth 1986). It formed the basis of the first six-week course in Colchester, in which learners who already had knowledge of Russian were able to advance at a chapter a day.[9] The following year, a Serbo-Croat guide was published in the 'Teach Yourself' series (Norris 1993). Both books were widely used, though teachers were also required to produce many of their own materials. Responding to the needs of their military learners, British courses adopted a more communicative approach, which had become the most widely accepted framework for language teaching (Brumfit and Johnson 1979). Focused on the needs of the learner rather than the teacher, the approach encouraged the active involvement of the learners, encouraged maximum use of the target language, and emphasized task-based activities related to relevant socio-cultural contexts and using authentic materials.

The Beaconsfield Serbo-Croat course followed this approach, offering learners a simplified understanding of basic grammar but equipping them to be able to follow conversations and formulate appropriate responses. It was particularly innovative in extending simple 'role-play' activities into more complex scenarios, where the learners were required to communicate effectively in the kind of situation they might encounter 'in theatre'. Nick Stansfield, who was the course leader in 1993–4, explained this in detail:

> *Nick Stansfield*: A lot of the course would be based on scenarios, so we would write scenarios based upon what I remembered from Bosnia, being stopped at a checkpoint, meeting a Bosniak liaison officer or a Serbian liaison officer, coming together on the front line, doing a body exchange, and simply scenarios. And then they were told to act out those scenarios using the words that we would give them, and they would go ahead and do that. We used to do telephone conversations with them, and pose problems to them. With someone ringing up, this is a real situation, they ring up, they say my father's just been killed by a sniper, what do I do? And the fact that the guy's still firing at the building, what shall we do? And the guy has to then explain, you know, wait there, we are coming, with our people, we will help, we are coming with our people, we will help you, you know, to safety, kind of thing.[10]

The scenario-based approach had several benefits. First, it was likely to motivate students by confronting them with situations they could expect to encounter on active service, and they could therefore understand the practical purpose of their language learning. Motivation is a fundamental factor in language learning and is recognized as promoting effective acquisition (Dörnyei 2003). Second, if the scenarios were carefully chosen, they would provide a script for the learner to use in real-life situations. The importance of this was recognized by military educators, who made a point of ensuring that the experience of people who had returned from active service could be incorporated in the courses. Louise Robbins recalled her experience:

> *Louise Robbins*: Towards the end of that course we did the military training, the pre-operational training, so we joined together with the infantry and all the other arms and corps to go to Salisbury Plain for two weeks, to stay up all night in the freezing cold...They included serials for the interpreters, so someone would come and drag me out of my sleeping bag at three in the morning, and you just have to pull your boots on and go and do the practice interpreting, so it would be a case where a refugee had turned up at the gate and they were asking for something but the soldiers didn't know what, so I would have to go, and we all did. And so that was how it turned out to be in real life, and so the exercises were based on knowledge of what had gone before, and that's how army exercises are developed, they look back at what happened on Op GRAPPLE 1 and Op GRAPPLE 2, incorporate it into the training for Op GRAPPLE 3 and 4 and subsequent operations.[11]

Operation GRAPPLE in this context was the codename used for the participation of British forces in the UNPROFOR operations in Bosnia-Herzegovina. Robbins's narration clearly situates her language learning scenarios in the military preparation rather than as a separate intellectual exercise. Scenarios and simulations are widely used in military training, for small-scale tasks and for larger operations, up to the level of military exercises. This approach was therefore recognized and accepted by the learners as an appropriate way to learn. As the Bosnian conflict developed, more elaborate scenarios were developed, and some use was made of the village on Salisbury Plain that had been modified to simulate a Bosnian village. Similar exercises were also conducted in Germany. Whereas the use of these simulations was commonplace in military training, this was probably the first time that language issues had been incorporated in such a simulation.[12]

Scenarios posed challenges for the language teachers. The majority of them were civilian native speakers, who had no previous experience of military service. It was difficult for them to devise appropriate scenarios and to assess the language resources they might require. Gregory Cook, an adviser to DSL, noted:

> *Gregory Cook*: The trainers were recruited, you know, in the normal way, an advertisement placed, people came for interview, and they were selected. So very little military teaching. Because we didn't really have many trainers who spoke Serbo-Croat, and so we were in the situation of having trainers who on the whole were non-military teaching military students a military foreign language. And that's one of the drawbacks of using civilians, of course, is that they don't necessarily know the military terminology either in English or in their own language.
>
> *Catherine Baker*: So what can you do to bring civilians up to speed on that?
>
> *Gregory Cook*: Ask them to read the (laughs) I mean basically, they're told that they've got to get up to speed. They're mainly lexical items, you know, types of weaponry, types of rounds, little bit on tactics, but on the whole, what you can do is you can produce a general military vocabulary, so that while it may be difficult for the personnel who first start, the next people that come along, they've got a basically a vocabulary list.[13]

The small number of military Serbo-Croat speakers, including Cook and Stansfield, were expected to provide technical advice on the specific military requirements of language courses. Vocabulary was perhaps the easiest gap to fill, but as the conflict continued, a more detailed specification was developed, based on experience:

> *Gregory Cook*: What was done was that a team went out to ... in theatre, and analysed the job that the linguists were actually being asked to do on the ground, as opposed to what we thought they were being asked to do. And that produced a whole set of what we call training objectives, and scenarios and various tasks, that the linguists at all levels were actually being asked to do in, in the operational theatre. And that then guided course design. And so course design was altered to make sure that those objectives were fulfilled, so that people could go out and actually do what they were being asked to do.[14]

The development of training objectives, tasks and scenarios put the language courses on a more professional basis and sought to ensure that the courses were fit for the purpose of equipping personnel to function effectively in the language situations they would meet. The extent to which the courses succeeded in their purpose is not so easy to assess.

The tasks of specialist linguists

The role of the specialist linguist was varied and often unpredictable. In a technical sense, they were graded as 'linguists' or 'interpreters', but the distinction was a fuzzy one. The British use of the term 'military interpreter' was particularly misleading, since it was used with at least three meanings. The first was a level of proficiency, closely associated with the Civil Service categories, indicating competence at STANAG level 4, roughly equivalent to degree level. The second meaning was a specialist function, designating military personnel who carried out the function of interpreting between NATO officers and speakers of other languages, mostly the local language. And the third meaning was a general function relating to military personnel who had a working level of knowledge of the local language, which could be called upon for any purpose as needs arose. Hence, Milos Stankovic, Nick Stansfield and Louise Robbins referred to themselves at different times as interpreters, although they had quite different levels of expertise and roles.

Stankovic was initially deployed as part of a group of 'interpreters', when this was understood in the third meaning, as one of his colleagues put it: 'interpreters, you know, anyone who can speak the lingo' (Stankovic 2000: 48). He was 'comfortable being the "mouth" informally or during low-key affairs', rather than doing formal interpreting (Stankovic 2000: 238). His profile corresponded to the tasks for which specialist linguists were trained to the STANAG level of 3 or above, which was the minimum professional level. The current version of the standard sets the expectation that people qualified at this level 'can converse in most formal and informal situations; discuss abstract topics; support opinions; hypothesise; deal with unfamiliar topics and situations; describe in detail; clarify points' (Lewis 2012: 63). In the Bosnian operations, this corresponded to routine levels of language use, as Gregory Cook explained:

> *Gregory Cook*: Well, if you look at an active operational theatre, leaving out intelligence completely, language duties would involve going out with a patrol, a six-man patrol or a ten-man patrol or something of that nature, maybe on foot, maybe in a vehicle, coming across a road block, an illegal road block, having to talk to the, you know, these people would be armed, so you've got a potential conflict

> situation, negotiating the removal of a road block, for example, or an illegal checkpoint... interviewing locals, if there'd been an incident, if you're going into a village, being able to talk to perhaps the local headman, or whatever he might be, mayor, or dignitary... generally finding out perhaps what the local population feel, towards the forces, so pretty hands on operational stuff. It could be to do with civilian matters, evacuating a civilian to a field hospital or to medical facilities or something like that. But fairly low-level active accompanying the soldiery out on foot.[15]

Low-level activities were considered to be within the competence of linguists trained for nine to 12 months, and would not generally involve sustained or intensive use of the language. They involved mediating between the military and the local population, where problem solving was at least as valuable a skill as linguistic proficiency. Louise Robbins, for example, encountered several incidents which tested her language and problem-solving skills. When a British soldier took a Croatian flag as a trophy, she had to negotiate with the distressed owner of the flag and arrange for it to be returned. When local militia were firing their rifles outside the gates of the army compound, she had to establish why and negotiate for them to stop. She also organized multinational sporting fixtures, including a five-nation football tournament and a three-nation rugby match:

> *Louise Robbins:* I organized some rugby, soldiers, officers, especially officers, they want to play rugby, they always bring their rugby boots. So I set up a rugby match with the French unit that was in the same base in Divulje Barracks in Split, and I found myself interpreting between... French captain, Croatian man, and I was going through Serbo-Croat, Croatian, through English (laughs) in my head, to French, and back. And I don't know how many languages that you have, but you know, L5 was interfering with L2, and you know, when you've had an intensive course in a new language it can interfere with your recall of the languages that you've spoken fluently for quite some time. That was interesting and challenging.[16]

The episode is a reminder that the role of military linguist is not confined to working between two languages, but frequently involves other languages. Robbins' second language (L2) was French and Croatian her fifth (L5). She also spoke German and Russian. On the one hand, this suggests that the role of military interpreter is more challenging than could be envisaged or prepared for. On the other hand, it emphasizes that linguists are often acting in multilingual contexts and bring a range of linguistic resources to the task. Most of the British linguists in the Balkans already had a good grasp of one or more other languages, usually French from their formal education, German from being stationed in Germany and Russian from military training.

Beyond the low-level support for operations on the ground, linguists were also required for a range of higher level tasks, as Gregory Cook explains:

> *Gregory Cook*: Then at the medium tactical level you would have a linguist in headquarters, advising the commanding officer, who might need advice on a range of matters, in his area. Somebody able to read local notices, newspapers, tell him what was going on. Maybe taken out to act as interpreter at the commanding officer's meetings with local leaders. That type of activity. And then if you go up another notch in the operational theatre, it would be mainly a static job within headquarters, a lot of translation, a lot of interpreting at official meetings, and making a synopsis of what's heard on the radio, seen on the television, in the press, newspapers, and generally giving if you like the native language side of the action to the headquarters.[17]

In the early stages of the campaign, there were very few military linguists with a sufficient level of proficiency in the local language to meet these requirements, and often they were met by locally employed staff with expertise in English. This had the effect of reducing the need for military personnel to carry out these duties and redirecting them into other roles. The military linguists might take a supervisory role in managing language services (see Chapter 3) but were more often directed into roles which used their problem-solving skills and military preparedness. In the case of Milos Stankovic, he saw his role as 'fixer', as he described to his therapist:

> 'Ian, I was a fixer.'
>
> 'A fixer?'
>
> 'Yeah, that's right – a fixer, a sort of go-between ... for the UN, for Rose and Smith ..., you know *'go-and-wave-your-magic-wand'* stuff.'
>
> 'That's the job they gave you?' He sounds incredulous.
>
> 'No, not really. It sort of just happened by accident. It evolved I guess ... by accident.' (Stankovic 2000: 35)

The fixer is a familiar role for linguists and interpreters, who are frequently called on to use both their language skills and their ingenuity to solve problems independently. In the Bosnian operation, it was unusual for military linguists to identify themselves as fixers, though in Stankovic's case he also had personal links with the Serbs and was able to use his ethnic background as a resource to solve problems. Stankovic's combination of language and culture made him a valuable asset and drew him into a much more complex role of liaison and intelligence. His perception was that this happened by accident. Indeed, he was not alone in this perception, as linguists frequently emphasized the unplanned nature of their duties. A potential risk of this broader range of roles was that linguists could easily find themselves in competition with others aspiring to be liaison officers, a highly prized role which offered good opportunities for recognition and promotion. Stankovic certainly encountered this risk, and his successor in post was designated as a liaison officer (Stankovic 2000: 425).

The uncertainties of role also brought opportunities for linguists to have some influence over their own duties, particularly where they held officer rank, as many did. Louise Robbins, for example, was able to find a suitable role when she was deployed:

> *Louise Robbins*: And we were looking around as interpreters thinking, 'Well what are we going to do?' You know, looking for work. And I was in the headquarters one day thinking, 'Well what am I going to do', and suddenly turned up Major T— R—, Royal Engineers, whom I had met on Salisbury Plain during that two weeks training before we deployed. And I had interpreted for him during the training. And we remembered each other, I was delighted to see him, he was delighted to see a familiar face, and I said, 'You're going to need an interpreter.' He said, 'Yes I think I am.' I said, 'Right you've got me.' I said, 'I don't know, they haven't got anything for me to do here, I'm going to support you.' He said 'Fine, stick with me.'[18]

Her success in finding suitable work was no doubt partly due to her officer training, which laid emphasis on initiative and the capacity to act independently. She was able to identify a need and persuade others to accept her solution. It was also of assistance that she was able to draw on a personal link in this case. Shortly afterwards, she met the commander of a second British unit and persuaded him to accept a further proposal:

> *Louise Robbins*: But they were going to need an interpreters' cell, and they needed someone like me to set it up. So that was accepted, you

> know, I found my own work, and it was the best thing ever, because it was hugely satisfying, and I made a difference.[19]

In practice, individual linguists were placed in roles where language expertise was needed, whatever the level of proficiency they possessed. This reflected the nature of conflict, which is often described as 'chaotic', since the needs may change suddenly, responses are based on available resources and decisions are made very rapidly. As the armed conflict subsided, the different roles became more settled and structured, but the military linguists were still deployed in a wide range of roles.

An important use of military linguists was in intelligence work, particularly in human intelligence work, known as HUMINT. This involved, as Eric Wilson, an intelligence officer, put it: 'going out, speaking with the locals and so on, just to gather information about what was happening actually on the ground'.[20] In view of the specialist nature of this activity, intelligence linguists were typically taught on separate courses, and their duties usually required them to operate independently, as Wilson explains:

> *Eric Wilson*: Well, their task, during IFOR, would be to make contact with people on the ground for intelligence purposes. It's not a matter of liaison between fighting units with interpreters... it would be, particularly for intelligence purposes, and possibly even in more informal situations, you know, in a bar, or what have you, rather than having to interpret as part of a street patrol all in full kit or whatever, which is where you're not working through an interpreter. You're using your linguistic skills, and so you, they would have had to improve their linguistic skills immeasurably to be able to do that.
>
> *Catherine Baker*: So what would they have had to do to get to the level they needed to be at?
>
> *Eric Wilson*: Ah... well, further linguistic training, and training in the particular job skills, and experience on the ground, right. Experience on the ground is hugely important, you know, being thrown in and (laughs) and having to do it for real.[21]

The nature of intelligence duties required greater language proficiency than 'low-level' operations, but Wilson emphasizes that the type of proficiency could not easily be learned on a training course. This perception is confirmed by Alma Kovač, who described one of her courses in 2001:

> *Alma Kovač*: But mostly they were very, very, students were very eager to learn. Very motivated, you know. Especially at the beginning.

> Because they felt, it's not just war, you know, it's a … they suffer, people suffer there, and some of them suffered with those people, so that they were eager to go there and to do something, like, you know, British government is not doing anything, but we want to go. Almost like they were, maybe they were volunteers, at the beginning, because they were not, I mentioned one who was a policeman, but they were reservists, so they joined and … yeah. Anything else you … ?
>
> *Catherine Baker*: What would these students of yours have been with their languages in Bosnia?
>
> *Alma Kovač*: Ah. You know, they are intelligence, so …
>
> *Catherine Baker*: Oh, sorry (laughs)
>
> *Alma Kovač*: I don't know (laughs). What they told us is, when the war was there, we want to collect the information about the atrocities, about war criminals, and I know that lots of those documents are in The Hague now. So, later on they were probably, I don't know what … [22]

Kovač could say little about the nature of her students' work, probably because she was given no specific briefing on the subject at the time, and clearly felt the work was too confidential to discuss in detail. She was therefore limited in what she could provide for them. However, if the soldiers maintained their high level of motivation in the field, then it is likely that they would ensure that they developed their language skills in the necessary directions.

Challenging roles

The combination of military and linguistic roles brought complexities to the role of these specialists. At times they might be thought of as being merely a linguistic conduit for the messages of others. Nick Stansfield felt this was a widespread expectation, shared by trained interpreters:

> *Nick Stansfield*: At Molesworth [US base in England], the Americans used to call the interpreters 'lips'. 'Hey, lips!' you know, and the lips would come over and do the interpreting and they were supposed to be invisible. They were simply a pair of lips, and that is the basic principle, that you stand behind the colonel, the Queen, John Major, you know, Margaret Thatcher, whoever it might have been coming out to see us. The Queen never came out (laughs). And just adopt a low profile, and simply do the interpreting, the interpretation, on behalf of this, you know, obviously very important person. It may

> not be such an important person. It may just be, let's say, a very mundane task such as laying gravel on a parking area. One of the logistics sergeants might be explaining to the tractor driver or the local guy, you know, that needs to know how to put this gravel down, how to do it, and the interpreter simply needs to be able to, in an efficient way, give that information across. It's very simple.[23]

This quasi-invisibility was a convention valued at the point of communication, where an untrained interpreter might introduce distractions by asserting their personal presence. It was closely aligned with the stance of professional conference interpreters. The role of 'lips', or in Stankovic's term 'mouth', often provided a more comfortable role for the individual linguist. However, this temporary invisibility while working on a specific interpreting task was also situated in a wider profile of tasks the interpreter might be required to undertake by virtue of their military status, whether in the immediate context of the operation or in the broader context of an individual's military career. The range of situations in which they might take a purely linguistic role was also bounded by their level of expertise.

Both the 'professional' and the 'expert' levels of functionality are characterized by proficiency in the four traditional skills of listening, speaking, reading and writing. Teaching was aimed at raising the level in each of these areas. However, it did not explicitly address the more complex skills of mediation: translation and interpreting. These are separately identified in the *Common European Framework of Reference*, which identifies distinct sets of skills that are required, beyond general oral or written competence (Council of Europe 2001). While the grammar-translation approach to language teaching normally provides some experience in translation as a language learning technique, the military implementation of it placed significantly less emphasis on written competence. And none of the prevailing approaches to teaching provide specific experience in interpreting, which is considered a separate specialist skill. As a result, when they were called on to provide formal interpreting, military linguists were often ill-equipped to respond. Louise Robbins recounts how she found herself out of her depth in a church service held for both British Army and local people:

> *Louise Robbins*: Then the next thing I knew was, our Catholic father called me up to the altar, gave me the microphone, and said, 'Will you interpret please'. And I was (whispers) 'This is a bit of a surprise, they're all laughing at me.' I said, 'OK, I'll do my best.' And one of

> the things he said was, 'Let us pray.' (laughs) I don't know how to say that in Serbo-Croat. And another of the things he'd said was, he wanted me to impart to the congregation how wonderful it is to have been received here so well into this country, and I made the most stupid mistake of not translating what he said, you know interpreters translate meanings not words, and I used the phrase *bivšoj Jugoslaviji* [former Yugoslavia]. And they all went (sucks teeth). And I thought 'Whoops, I mean *u Hrvatskoj* [in Croatia].' Right, so that was one mistake. So that was hugely embarrassing, and it just shows we weren't ready; we weren't ready for those sort of tasks.[24]

It is unlikely that the vocabulary of liturgy would figure in a training scenario for military interpreters, though the sensitivities surrounding the names of emerging countries in the region may well have done. The interpreter was aware of her limitations, but, as the only available resource, she had to perform the task to the best of her abilities. Her mistakes caused embarrassment at the time, though it might well have been even more embarrassing if no language capability were available. As with the colloquial linguists, the roles allocated were frequently beyond the expertise of the military linguist's competence. Stankovic recounts that he was required to undertake a formal interpreting role, as the language intermediary for the British commander, General Sir Michael Rose, and despite being a proficient linguist, he found the interpreting difficult, especially at a meeting with General Ratko Mladić:

> When you're struggling to interpret you can hardly remember a bloody thing that's been said. From my point of view the meeting was a total disaster. I just couldn't keep up with Rose. He rattled away like a machine gun, almost without pause. Forget being able to speak a language. That has no relevance whatsoever when it comes to simultaneous translation. You've actually got to be trained to do that and then you've got to have an almost computer-like brain to do it. I had neither the training nor the brain. It was a nightmare – you'd miss something, panic about missing it and before you know it you've missed the next bloody sentence and then you'd be locked into an unrecoverable, terminal death dive. (Stankovic 2000: 238)

The anxiety of interpreting in the specialist sense is palpable in this description. His lack of training as an interpreter was compounded by the high level of the meeting between Rose and Mladić, and by the fact that the commander made no allowance for the interpreter in his delivery. The experience prompted Stankovic to extract himself from the role of 'formal interpreting', which he felt should be taken by skilled professional interpreters. Given the complexity of the situations they had to confront, it is not surprising that specialists like him and Robbins were plunged into tasks that far exceeded their knowledge and proficiency.

As operations became less hazardous, commanders increasingly found the locally employed civilian interpreters better equipped for the spectrum of specific language support tasks. They also often developed great loyalty to them and preferred to work with them rather than with the military linguists. The preference of commanders for local interpreters often reinforced the uncomfortable position of military interpreters within the operational structure. The experience of Louise Robbins was that she had to find jobs to do, such as attaching herself to a suitable officer. Their position was often compounded by their position in the unit. As Robbins describes:

> *Louise Robbins*: They had some sort of idea where they were going to put us. And the Op GRAPPLE 2 crowd of interpreters, they were already out there, feeding back, saying don't put an interpreter here because there's nothing to do, but we need more interpreters here because there is a lot of work to do. But the plight of... military interpreters is, we get, not literally, but parachuted in. We get plucked out of our wherever we are, our education centres or whatever job we're doing, and dumped in a whole environment with people that we've never met before, whereas, when we went to a brigade headquarters all of the brigade staff knew one another, because they'd worked together in, they were from Germany actually, so I'd deployed from Britain to a German unit, and so they already had their friendships, their protocols, and here we were, these odd people who had different cap badges, they didn't really understand what we were about, and that is the nature of the work. And at the end of the operation you're parachuted or airlifted back out, plonked back in your education centre, never to see any of these people again.[25]

As specialists, they were deployed to wherever their services were thought to be needed. They were therefore not an integral part of the unit and had to work hard to establish their role. This was difficult when the unit's officers did not have a clear grasp of what the specialist could do and may not have been party to the decision to send one. It was even more difficult when the unit already had the services of established local interpreters, who could meet most of their more obvious language needs. And military interpreters were often glad to have the support of the more proficient local specialists. It is interesting to note that Robbins has a slight hesitation before using the term 'military interpreter' to describe herself and her colleagues. She explains further how, when confronted with a particularly difficult meeting, she was delighted to have the support of a local interpreter:

> *Louise Robbins*: D— had been sent by the outgoing G5 person, she was about to get on a plane home, I went, 'I need some help with this meeting, can you tag along?' And she just appeared out of nowhere, sat there, of course she was beautiful, wooed the men, did the interpreting, and again it just proved, we're not ready as interpreters, we're not really interpreters, in five months you just cannot get to that standard, some people could, I was a pretty good linguist, but Slavonic was, you know, that was tough.[26]

The fact that many local interpreters were women, often young and attractive, was certainly a factor in officers preferring to use them for language support (see Chapter 3). But it may have been more important that they had a higher level of expertise in specifically linguistic tasks. They were native speakers of the local language, and they were able to develop their skills in English through constant interaction with the personnel of the unit they worked with. They also generally had no other role than linguist in the unit. In comparison, the military interpreters generally had a lower level of language proficiency in the local language, acquired through training, and had more limited opportunities to develop their language through their work. By contrast, they had a wide range of other skills which could be put to use in the operation. The combination of limited linguistic proficiency with broader military capability led Robbins, at least, to suggest that military interpreters like herself were 'not really interpreters'. No doubt others who had reached a higher level of proficiency and had undertaken longer periods of training may have been more confident in their role as military interpreters. Nick Stansfield, the first military interpreter with the British forces, had no qualms about his language skills, which were at degree level, but did not consider his job to have been solely one of interpreting. While attached to Colonel Bob Stewart, he was 'his driver, interpreter, aide, confidante'.[27] And he recognized that even the very gifted linguists among the military might have more important roles, drawing on their specialist expertise in other aspects of operations, particularly in liaison work.

Conclusion

The work of military interpreters, translators and linguists was challenging and complex. In the first instance, acquiring high-level competence in a foreign language normally required intensive training for a long period. In the case of Bosnian/Croatian/Serbian, it was difficult for native English speakers to learn, even if they already knew two or three other languages. When they were deployed, they were confronted with tasks that called on all of their linguistic and non-linguistic expertise. Their responsibilities were often unpredictable and drew them into wider roles as problem-solvers and even fixers. Even with rigorous and well-designed training programmes, military linguists were often acutely conscious of the limits of their language proficiency and were happy to be supported by locally employed interpreters with native competence in the local language. However, military linguists sometimes had difficulty in finding a suitable role in their deployment. The breadth of their capabilities, the limitations of their language proficiency and the presence of more specialist local linguists challenged their role as military interpreters. Unlike specialist linguists in other walks of life, their professional role was always wider than providing language services, and in many cases their other roles were more highly valued, for example in the area of liaison, where they might be seen as close to the role of designated liaison officers, perhaps uncomfortably so at times.

As the level of violent conflict declined, civilian linguists were able to take over routine work such as accompanying patrols. Military linguists typically assumed a wider range of military roles, many of them focusing on intelligence work and promoting better relationships with the local population. They were particularly valued for their ability to solve problems. In many respects, this was advantageous for the linguists themselves, since they were more likely to gain recognition and promotion for their contribution to military objectives than for their specifically linguistic expertise. The shifting balance between expertise in language and in other military disciplines meant that military interpreters rarely functioned as invisible language intermediaries and were often most comfortable when they were called upon to deploy all of their different capabilities.

3
Language Support on the Ground under UNPROFOR

Viewed from the perspective of members of a foreign military, the process of deploying to Bosnia-Herzegovina or a new area within it represented the performance for real of the tasks, duties and practices they had begun to learn during pre-deployment preparations and training. Among these preparations were the decisions about the length and content of language training, and about who should receive it, discussed in Chapter 1. The work of arranging for language support 'on the ground', at headquarters, battalion or company level, was thus for foreign soldiers a second phase of a language encounter that had originated in their home country. However, the militaries that took part in peace support operations did not meet their language needs universally or even primarily from their own ranks. From 1992 onwards, they would recruit thousands of native speakers of Bosnian, Croatian and Serbian to work as 'interpreters', language intermediaries whose roles sometimes in fact blurred written translation and spoken interpreting. Foreign militaries thus became one of the most significant international employers in the new economy that emerged in Bosnia as a result of conflict and intervention. The language encounters of the locally-recruited language intermediaries – which could last up to twenty years for the longest-serving interpreters – began when foreign troops moved into a town, opening a new base and beginning to offer work.

The trade-off between meeting language support needs internally and hiring local people to interpret and translate was faced by every military that participated in the multinational force. Using one's own soldiers as the language intermediaries provided advantages of trust both in terms of operational security and in terms of relying on the linguist to be able to defend themselves in a confrontation. However, this choice brought disadvantages of number (insufficient military linguists and colloquial speakers had been trained) and quality (apart from a few heritage speakers, militaries' own language intermediaries did not have native-speaker-level proficiency in the local language). Locally hired language intermediaries, though citizens who could not be security cleared, had proficiency in the local language that very few foreign language intermediaries could match. Logistically, they were cheaper to recruit and would free a trained soldier up for other tasks. Expeditionary forces throughout history have been faced with the same tense decision (see Footitt and Kelly (eds) 2012a): how far to spare their own personnel for language duties, how far to trust local people to deliver an accurate interpretation and keep their work confidential and how far to mediate their communication through a native speaker of the troops' own language or a native speaker of the locals' language or languages?

The power relations involved in this decision have been explored by the Translation Studies scholar Michael Cronin (2002) through the lens of colonial occupations. The power-exerting institutions of any occupation need to gather information on the basis of knowledge expressed in the languages that are foreign to them and local to the indigenous inhabitants; in exerting power, they must also interact through language with those they govern and dominate. Two approaches were open to imperial powers, and were often blended. One was for the occupier to train its own agents 'in the language or languages of the colonized', what Cronin refers to as an 'autonomous' system. The other was to teach 'the imperial language' to the local people, a system Cronin terms 'heteronomous' (Cronin 2002: 393). Either of these solutions has one party operating in a non-native language and thus communicating in a medium that is relatively foreign to them.

The scales and time frames of these approaches could vary. Language encounters could be managed entirely through a class of intermediaries, whether recruited autonomously or heteronomously; more ambitiously, education (in schools and other institutions such as the Church) could train locals in the imperial language as their first language with the effect of eradicating other, indigenous languages and systems of knowledge (Comaroff and Comaroff 1991, 1997). Peace operations in Bosnia-Herzegovina and other such sites are, of course, towards the more temporary end of this scale. Their impact on local languages was nowhere near as total as the education projects of colonial missionaries had been, even though some interviewees expressed concerns about the spread of anglicisms and English-based neologisms into the wider local language from what Steven Sampson (1996: 123) has described as 'project-speak'. Peace operations contain an overt drive to reshape local societies around norms that are considered preconditions for a lasting peace (Paris 2002), but they are not framed by those who carried them out as occupation or colonization (Higate and Henry 2009: 56), even though people inside and outside the region who reject the force's mandate may consider them to be either or both. Nonetheless, a common challenge of enabling an international staff of thousands to communicate with a local population is present in peace operations just as it was in the much more pervasive exertions of power described by Cronin.

As a site for peace operations, Bosnia-Herzegovina threw up the additional challenge that the local language was little spoken in the troop-contributing nations. The language training programmes discussed in Chapter 1 could not, and were not designed to, produce enough personnel to meet the militaries' needs in Cronin's 'autonomous' way, and it was thus essential to hire interpreters locally. The addition of US ground troops to the military coalition in Bosnia-Herzegovina after December 1995 would bring with it a middle-ground solution of hiring civilian contractors, citizens of the home country who were also native or heritage speakers of the local language: they received a rudimentary level of training to enable them to function in a military environment, were kept separate from locally recruited interpreters and could be used for intelligence-related tasks in the same way that foreign militaries used their own linguists (Rovegno, Hajdari and Perezic 2003). However, this later practice was not in use when the UNPROFOR members acquired their own experiences of establishing language support in the field. These early language services were heavily dependent on locally hired interpreters and were characterized by a high degree of improvisation.

British language support in central Bosnia

British forces began contributing to peace operations in Bosnia-Herzegovina in November 1992, after a United Nations decision in August 1992 to extend its peacekeeping role in former Yugoslavia to that republic. This deployment expanded the scope of the multinational United Nations Protection Force (UNPROFOR), which had been stationed since February 1992 in four demilitarized zones of Croatia, on the front line between Croatian forces and the JNA, since February 1992. The UN Security Council had initially hesitated to send a peacekeeping force to Bosnia-Herzegovina when hostilities broke out there in April 1992. In August 1992, after the exposure of concentration camps in territory held by Bosnian Serb forces, a Security Council resolution authorized the UN to use 'all measures necessary' to deliver humanitarian assistance.[1] The British contribution began with a battalion (BRITBAT 1) based in the central Bosnian town of Vitez, and before the reorganization of foreign forces in December 1995 would gradually extend into Gornji Vakuf, Tuzla, Maglaj, Bugojno and Goražde.

UNPROFOR's mission required the units that composed it to move as far into Bosnia-Herzegovina as possible, setting up bases on the way; to establish a presence in contested territory; to talk their way through checkpoints (a source of high stress for local interpreters); and to cope with the shifting front lines as local forces gained or lost ground and alliances broke down. Controversially, the UNPROFOR mandate did not allow it to impose a settlement through prevailing force on what the intervention termed the 'warring factions' (see Gow 1997; Burg and Shoup 2000). Contributing a battalion to this endeavour in Bosnia-Herzegovina placed logistical demands on UK forces that greatly exceeded the demands of its contribution to UNPROFOR in Croatia: this had been a medical battalion, 24 Field Ambulance, which was based in Zagreb and available to support other countries' UNPROFOR battalions in the Protected Areas. The hinge of knowledge that enabled a transfer of experience from deployment in Croatia to deployment in Bosnia-Herzegovina turned out to be Nick Stansfield, who was later to become the Serbo-Croat course leader at DSL (Chapter 2). Stansfield was a captain in the Royal Army Educational Corps (RAEC) who had studied Russian and Serbo-Croat at the University of Nottingham and joined the British Army in 1986. Between 1986 and 1992 he had been a military Russian interpreter and arms control inspector with the Joint Arms Control Implementation Group and then an instructor at the Army Apprentice College in Harrogate. In 1992, his self-reported language skills saw him sent on a six-week refresher course in what the Army still routinely called 'Serbo-Croat' and deployed to Zagreb with 24 Field Ambulance (where he produced the Army's first set of language cards for former Yugoslavia). In August 1992, he was included in a UK Land Forces (UKLF) reconnaissance party to Bosnia-Herzegovina that marked the beginning of what would be many months of involvement in Bosnia as British forces' major source of linguistic and language-management expertise.

Stansfield considered he had been included in the reconnaissance party, which sought to find base locations and supply routes for the future BRITBAT 1, as a 'known quantity' who would be 'reliable', 'trustable' and 'unbiased' in interpreting between locals and the senior British officers. This more than outweighed his local language proficiency, which was excellent by British standards but still not that of a native speaker:

> *Nick Stansfield*: [I]f you ask my own opinion on it, obviously my skills were still developing at that stage, so there were clearly... better English, well, perfect Serbo-Croat speakers who were from the country, but really good English speakers who could do a fantastic job, but the belief was then that a British officer or British service personnel would be more reliable to do that.[2]

UKLF's summer reconnaissance missions in 1992 established many of the key sites for the British military experience in Bosnia-Herzegovina. The rear headquarters would be Divulje Barracks in the Croatian port city of Split, and thousands of British troops, including dozens of military interpreters and colloquial speakers, would enter 'the Balkans' or 'theatre' through this location. They would then cross the Croatian/Bosnian border transfer along what the reconnaissance missions established as the Main Supply Route to their destination bases in central Bosnia such as Vitez, Travnik and Gornji Vakuf.

As interpreter to BRITBAT 1's first commanding officer, Lt Col Bob Stewart of The Cheshire Regiment, Stansfield viewed his role as 'making sure he [Stewart] got as much information in order to make his command decisions on the ground.'[3] Other duties ranged from ordering a sniper to vacate the grounds of the British base to translating medical reports, instructing local maintenance workers, negotiating at checkpoints and arranging liaison meetings between local military commanders and Stewart. In the long run, however, Stansfield was a strong advocate of the use of locally hired language intermediaries for any tasks that did not require a military-trained UK citizen.[4] As a military educator, he developed a language support model with an element of training that would often be absent from later language services managed within a logistics chain of command:

> *Nick Stansfield*: It was really challenging. And I think I was instrumental in proving that – not proving but convincing them, really – that actually: local guys, you just need them, because we simply don't have enough in the British forces to put out, and there are many officers who are very gifted linguists – and non-officers, NCOs and so on – soldiers who are very gifted linguists but who have got very important jobs to do, and they can't be necessarily used as, they're better used in their actual roles, whether it be tank commander or

> Royal Signals specialist or whatever, they're better in those roles than actually being used as an interpreter. The whole point is about training, if you like, younger people, or people with a basic ability to become really, really good at interpreting.[5]

British forces' first locally hired interpreters were recruited from the Vitez area as soon as the troops arrived there in November–December 1992. The work of expanding and training this interpreting team in early 1993 would coincide with the outbreak in central Bosnia of a separate conflict between the Sarajevo government's forces (ABiH) and the Croat Defence Council (HVO) over territories the HVO had expected to be awarded under the newly published Vance–Owen Peace Plan. This confrontation began in Gornji Vakuf and spread out along the towns of the Lašva valley, including Vitez and Travnik, making BRITBAT 1's negotiation and liaison tasks more complex and the situation for its troops and local interpreters more dangerous yet.

Against this background, Stansfield and the Cheshire Regiment's technical quartermaster undertook the work of assembling a team of local interpreters – a job with very little precedent. The Cheshires' urgency in recruiting interpreters had been increased by advice given to Stewart by Lt Col Michel Jones, the commanding officer of a Canadian battalion from the Royal 22e Régiment whom Stewart had met during the first reconnaissance. Hiring approximately 15 interpreters, Jones recommended, should be one of the battalion's first priorities, along with selecting skilled and trustworthy liaison officers, making use of a national intelligence system to circumvent the shortcomings of the UN information network and impressing the local forces with the noise, size and numbers of its armoured personnel carriers (Stewart 1993: 37). BRITBAT's very first interpreter was hired informally when the Cheshires' advance party entered Vitez:

> Luckily Major Alan Abraham, B Squadron Commander, had located a woman who might be able to do the job and so we went around to her flat close to Hotel Vitez. After coffee, she agreed to a salary of 200 Deutschmarks – the best currency to use in Bosnia – and we had our interpreter. (Stewart 1993: 83)

The process that began with this very informal agreement was characterized by Stansfield as 'very ad hoc'.[6] He noted also that '[p]eople were not trained to recruit interpreters' or to evaluate the skills of prospective interpreters who approached the battalion for work.[7] Interpreters in this model were paid from battalion funds, given a British Army uniform (without flags or insignia) for purposes of practicality and anonymity and accommodated in houses rented by the battalion for officers' use (later British bases housed interpreters in the same Corimec containers used for enlisted soldiers' accommodation). Interpreters spent duty hours in a translation office from where supervisors would call them for particular tasks, for instance to accompany a liaison officer and driver on an off-base visit (this was considered to require the highest standard of English from interpreters) or to go out with the regular foot and vehicle patrols.

The reproduction of experience

Stansfield's supervisory role, explaining what it meant to be an interpreter and what BRITBAT 1 was in Vitez to achieve, was passed on to the military interpreters posted to Vitez to replace him. These included Milos Stankovic, a captain in the Parachute Regiment, and Fred Whitaker, one of the most experienced language instructors in the British Army. The differences between Stankovic's and Whitaker's narratives of this aspect of their posting make clear that language knowledge was not sufficient to make a suitable interpreter trainer. Stankovic, who stayed on in Vitez as the military interpreter after 1st Battalion, Prince of Wales's Own Regiment of Yorkshire (1 PWO) relieved the Cheshires, chafed at the supervisory responsibilities such as drawing up leave rotas which prevented him getting out into the field on exciting missions that, with his Parachute Regiment background, he found most fulfilling: 'my main preoccupation was being mother to the local interpreters, of whom I'd been put in charge' (Stankovic 2000: 174). Claire Duncanson (2009: 67) reads Stankovic's memoir, in common with other published British UNPROFOR memoirs, as expressing an 'idealized notion of the brave, heroic, strong warrior' which rested on a 'hegemonic military masculinity' opposed to femininity. His reference to 'being mother' suggests that he saw the supervision of interpreters as an outright opposite to what he believed the core tasks of soldiers should be.

Whitaker, in contrast, was a career Army educator and thrived as a supervisor of interpreters. He exemplified the observation of Rachel Woodward and K. Neil Jenkings (2011: 258–9) that, viewing the military from a wider perspective than the specialist domain of combat soldiers, '[t]he possession of professional skills and expertise', combined with 'an aptitude and willingness...to use such skills in extreme and hostile environments, for the sake of a wider military objective', is itself a marker of military identity. Whitaker thus spoke at length about the improvements (including rudimentary language testing) he had made in collaboration with the unofficial senior interpreter, a former teacher named Dobrila Kalaba. Whitaker considered that failure to brief interpreters affected the quality of their work and thus the quality of what could be achieved by British forces, who depended on their language mediation:

> *Fred Whitaker*: [T]here were times when interpreters would be picked up, if I can use that expression, in the morning, somebody would come by the room where all the interpreters sat, and say 'Right, we're off,' and put them in the back of a Warrior armoured personnel carrier, and then they'd drive off somewhere, and then they'd arrive wherever they were going, and they'd open the door, and out would come the interpreter. And the interpreter wouldn't know where they were, who they were going to meet, what the reason for the meeting was. This sort of thing, I think, was common. And it – I think it did get a little better, but I don't think it went nearly so far as it should have done, and I think that lack of proper briefing of the interpreter was a drawback.[8]

Whitaker also identified a number of obstacles to effective language support management. One of them was the killing of Kalaba by a sniper in July 1993, a sad event noted in many published and oral British narratives from Vitez. Others were potential 'clash[es] of interests between what the battalion wanted and what the interpreters were capable of doing', supervisory conflicts where more than one officer wanted to work with the same interpreter, and the endemic problem that British (and most other foreign) tours of duty only lasted six months:

> *Fred Whitaker*: For the first month you're learning your job. If you were like me, and the situation in Bosnia was completely unlike anything I had experienced before, then finding your feet in that did take a little time. And then you got drawn into all the operational activities of the unit, and so there were times when you were very busy. And some times when you weren't very busy. There were also times when you were away for a period on extended patrols, I spent quite a lot of my time with the United Kingdom Liaison Officers, who tended to go out for much longer, to various locations in the British area, and so…there was no real opportunity to have a concerted development plan for the interpreters. All you could do was

> what you could in the circumstances, and...more could have been done, certainly.[9]

After the initial phase of set-up, maintaining a language service in a military context where troops rotated in and out meant learning from others again and again. This was particularly important when the British contribution to UNPROFOR expanded from one battalion to two in February 1994 and the Vitez model had to be reproduced in a new battalion headquarters. The opening of any new base, whether through an expansion of forces or a change in a unit's area of responsibility, began with a similar reconnaissance process to the UKLF expedition of August 1992 but on a smaller scale. A location had to be found, usually in an abandoned factory, subsidiary bases and outposts would have to be located too, and the logistics team would have to identify suppliers for goods and services that it was most practical to buy in the local area. Among these requirements was the work of local interpreters, who would supplement the limited number of military personnel able to communicate directly with the population.

The second British battalion (BRITBAT 2) was based first in Bugojno and later in the UN Safe Area of Goražde, and was first constituted by 1st Battalion, the Duke of Wellington's Regiment (1 DWR). As the first standing UN presence in Bugojno, 1 DWR had to recruit its interpreters from scratch. The military linguist attached to 1 DWR, Capt Louise Robbins, was one of the graduates from Stansfield's course at Beaconsfield and had been serving as a military linguist at Divulje Barracks until she was recommended to the battalion (Chapter 2). Her duties in Bugojno, recruiting a new team of local interpreters and carrying out some assignments of her own, were similar to those of the military colloquial speakers in Vitez. Robbins, like Whitaker, was a serendipitous choice for this type of role, having worked as an Army language advisor at the Tidworth education centre who organized colloquial-level courses and oversaw all Army language training in her military district. She was able to pass on teaching and learning experiences from the Beaconsfield course to the local interpreting team:

> *Louise Robbins*: I trained them, during quiet times, when there weren't many patrols, we would sit and do training exercises. I would do what we'd done on our Serbo-Croat course, set up a situation and say, 'OK you're the local, you're the interpreter, and I'll play the military,' and we'd run through a dry run. Because...people need training in using interpreters, because otherwise how would they know?[10]

Robbins understood the supervisory role as a protective relationship standing between young, vulnerable civilian interpreters and bureaucratic military procedures. She considered, for instance, that the supervisor should take personal responsibility for the safe equipping of interpreters:

> *Louise Robbins*: But I got them boots, combat trousers, combat jackets, helmets, flak jackets. I had to do a lot of arm-twisting of the quartermaster and the quartermaster's staff. He said, 'I know what you're doing, you're looking after your troops, it's what no-one else will do.' And I said, 'well, they won't work without this.' You can't send soldiers out with flak jackets on and protection and the interpreters without, because a bullet will go straight through them, you know, it's not fair.[11]

On other occasions, this might involve bending rules or exploiting gaps in policy for the sake of interpreters' wellbeing:

> *Catherine Baker*: What was the age limit [to work as an interpreter]?
>
> *Louise Robbins*: You had to be 18 to work for the UN. And the UN always asked on the employment forms, 'do you have a member of your family already employed by the UN?' And I used to tell them to write 'no'. Because the UN had a policy of, I suppose they called it fairness. Only one family member was allowed to have a job with the UN. And I said yeah, just write 'no' and plead ignorance. Because otherwise you won't get the job. And I needed them. Every patrol needed an interpreter.[12]

In the British Army, the role of the military interpreter in Bosnia-Herzegovina had clearly emerged through practice rather than policy, initially in as informal a way as a dialogue about expectations between Stansfield and Stewart. Everyday interpreting tasks were performed by the local interpreters and military colloquial speakers who provided most of the British forces' language support in numerical terms. However, senior British officers, up to and including the British generals who commanded UNPROFOR in Bosnia-Herzegovina (Gen Michael Rose and Lt Gen Rupert Smith), depended on a small number of individuals like Stansfield with fluent 'Serbo-Croat', who operated at a higher level of proficiency than the short-course graduates (Chapters 1–2). These interpreters would blend interpreting duties with a liaison role, reporting directly to the commander, and they generally spent much longer in Bosnia-Herzegovina than the usual six-month tour of duty.

Stansfield was all but alone in the British forces in having a degree-level education in Serbo-Croat. Stansfield's successive replacements, Nick Ilić and Milos Stankovic, had instead acquired their language knowledge as heritage speakers, the sons of Serb fathers; however, they deployed under pseudonyms (Nick 'Costello' and 'Mike Stanley') in order to conceal their ethnic origin and protect their neutrality. In principle, with their South Slav backgrounds concealed, they would be insulated from intimidation, exploitation or mistrust at the hands of local power-holders. In practice, their local interlocutors tended to assume that internationals must be ethnically South Slav in order to attain fluency at all and smiled at the subterfuge.[13] If the local force's relationship with the peacekeepers broke down, however, they would challenge the pseudonym and threaten the military interpreter. The British Army's third heritage speaker, a corporal in the Royal Anglian Regiment ('Nick Abbott'), had to be sent home after three months when the HVO exposed him as a Serb. Stankovic's memoir retells an incident where a VRS colonel in Srebrenica accused him of being a Bosniak spy and he reluctantly told the story of his Serb relatives' gravestone in southern Serbia. At the end of the visit, a powerful Bosniak threatened to kill him if he returned because 'we know all about the graveyard' (Stankovic 2000: 161–6). The heritage speaker was a prized but risky resource, scarce in number and all too easily burned out.

The tension between the advantages and disadvantages of using a local or international interpreter was at its sharpest during the UNPROFOR years, when the risks were greatest and the violence worst. Local interpreters did go on some liaison visits, but for them to accompany a liaison officer on information-gathering tasks could cause, Fred Whitaker recalled:

> *Fred Whitaker*: ... problems with ethnic allegiances, and also the worry sometimes of putting an interpreter in a difficult position ... and so to take a member of the British forces, who had at least a knowledge of the language sufficient to carry out the task, was probably better.[14]

Local interpreters might also be tempted to intervene in the transfer of information or pass that information on in order to benefit 'the people from their own community' rather than 'the job they were doing', so that the military could never have full trust in their activities.[15] Whitaker further considered that local interpreters' generally young age and lack of military training might put them under too much pressure when they accompanied the first British battalions on their most harrowing tasks, such as clearing up the site of the infamous massacre at Ahmići or arranging a body exchange between manipulative local commanders. These reservations were echoed by other British military linguists who had served during and after the UNPROFOR period (Chapter 6). Nonetheless, the basic operational standard of military colloquial speakers, who were the backbone of the Army's internal language support, did not leave them fluent enough to cope with complicated interpreting tasks over a wide range of unprepared topics, making communication through a local interpreter more comfortable.[16] The burden of negotiating the balancing act between accuracy, security, skill, cost and availability fell on the multinational force at every level, from headquarters to observation posts.

The supervisory relationship and its limitations

Improvisation was the watchword as the British Army established itself in central Bosnia. The unprecedented demand for language support, met by the instruction to 'just crack on'[17] (as Stewart had told the Cheshires' technical quartermaster) and devise a system, was simply one dimension of the challenges described by Col Alastair Duncan, the commanding officer of 1 PWO, a year after returning from his regiment's stint as BRITBAT 1:

> On reflection back in the Battalion's base in Germany I realised that Bosnia was a very unique area and the task equally unique. There was no template to be drawn from my experiences in the Army and the easy solution of 'it has worked somewhere else so it will work here' was clearly a non-starter. It wasn't a task the British Army had done before. It was unusual to be in a war but not at war; we were effectively sitting right in the middle of somebody else's civil war. (Duncan 1994: 47)

Over time, a growing awareness of the nature of the mission and the fortunate presence of experienced language instructors as military linguists in Vitez enabled a rudimentary set of management norms to be developed. Supervisors learned when interpreters were likely to be in most demand and came to understand the potential for interpersonal conflicts in interpreter allocation. They attempted to limit the civilians' working hours, insofar as possible in the unpredictable environment of a military base during wartime. Whitaker, in collaboration with Dobrila Kalaba, attempted to establish a more rigorous recruitment and testing procedure than had existed previously, and drew on his own understanding of linguist performance to make the recommendation that local interpreters should be briefed in advance. Sometimes this last provision would be sacrificed to the operational security recommendation not to brief interpreters until the last minute in case plans leaked out and put troops at risk: even some local interpreters who had not started work until the mid-1990s reported setting off on jobs with no idea of their destination.

Linguist–supervisors, meanwhile, faced severe pressures in the competing demands on their own time as well as the stress of many interpreting situations. Their duties in Bosnia-Herzegovina fell into an awkward middle ground between the traditional concept of a military interpreter and the highly prized role of a liaison officer, which regiments sought for their own captains. Educators flourished as supervisors, but military interpreters from other units might struggle. Stankovic, a particularly reluctant supervisor, noted that by the time he left theatre in January 1995 his replacement, Capt Tom Dibb, was officially described as a liaison officer to the VRS rather than an interpreter (Stankovic 2000: 425) – implying that by then it had been recognized that the person in that role was not supposed to waste time as an interpreter supervisor. Dibb was not expected to manage a team of interpreters in addition to his liaison work – although, ironically enough, his own replacement later in the year would be none other than Fred Whitaker, on his second of three tours of duty in former Yugoslavia.

The institution of the responsible and protective military supervisor, created in Vitez by a core of British Army language instructors, was reproduced through time as new military interpreters rotated in and out. The institution was also transferred through space with the establishment of BRITBAT 2 in 1994. A further transfer of experience and practice then took place when two companies from 1 DWR deployed to Goražde in May 1994, bringing several local interpreters from Bugojno along. The mismatch between 1 DWR's tour dates and those of their interpreting supervisor Robbins, an individual attachment, meant that she had already returned to the UK by this point. However, the practices she had instituted did not immediately vanish when she left. An account by the first resident of Goražde to be employed as an interpreter alongside the Bugojno team reflects strategies for improving speaking skills and suggests that the supportive disposition of the Bugojno working environment had travelled with the group: 'Start thinking in English,' he remembered them telling him. 'That was the first time ever to hear something like that from anyone.... So instead of thinking about a cake on a plate in your own language, start thinking into English about that.'[18] At the same time, the Bugojno interpreters passed on their coping strategies for adjusting to the alien everyday culture of the British garrison, from advice as to which foods to pick in the mess hall to a warning about the inexplicable British custom of putting milk in tea.

However, a less pleasant theme of Robbins's experience in Bugojno, the troubled relationship between UN procedure and the reality on the ground, was magnified in Goražde. Local interpreters were not supposed to receive an employment contract before they had passed the UN test. In the absence of Robbins or a replacement, no military interpreter was available to administer the test in Goražde, and BRITBAT 2 had to wait four months before a UN testing team came from Sarajevo. In the meantime, the employee from Goražde was hired informally with payment in kind, on the understanding that he would be sacked if he eventually failed the test. The bureaucratic technology of identification, meanwhile, continued to prove itself unsuitable for a conflict zone and a refugee population. Robbins had reported in Bugojno that the procedure for obtaining a UN ID card required interpreters to supply a photograph, which a refugee might not be able to supply: one interpreter had had to cut up a cherished family photograph for this purpose. In Goražde too, an interpreter used an elementary school photograph for his ID card, which went back to HQ UNPROFOR Sarajevo for processing.

A third actor in the employment relationship, the local authorities, made its interfering presence felt in both sites. The local authorities in Bugojno forced the UN to pay half the local employees' salaries to the town hall on the pretext of reducing the disturbance to the town's economy. Even more seriously, the ABiH military command in Goražde was so suspicious of local interpreters – because they frequently crossed front lines with the British and had contact with the VRS – that they harassed one female interpreter into quitting her job and imprisoned two male interpreters in the spring of 1995. Emir Suljagić, who worked as an interpreter for UNPROFOR in Srebrenica, recalled similar experiences in his memoir *Razglednice iz groba/Postcards from the Grave*: soon after starting work, he states, he was confronted by the town's military commander Naser Orić who accused him of passing on information to one of Orić's rivals in the local power struggle. Orić and his closest allies interviewed him the next day, but he recorded no further interference from the local elite (Suljagić 2005: 115–16).

The imprisonments in Goražde were the most extreme cases of harassment the authors heard themselves. In many more towns, however, the multinational force's civilian staff were vulnerable to local authorities' attempts to frustrate and confound the UN. For instance, one woman who had worked during the war for the UN Military Observers' office in Pale, the site of the VRS headquarters, remembered that the local authorities had forced the UN to break its policy that local staff should not have other employment in order that she and a colleague should teach at a nearby primary school on top of their eight-hour shifts as interpreters.[19] Effective military supervisors could protect the interests of their local employees on the army base itself, but during the instability of the war they had far less power when faced with antagonistic local commanders and mayors.

Spatial, social and sexual relations

A full understanding of how interpreting teams functioned requires consideration not just of their interpersonal relationships but also of the spatial contexts within which they worked. Field interpreting, where interpreters were used primarily for visits and patrols rather than on-site work, was a distinctive spatial experience situated within the space of a foreign military base. The participants in peace operations can be viewed as 'actively and necessarily creat[ing] and maintain[ing] spaces of security and insecurity' (Higate and Henry 2009: 17). This perspective is well illustrated by the close-knit environment of the base at Vitez, which represented an immersive workplace, living quarters and social space for interpreters as well as soldiers and became a model for the spatial management of interpreters on other bases. Both during and after 1992–5, bases that required interpreters to be available around the clock would provide them with accommodation, typically two or four interpreters to a single-sex room or accommodation container. The improvised nature of the Vitez base also saw interpreters put up in one of several houses rented from local residents by the British Army. Improvisations were made by other components of UNPROFOR in similar ways. In besieged Sarajevo, sleeping quarters were set aside for interpreters in the former telecommunications building where UNPROFOR had its HQ, though some still chose to return home every night and stay with their families.

Arrangements for interpreters' accommodation and access to areas of the base were worked out at the discretion of base commanders (which could be delegated to the officer in charge of the interpreters' cell), within the broader security policies of their national contingent. Experiences could therefore differ between two nearby bases belonging to one force or even on the same base when troop rotations placed a different commander in charge. Interpreters in Vitez had been allowed to join the officers' mess, but the same practice did not take root among 1 DWR. In Louise Robbins's account of Bugojno, the officers' mess was the limiting point of the equality between troops and interpreters:

> *Louise Robbins*: I housed some of them, because they were refugees and just turned up, we fed them, they even got ration cards just like the rest of us for their two cans of beer a day and a packet of cigarettes. So we treated them as well as we can like one of us. Those in Vitez, the interpreters' cell in Vitez that was well established, those interpreters were members of the officers' mess in Vitez. Now my interpreters got wind of that and wanted to be members of our officers' mess too. When there were only two of them it was fine, thereafter it became problematic. The Duke of Wellington's Regiment are very – I'll say it, some of them are quite stuffy, and didn't want their officers mess overrun with local interpreters. I suppose quite rightly in a way, it's where they relax, and they want to speak freely, and anything they say in front of a local interpreter, they [the interpreter] could be feeding it back to the Serb confrontation line, you just don't know. But, anyway, that was another issue.[20]

In Vitez, by contrast, memoirists and new interviewees alike emphasized a spirit of informal congeniality. A lieutenant was able to invite three female interpreters, apparently displaced from their homes, to live in the house rented for the Cheshires' junior officers; the military diarist who recorded this commented on how difficult the women's beauty practices made access to the bathroom (Woolley 2004: 78). The commander of 1st Battalion, the Coldstream Guards (1 COLDSTREAM), stationed in Vitez between November 1993 and May 1994, fondly remembered the soundscape interpreters created in the officers' mess while he showed one of the authors his photographs from his tours of duty in Bosnia-Herzegovina:

> *Coldstreamer*: I said to them once, and the middle photograph on this page explains what it's all about, I said to them once, 'Why did you learn, you know, why were you as enthusiastic about learning English?' 'Abba,' they said. I said, 'What?' 'Abba,' they said, 'we all fell in love with English because of the songs of Abba.' And they said – and of course whenever you bought the cassette or the record or whatever it was in those days it always came with the words, and

> the words made sense. And I said to them, 'Yes, it's a very good thing you didn't learn English from the songs of Bob Dylan, or we'd really have a problem.' But they were obsessed by Abba. And whenever, in the evenings in the officers' mess, whenever there was a quiet moment, they always insisted on putting Abba CDs on to the music-playing thing. And so we were very into Abba. And then they reproduced all the words and we all had to sing the songs of Abba, and things like that. So Abba held a sort of semi-religious position in the lifestyle of Yugoslavs in central Bosnia as far as I can make out. But, Abba has a lot to answer for, but it did a good job there.[21]

In Alastair Duncan's account, the officers' mess in Vitez – remembered here as a space solely containing military personnel, even though interpreters would also have had access – was where the disorder of serving on a front line became routinized in everyday life:

> [T]he soldiers' perception of normality was changed. Standing in the Officers' Mess there would be a party of visitors who had just arrived. At the same time bullets were striking the sides of the Officers' Mess, which was quite normal for us, and a visitor would hear one of my soldiers say 'Sorry was your drink a Guinness or a lager?' and this just as another bullet whistled overhead. Or people sitting upstairs watching the television as dust fell down from the roof above, and all those watching the television were doing was sitting there holding a hand across the top of their beer so it didn't get dust in it. Our perception of normality had moved but when we got back I think we all became normal again. (Duncan 1994: 55–6)

The banal details of space on military bases took on transformed meanings in the accounts of local interpreters themselves. For soldiers, the base was a familiar place where their own laws and discipline applied, they were protected from attack by fences, Hesco Bastion walls and shelters, and they had access to their own food, drink, media and language. Local civilian workers' experience of the base, on the other hand, involved negotiating permitted and non-permitted spaces: their working area, rest area and accommodation and the shelters were permitted, but sensitive areas such as the operations room were off-limits for reasons of operational security, while social areas were liminal spaces in need of resolution, under regulations subject to change. To work on a military base during the war offered access to heat, light, food, electricity and an expectation of protection, even though that expectation was not always fulfilled. English-language popular music, present in social spaces and on forces radio, made an aural contribution to local workers' perception of the foreign base as a sanctuary from the ethno-nationalist dominance of wartime media in Bosnia-Herzegovina. Outside the base, local radio and television were dominated by nationalist and patriotic songs that positioned listeners as ethnic subjects and aimed to break up inter-ethnic social ties (Laušević 2000); within the base, interpreters sustained their accustomed listening practices involving foreign as well as local music, just as they formed lasting friendships with other interpreters regardless of ethnicity in the manner of pre-war Yugoslav life.

Military bases were also a gendered space. Masculinity remains 'an integral part of...military culture', including the military culture of peace operations (Kronsell 2012: 13). Bearing in mind that bodily performances are what constitute or produce space as it is experienced (Higate and Henry 2009: 99), the predominance of men in deployed military forces means that the dominant gender subjectivity is defined by the 'sheer numbers and uniform bodily presence' of young men (Valenius 2007: 517). In the early 1990s, the British Army in the early 1990s was a 95 per cent male organization adapting to the very recent integration of the Women's Royal Army Corps into Army regiments, which had opened up many non-combat roles to women (Woodward and Winter 2007: 32–3) – although the exclusion of women from combat did not remove female soldiers, such as a military interpreter accompanying an infantry patrol, from the dangers of front-line service. While every local interpreter working for a foreign military had to come to terms with the base's cultural and linguistic strangeness, women experienced the added pressure of adapting to a masculine-gendered environment. In December 1995, when British forces held recruitment days in Banja Luka for a new tranche of interpreters (Chapter 4), women commonly attended in groups or went through the recruitment process with a male friend. This practice maximized one's chance of starting the often-daunting job alongside a familiar and trusted person and helped women manage the risk to their reputation that might ensue in neighbourhoods policed by gossip where the international military was often perceived as an occupying force.

The feminist International Relations scholar Cynthia Enloe argues, in comments on US bases in the United Kingdom, that the sexual politics of military bases are usually invisible yet integral to their legitimacy in the host country and community:

> The normalcy that sustains a military base in a local community rests on ideas about masculinity and femininity. A foreign base requires especially delicate adjustment of relations between men and women,

> for if the fit between local and foreign men and local and foreign women breaks down, the base may lose its protective cover. It may become the target of nationalist resentment that could subvert the very structure of a military alliance. (Enloe 1990: 67)

In Bosnia-Herzegovina, commanding officers and the supervisors of interpreters took steps to guard against the potentially disruptive effects of introducing attractive young female civilian employees into all-male or mainly male groups of soldiers. The first two British battalions in Vitez had seen a number of sexual relationships develop between male soldiers and female employees, sometimes leading to the breakdown of army marriages in the United Kingdom or Germany. The commanding officer of 1 COLDSTREAM decided to intervene in this practice after replacing 1 PWO:

> *Coldstreamer*: When I arrived, I got all my officers together, and I got the regimental sergeant-major to get all the other ranks together, separately, and I said to them, we're all here together, and we will all behave like a bunch of monks who have all come to war. We've left 350 wives behind, in Germany, and I don't want anybody misbehaving. And if you do misbehave I will send you home. And after about two weeks one of my corporals was found in bed with one of the Bosniak cleaners or something. And he appeared in front of me and I said to him, 'You're an idiot.' And he agreed he was an idiot. And I said, 'You've now got 48 hours to work out what you're going to say to your wife when you get back to Germany, because you're going straight back to Germany. I'm not going to take your rank off you, I'm not going to fine you lots of money, but you're going to have to work out what you're going to say to your wife, and you're going to have to work out what you're going to say to your chums the rest of your life as to why you haven't got a medal for being in Bosnia, but you knew this was unacceptable, and: go home.' And so, after that, either people behaved or nobody brought it to my attention. But, generally speaking, people knew that there was a limit, and that they had to stick with that limit.... it was important to have a clear moral standard, and then to impose it on people when they stepped out of line. And I think it was appreciated by all concerned that it was (a) necessary and (b) applied evenly and fairly.
>
> *Catherine Baker*: Did the Army as a whole have a policy on fraternization, or...
>
> *Coldstreamer*: No, I don't think the Army had an official line, certainly nothing I've ever seen in writing about fraternization. I

mean, there were a number of interpreters who did sort of fall in love and end up marrying officers with whom they worked, but no different from any other sort of office romance, I suppose, over a longer term. But, basically we were too busy to allow people to give way to that sort of activity. And it really wasn't a major issue for my battalion.[22]

The change in culture between 1 PWO and 1 COLDSTREAM was marked enough for another military interpreter who had served in Vitez during the Coldstream period to remark on it in his own interview:

Fred Whitaker: I do know that there was a problem when we arrived in Bosnia, the previous regiment had taken a number of the interpreters back to their home base in Germany. As a reward for their work. Inevitably, the interpreters they took back were young, female and personable, and several of them never returned to Bosnia. And that caused a lot of problems, actually. And so people were warned very carefully, look, you know, this is – you have to understand that you can't just take somebody out of here, and assume that they're going to come back again, because of course they could simply ask for asylum (laughs) in wherever they were, and that was the end of that. So I had to go and recruit more interpreters. So you had to, I think, be conscious that relationships – though they could be friendly, cordial, close – had, you know, a boundary beyond which [one] should not step, really. I do remember the commanding officer of the Coldstream Guards coming in and saying to his assembled officers – I don't mean this in the sense that the previous battalion had any difficulties, as I say – but he made a point right at the beginning, you will not have any personal relationship, not any intimate personal relationship with the interpreters. That's that. That's absolutely out. If you do, you're out, and that's that. You know, it has to be a professional relationship, friendly, yes, but it has to be professional. And I think it was. He was an unusual commanding officer, in fact, he was quite a good linguist himself, and had an understanding of how things worked. But I think that was it.[23]

In Bugojno, meanwhile, Louise Robbins conceived of the prevention of inappropriate sexual relationships as a caring task which formed part of her role as a responsible military supervisor:

Louise Robbins: And I counselled them. I struggled to keep the women interpreters out of bed with the soldiers. It's inevitable, war does

> funny things to you, but where women were married to Serb army commanders, not a good idea. Soldiers don't care, out on patrol, they do their best to get her in a shelled-out building...and the girls are up for it, because, you know, they might get something out of it. So I disciplined them, that's why the word 'discipline' [referring to notes] is there, yes, get them in straight away, what do you think you're doing? (laughs)
>
> ...[A female interpreter], who was married to a Serb army commander, actually came to me to ask privately, do they put something in the soldiers' tea to dampen their ardour that might stop me getting pregnant, because nothing's happening. And I said no, no they don't, and anyway it wouldn't affect you, you know, they don't put bromide in soldiers' tea any more, but perhaps they should actually![24]

Policing the sexual order extended to regulating the body (Baker 2010a). Whether deliberately or fortuitously, among the many reasons for issuing interpreters with uniforms – concealing their local civilian status from snipers, practicality when accompanying missions on dirty or muddy ground, signalling to interlocutors that the interpreter was part of the military team – was the masking of the female body shape, following long-standing practices of downplaying sexuality through uniform.[25] This practice was force-wide, not just British. An interpreter for Swedish troops at Srebrenik in 1994 experienced a change of policy when her unit's military supervisor decided to uniform the interpreters. The supply system had difficulty satisfying her requirements (a frequent problem for smaller-bodied female soldiers), while the uniform remained open to a degree of customization and individualization.

> *Catherine Baker*: And what did they give you in terms of uniforms and equipment?
>
> *Azra Bajević*: Oh, we got everything. We were obliged to – initially when I started working it was OK to walk around the camp in civilian clothes. But it was only a couple of months, at the beginning of me working for the Swedes, and then of course (laughs) it's kind of normal, because there were so many men and very few women, that...I started feeling uncomfortable, and of course the major of the company said that perhaps it would be more appropriate if I would wear a uniform as well. So we got orders that whenever we come

> to the camp we go straight to our room and we have to switch to the uniform. It was of course difficult to find uniforms for girls of my size, so I would have really big boots, so that I would have to wear like two or three thick socks inside and still have enough space (laughs). It was really funny. And, we had to wear flak jackets and everything. They were quite heavy, and I have to say that we cheated a bit, we would take out the plates from the flak jacket. Which of course did not provide us with the protection that it was intended for, but it was really difficult to walk around with those flak jackets. And especially in the summer. And ... the uniform that I got when I started working, I think that I had it until the end, through three years of me working for them. I did not change it. They did not have it in my size anyway (laughs).[26]

Writing on Swedish experiences of gender and peacekeeping, Annica Kronsell (2012) suggests that taking account of gender at a high policy level (gender mainstreaming) is easier to achieve than day-to-day integration in masculinized military spaces. Once militaries start attempting to incorporate women, the point at which contradictions become apparent is when gendered military norms are 'challenged by the female soldier/officer in day-to-day practices', not least the practice of fitting into a military uniform (Kronsell 2012: 48). Bajević's account is in line with these observations, yet it also shows that gendered everyday military practices do not solely affect soldiers but also civilians who work with them within military spaces. One cannot therefore conceive of military spaces and their constitution through bodily practices without considering their civilian population as an integral, even though non-normative, aspect of the space.

The end of BRITBAT in central Bosnia

The February 1994 ceasefire which led to the Washington Agreements and ended the Muslim–Croat conflict in central Bosnia occurred near the end of 1 COLDSTREAM's tour. At this point, the work of BRITBAT 1 became more stable and the ability to enforce a validation procedure at recruitment improved, while the need for language support in liaison and negotiation became even more demanding. A number of new interpreters were therefore recruited in Vitez. The commander of 1 COLDSTREAM perceived a certain tension between the new interpreters and the team who had been working during the hardest months of the war (and who had nicknamed themselves 'Tito's children', comparing their own ethnic mixture to the disintegration of Yugoslavia):

> *Coldstreamer*: Just before we left Bosnia, the peace agreement brought about the employment suddenly of a lot more interpreters. Suddenly we had a lot more people moving around trying to pin down front lines, trying to negotiate bus routes and all sorts of things. And so, there are the four 'Tito's children,' and then there are about another ten that we took on who were known as 'Tito's grandchildren,' but they were viewed by the experienced interpreters as interlopers and amateurs and not up to scratch at all. And some of them weren't ever going to be very good. But it was a challenge to have to take on another dozen interpreters at very short notice, to find people who were going to be able to make sense in English to the extent that we required.[27]

A strong sense of camaraderie, born out of shared danger and grief, echoes from the interviews and memoirs of many soldiers who worked with the interpreters at Vitez. Sometimes, as Nick Stansfield hinted, the connections have lasted until the present day:

> *Nick Stansfield*: And the team that we built, I think, in central Bosnia was really really good. I'm still in touch, even on [the internet] I get contacted sometimes by people, by former interpreters who have now married people in the west, or are still in Bosnia, and they say 'Do you remember the days when we were in central Bosnia?' And there was a great camaraderie between the guys. So, you know, the team was built, and, yeah, it worked well. It worked well.[28]

The military topography of Bosnia-Herzegovina changed significantly in December 1995 when UNPROFOR handed over to the NATO-led Implementation Force (IFOR). All contingents' areas of responsibility were rearranged to accommodate new troop contributors, notably the USA, and to divide the whole country into three Multi-National Divisions. For British forces, this meant that their presence would centre not on central Bosnia but on the northwest and particularly on Banja Luka, the site of their divisional headquarters in what was confusingly called Multi-National Division (South-West). Certain towns took on dramatically different roles on the military map after 1995, notably Tuzla, which transformed from a British and Nordic outpost to the bustling centre of the new US military mission in Bosnia-Herzegovina and the headquarters site of Multi-National Division (North). At the same time, the nature of language support requirements across the force was also to alter. There remained a need for field interpreters to accompany troops on patrols, liaison visits, weapons inspections, mine clearances, mass grave site visits and other such duties, and on new assignments such as providing security for election days and refugee returns. The demand for headquarters-level language intermediaries to produce high-quality translations of documents for use in negotiation, liaison and document analysis, meanwhile, greatly increased. The challenge for the multinational force after 1995 was therefore to improve its language support provision in order to meet these new needs.

4
Improving Language Support

After the Dayton Peace Agreement in late 1995, the armed conflict was formally ended. Over the following months, an uneasy peace was achieved, which enabled the first steps to be taken towards rebuilding the country. The language support arrangements, which had been set up in a hurry, slowly evolved to deal with the new demands. But increasingly they struggled to provide the professional language services that the new conditions required. The emerging difficulties can be understood in terms of quality management, a conceptual approach which was being developed energetically in relation to business and public services during the 1990s (Martin 1993). The principles underlying this have since been widely adopted for management purposes in Western countries (Hoyle 2006). This approach defined quality as 'fitness for purpose', which meant that the first step was to analyse the needs for which the product or service was required and to develop a set of explicit specifications. It then argued that the achievement of quality outcomes was dependent on a whole system rather than a single variable. These concepts are useful in analysing the development of language support for the military in Bosnia-Herzegovina. They direct inquiry particularly towards understanding the changing needs for language support, the organization in place to provide it, the work processes undertaken and the profile of people carrying them out, especially their qualifications and training. They also inform the actions that NATO eventually took to improve the quality of language support.

The need for language support

When the Dayton Agreement was concluded and the Paris Treaty was signed, the UN forces that constituted UNPROFOR were replaced by the NATO-led IFOR, subsequently SFOR. The size of the force as its peace operations converted to more energetic peace enforcement was initially much larger and made more demands on language support. The forces took on a different range of tasks, and the profile of language needs began to change. In the year of its operation, IFOR implemented the military provisions of the Dayton agreement: overseeing the end of hostilities, separating the different armed forces, transferring areas of territory between the two main entities, supervising the removal of heavy weaponry, patrolling boundary lines and repairing and replacing infrastructure. The IFOR mission involved some 80,000 troops, twice as many as its predecessor, and therefore had an increased demand for language support. In addition, the much broader duties of the force required more intensive engagement with local civilian authorities, which further increased the language needs. Tony French, an artillery officer with IFOR, described his experience:

> *Tony French*: Post the elections, my role changed a great deal, from peace implementation, I think it was called, which was basically, OK, they're firing at you, you might fire back once or twice, with small arms – I never used artillery. Came close, but never actually had to use artillery. It went from that kind of thing through to a more peace ... keeping type thing, where I was out in the local community, talking to people.[1]

Towards the end of 1996, the priority of the mission shifted towards a 'hearts and minds' operation, as French put it. And, although this still involved some danger, the forces were required to engage with the local community:

> *Tony French*: In the short term, for your own personal security, it would have been better to talk from the top of my Warrior, with my gun pointing directly at them, and say (laughs) 'How about it', rather than getting off and going and speaking to them, which I always found a bit (laughs) dangerous, getting out, and they're brandishing all their weapons and looking at you, and still you just had a natural feel to, you know, I'm not going to talk to them from up here, I'm going to have to go and talk to them down there at their level, which puts you at personal risk an awful lot of the time.[2]

The closer contact with the local people required more sophisticated language skills than were needed from the top of a Warrior armoured vehicle, and the NATO forces therefore needed stronger language support. For part of his activity, Tony French worked with a Czech unit, and found that their own language enabled them to liaise with the local people with little difficulty. He also felt that the demeanour of the Czech soldiers was better understood and respected by the local Serb population. The cultural similarities were an important aid to effective communication. As the tensions eased further, the extent of interactions increased:

> *Tony French*: I could walk through Prijedor on foot, which to start with that would have been impossible. And when I started doing that I started getting local people to become interpreters for us, who were supplied by our battalion headquarters. So they would supply somebody, if I said I was going to do something, mostly on a daily basis, I would get somebody new, who would wait for us outside the camp. We would then pick them up, put them in our armoured vehicle and off we'd shoot.[3]

With the reducing risk of violence, he was able to use the services of locally employed civilians, who were recruited in large numbers by his headquarters. The extent of the need for language support during the mid-1990s was confirmed by Armin Kosarević, an interpreter for the US military police in Tuzla for SFOR:

> *Armin Kosarević*: I'm not sure, but at that time there was a lot of interpreters, in every base. In this camp, maybe, thirty–forty. Maybe even fifty. Because they were going every – they had a rule that no military convoy could leave a base without the interpreter. So even if they were just going from one camp to another, they had to have an interpreter with them. And they were going quite a lot. So, I was pretty sure it was very close to fifty in each camp. Maybe in the airport was over, maybe, a hundred, two hundred. I'm not sure.[4]

Tuzla was a large base and had an unusually large pool of interpreters. Its airport was a major arrival point for UN and NATO troops. Most of the smaller bases distributed around the country had much smaller groups of linguists, as Azra Bajević, a local interpreter in the Tuzla area between 1994 and 1997, suggested:

> *Catherine Baker*: And how many interpreters would each company have?

Azra Bajević: It depends on the period, but I think three. Three for the companies, and HQ had more, maybe six or seven, I think. And I'm talking only of the locals, of course. They also had one military interpreter per company, and they had maybe three or four in the HQ.[5]

On this reckoning, a company of perhaps a hundred personnel might have three or four local interpreters and a military linguist, though numbers are impossible to establish with certainty, since they varied at different periods and with different military contingents. At the end of 1996, IFOR was replaced by the Stabilization Force (SFOR), which initially comprised 32,000 troops, less than half as large as IFOR. A significant proportion of these personnel were based outside Bosnia-Herzegovina itself, mostly in neighbouring countries. Over the 10 years of its mandate, the force was restructured several times and gradually reduced in numbers, reaching 12,000 in 2003.[6] The number of local interpreters cannot easily be extrapolated from these figures, but was almost certainly several hundred for most of the period, perhaps rising to more than 2000 at the peak.

In the early period after Dayton, there was little difference in the tasks for which language support was needed. Tarik Begović, a Bosnian interpreter with a Swedish unit in 1998, described his work in the Tuzla region:

Tarik Begović: In the very beginning I worked with light infantry units. They went on, they used to call it patrols. We were patrolling returnee areas in the area of Lukavac, which is approximately 15 to 20 kilometres west of Tuzla. We were checking that the returnees are doing OK, that they have no security issues, talking to them. Inspecting military sites, making sure that they have the exact amount of ammunition and weapons as they are supposed to have, that everything is lying in accordance with the agreements between former warring parties. I was going to meetings with the liaison officers, who were speaking, who were talking to local officials, party leaders, political party leaders, mayors, police officials, people like that.[7]

While most of the work of interpreters was initially concerned with accompanying patrols, the amount of liaison with civilian authorities was considerable. This was also accompanied by a growing volume of documentation that required translation services. Begović's perception was that the numbers of interpreters continued to increase throughout the 1990s and only began to reduce from 2003–4. If this pattern were repeated throughout the operation, it would mean that the work of liaison and negotiation with the local population continued to increase, placing greater demands on language support.

Over time, the duties carried out by the military became less broad, since reconstruction and civilian liaison work was increasingly taken in hand by civilian agencies, particularly the Office of the High Representative (OHR), but also by agencies such as the UN High Commissioner for Refugees (UNHCR), the Organization for Security and Cooperation in Europe (OSCE) and the International Criminal Tribunal for the Former Yugoslavia (ICTY). Many other intergovernmental and non-governmental organizations also played an important role. As a result, the language needs of the NATO-led forces changed in nature.

Organization of language support

The crisis-led operations of 1992–6 were gradually replaced by more routine processes. Ad hoc arrangements changed into settled structures. Responsibility for providing language support was delegated to individual contingents, and ultimately to the commander of each unit at any one time. As a result, the approaches taken were very diverse, since each country had its own traditions, and each commander could implement arrangements to suit the situation in which they found themselves. Military units were deployed for a limited period, ranging from three months in the shortest cases, through the more usual six months, which was the case of British units, to 12 months in the case of some US forces. At each rotation, the language support arrangements were handed over and could be changed by the incoming commander. In practice, it was unusual for arrangements to change significantly unless the unit was reorganized or relocated, although day-to-day working practices might change (see Chapter 3).

The ways in which the language services were managed could vary considerably. In some cases, they were managed by a military officer, who might be a linguist but was often not. In other cases, they were managed by a civilian under military supervision, or particularly in the case of US forces, contracted through commercial companies. The NATO headquarters in Sarajevo was managed by an officer, as described by Edin Selimović, and interpreter with the unit for Civil–Military Co-Operation (CIMIC) from 1996:

> *Edin Selimović*: Every six months I would have a different military, called a military supervisor. It would be one military personnel who

among other things that he or she would be doing, would be also handling interpreters.

Catherine Baker: Oh, right. So what sort of other things would they do?

Edin Selimović: Well, I don't know. Mostly, it was people working at the personnel office, administration office, of the CIMIC unit. And they would also be, as I said, managing work of interpreters.

Catherine Baker: OK. And that person would change sort of...

Edin Selimović: Every six months. Whenever the unit changed, we would get a new military supervisor.[8]

This model of organization was common to several contingents, including the British forces, who typically assigned an officer to oversee the language service. The benefit of this approach was that the service might be more responsive to immediate military requirements. The main disadvantage was the lack of continuity in supervision as the military contingents came and went. In Selimović's case, the officer responsible was usually managing several other activities, and was not necessarily a specialist. In other cases, the officer in charge might be a trained linguist, with no other duties. The benefits of having a specialist supervisor were considerable, as seen in the case study of language support in BRITBATs 1 and 2 (Chapter 3). Some forces achieved similar benefits by using civilian linguists as supervisors, as Tarik Begović found when working for a Swedish battalion:

Tarik Begović: They had a kind of a chief interpreter, who was a Swedish citizen, with Bosnian or Croat or Serb background, who spoke one of, actually, who spoke local languages, but was born and raised in Sweden, and he was given a military rank of first lieutenant. And he was our boss or chief. He was also doing interpreting part, but at the same time he was managing the whole interpreters' office, so to speak, you know.

Catherine Baker: What sorts of situations did he interpret in?

Tarik Begović: He interpreted for higher officers, such as generals or something like that, you know. I'm guessing that he was also in charge of interpreting things that we had no security clearance for, so to speak. Maybe there were some things we were not supposed to know about, he was in charge for those.[9]

The Swedish supervisor was a civilian language specialist, who was allocated an equivalent officer rank and reported to the military commander. He also provided language support directly in some cases.

Begović later worked with a US battalion, who employed a civilian contractor to manage their language services. The supervisor was not a linguist, but was a specialist manager whose job it was to supervise the interpreters and deliver language support. The principal benefit of this approach was that there was a degree of continuity between successive units, though this was not guaranteed, since the forces could well change to a different contractor. Begović was also impressed by the high level of organization of the Americans, who made much more systematic use of interpreters and paid significantly higher wages. He was aware, though, that there were two different types of interpreter:

> *Tarik Begović*: They had two different categories of interpreters. Cat I, Category I and II. Local people, Bosnians, Serbians, and Croatians, were Category I. But they had their own interpreters that they brought from the United States, who were American citizens who could speak Bosnian, Serbian or Croatian. Most of those people were actually people of Serbian, Bosnian or Croatian origin, whose parents moved to the United States. And since these people were American citizens, they had a security clearance, and they translated more classified information, and at meetings that were not, so to speak, available to local interpreters and local population.
>
> *Catherine Baker*: Did Cat Is and Cat IIs ever work together, or was it completely different?
>
> *Tarik Begović*: We both worked for the same company, the civilian company I told you about. We were pretty much doing the same job, interpreting, like nothing else but interpreting. And sometimes we worked together. But together in the sense of on the same convoy, but translating, interpreting different things. I never had experience of working with Cat II together, I mean, directly at the same meeting, or something like that. They were, I'd say, separate.[10]

The security issues were recognized by all the forces, though treated in different ways. In the US case, a strict segregation of roles was in force between local and international linguists. The Swedish company appears to have been more relaxed, but most contingents had some restrictions on what or how material might be accessed by local linguists.

Quality assurance

The great variety of arrangements for language support meant that there was no common framework for provision across the forces, and therefore a variety of processes. Each contingent was responsible for its own arrangements, and day-to-day responsibility was delegated to individual commanders. There were no formal guidelines at the level of NATO. Its work in the area of languages was overseen by the Bureau for International Language Co-Ordination (BILC) which reported to the NATO Training Group. However, the Bureau's remit focused on collaboration in the area of language training and education for the military forces. It therefore dealt mainly with teaching English (and sometimes French) to non-native speakers, setting linguistic proficiency standards and language testing. Its responsibilities did not extend to language support in the field (NATO 2004: B4). In consequence, there were no general arrangements for assuring or enhancing the quality of the language support provided.

The area of quality assurance was a well-established part of military practice. It normally included a requirement that an item or equipment be produced or maintained according to reliable procedures (quality assurance), and the finished product checked by a competent person before being issued or brought into service (quality control). In general conversation, the terms quality assurance and control were often used interchangeably. Maintaining an effective quality regime was a high priority in the military as a means of ensuring that equipment was in good working order and fit for its purpose. By contrast, the concern for quality in the delivery of language support services was distinctly uneven. Quality assurance was a local matter, and practice varied a good deal from place to place. Gordon Schofield, a RAF officer on a civil affairs posting in Gornji Vakuf in 1999, found that they had effective processes for translation:

> *Gordon Schofield*: You would give them a draft of a letter in English, and they would put it into that language. And it would always be ratified, because there was a senior interpreter that would check to make sure everything is as it should be, so it's almost like a quality control within their own interpreting cell.[11]

The quality control procedures were well established for translation, with a two-stage checking process similar to what might be found in a professional translation agency. Schofield was also reassured that the senior translators were 'overqualified' for their position, since some of them were experienced university lecturers who could earn four times as much by translating than they could earn in university teaching. Schofield understood that a similar quality control procedure was followed in Sarajevo, though that was not the experience of Nikola Andrijašević, a British military interpreter, based at NATO's SFOR headquarters in Sarajevo at the same period.

> *Nikola Andrijašević*: Unfortunately the limited amount of independent speakers available, and the sheer volume of documents being translated did not lend itself to any form of quality assurance, a great deal of quality assurance, short of random sampling of documents. And so there was quite a lot of potential for misunderstandings in those.[12]

The lack of quality assurance in translation was attributed to the sheer volume of work, which did not allow the output to be checked. However, it seems likely that it mainly reflected the low level of priority given to checking translations, and the absence of an organizational structure that would make this a normal practice. The consequences of poor translation could be significant, as Andrijašević pointed out:

> *Catherine Baker*: If there was an error in translation? What could that lead to?
>
> *Nikola Andrijašević*: It led to confusion, and delays and misunderstandings. Personnel not conducting tasks in accordance with the vision of the higher commander. If you're translating simple things like times and grid references, that's difficult to mistranslate, because that's just replacing figures into another document. But when it comes to little nuances in let's say an intelligence report that says possibly or probably, each has a slightly different meaning, but you can see how easy it is to mistranslate a probably into a possibly, which would then lead the recipient of the mistranslated document to come out with a different conclusion than was intended.[13]

The scope for mistranslation was considerable, and would be particularly crucial in documents relating to qualitative assessment, where nuances of meaning could be crucial. Quality control procedures were clearly implemented in some translation units, but were not adopted as general practice in all circumstances. The quality control of interpreting was more difficult to achieve, as Schofield explained:

> *Catherine Baker:* What sort of quality assurance was there for interpretation?

> *Gordon Schofield*: Well, interpretation is ... it's a lot harder, to quality ensure. What we came down to was, we had two very good interpreters. On occasions when they had gone on leave we ended up with different interpreters and the quality of those would be different. I won't deny that. And that was just, it's like anything, you find a good tradesman, you work with the good tradesman. We tended to know who the good tradesmen were and in their absence we knew the names of other very good tradesmen. So you would actually specifically ask for interpreters, as opposed to throwing yourself open to the interpreter pool and being given whoever.[14]

In the circumstances, it was not feasible to operate a structured quality control process for interpretation. To a large extent, it was left to the customer, the personnel using interpreters, to operate their own quality control. In some cases, where officers had some knowledge of the local language or a cognate Slavonic language, such as Russian, they could make some judgement of the interpretation offered. But in most cases, they had no way of doing this. As Andrijašević commented:

> *Nikola Andrijašević*: Ultimately a company commander or indeed any rank that was with an interpreter had to rely implicitly into the ... had to defer entirely to the interpreter, because they had no knowledge, and no way of conducting quality assurance.[15]

Military personnel could normally only affect the quality of the work by selecting individual interpreters they considered more reliable, though this would not necessarily result in any overall improvement in support for the unit as a whole. Andrijašević pointed out that the result of low-quality interpreting was likely to be misunderstandings:

> *Nikola Andrijašević*: If I'm walking to a village and I'm portraying an image, and ask questions, if the questions are not translated properly, instead of a benign question it can it can easily be misinterpreted into almost an interrogation. And you think you are talking to a chap and merely asking him a few questions, but because the way the interpreter has constructed the sentence, his tone of voice, the guy who is hearing the questions is hearing a totally different set of questions than the ones you intend. So if you're going in and you're intending a nice friendly chat, and that's your demeanour, if the interpreter misinterprets it, and it becomes an aggressive style of

questioning, then the feedback you get is not what you expect. And you've got this whole dislocation of your expectation of going in for a nice chat, all of a sudden you've got a very defensive individual, and you've got no idea why he's become defensive. The reason is because the interpreter hasn't carried out the task properly and has been misinterpreting at some stage or another. And unfortunately that's very difficult to spot, unless you've got somebody auditing every single piece of translation that's happening. It's one of the hazards of the job.[16]

The ability of interpreters to have a decisive influence on encounters and relationships made them a key asset or potentially a liability. If the quality of their work could not be controlled at the point of delivery, then it was all the more important that their quality should be ensured in recruiting them and in enhancing their skills.

Recruitment and training of people

Quality assurance depended heavily on processes being carried out by competent and trained personnel. In technical and administrative areas of support work, it was a constant concern of the forces to ensure that the staff they employed were suitably qualified. In language support, however, recruitment was generally more haphazard. Local translators and interpreters were engaged in a similar pattern in most units. Potential recruits were typically asked to take a test before being engaged. Azra Bajević described her experience:

Azra Bajević: I was the first time tested maybe end of '93, beginning of '94, for a position of language assistant with UNPROFOR, but I failed that test. And then the – maybe a couple of months later, I was called again for a testing. At the time they were employing a lot of people, whoever knew a bit of English could get a job, basically. And the second time I passed the test. And I was first called for an oral exam for a position with the Pakistani battalion. And at the same time they were recruiting for the Swedish battalion as well, because they also needed one interpreter, and I got an offer from Swedish battalion. So basically that's it.[17]

Bajević had invested in a course of English study before applying for the post, but still fell below the required standard. Her perception was that the standard was set low because of the urgent need for interpreters, but the fact that she failed the test at the first attempt suggests that some degree of selection was taking place. Tests normally examined language proficiency, and the scale and scope of tests varied greatly according to the context. During the UNPROFOR operations, there was a standard written test, though unit officers could exercise flexibility in determining the pass level. The UN test was not used by the NATO-led forces after 1995, and although they sometimes used other written tests, they often based recruitment solely on an interview, intended to assess their proficiency in speaking. In both cases, the tests were confined to examining the interpreter's proficiency in English rather than their expertise in translation and interpreting. Tarik Begović, an interpreter for SFOR and later EUFOR in Tuzla, was typical:

> *Tarik Begović*: We had different trainings, but nothing related to translations. We had a test once we had to pass. It was a TEFL test, test of, you know what a TEFL test is. But never, we never had trainings. Because before hiring, we had to pass the test. So they are sure that we actually already know enough English so that we could work.[18]

The reference to a TEFL (Teaching English as a Foreign Language) test is not entirely clear, but in context it suggests that it was one of the standard tests of English as a Foreign Language, which are offered by several international agencies. In areas where units used another language for internal purposes, that language was also the subject of testing. It often proved difficult to find local people with knowledge of languages other than English, particularly outside the capital, Sarajevo. Non-English-speaking units were more likely to draw on the resources of their own country to meet their language needs. Local interpreters were therefore selected for their level of language proficiency in English, and the urgency of the need meant that they were sometimes hired with relatively low levels of proficiency. Several locally employed interpreters confirmed Bajević's impression that jobs were offered to anyone who had some knowledge of English. People with low levels of competence, once employed, very often remained in post for several years. This was particularly the case for interpreters who had been recruited to UNPROFOR, under difficult conditions, where any level of language support was precious. In most cases, they remained in post after the handover to IFOR and then SFOR. Some learned to improve their proficiency, but many continued to serve with the same level of skills.

With uneven quality criteria at the point of entry into their post, it is clear that many interpreters needed a good deal of support and training to ensure that they could enhance their skills and knowledge so as to provide an adequate quality of service. Quality enhancement of this kind appears in fact to have been relatively rare. It was a potential benefit of management by specialist linguists that they might be better equipped to offer advice and development to the local interpreters, most of whom were recruited without any previous experience or training. However, very few of the local staff received specific training. Jelena Vlahović reported that, as an interpreter with the British forces in Šipovo in 1997–8, she received no training at all. By contrast, when she moved from this to a position as financial assistant on a similar salary she was given three separate training courses in the UK and Germany.[19] Slađana Medić, an interpreter in Mrkonjić Grad, followed a similar path at the same period, receiving no training in her three years at an interpreter but three courses in the UK in connection with her clerical role in procurement.[20] Bojan Dragović, who served as an interpreter for SFOR in Banja Luka, reported that he had been offered a training course in Britain but had had to decline the opportunity. Shortly afterwards, he withdrew from his position with the forces.[21] Although training opportunities were relatively few, and largely left to self-improvement, there was sometimes provision for appraisal and evaluation of the linguists' progress. Azra Bajević explained:

> *Azra Bajević*: They would do the evaluation. The liaison officer would do it. Then he would sit with us, he would say with what he is satisfied, which things he thinks could be done better, with which things he is not satisfied at all, and then you would, he would write that down on a form that was prepared and we would both sign and that was it. We had the grading in..., our salaries were basically levelled in several grades, and each grade had several steps. I don't remember how that worked, but I know when you just start working I think you are grade 2, and then you go to grade 3, but of course you have to go through all steps in that grade. And it all depends on this appraisal by this liaison officer.[22]

The liaison officer was the direct supervisor of the team of interpreters working for the Swedish unit in Tuzla. He or she was responsible for allocating work and for evaluating the performance of the individual linguists. The report submitted by the liaison officer to the headquarters then determined the pay grade of the interpreter. Although this was not directly training, it nonetheless provided the individual linguist with feedback on their work and suggestions for how they might improve it.

The NATO quality audit

The changing nature of military responsibilities was combined with a gradual reduction in the scale of operations. With the reducing level of tension, military planners at NATO headquarters began to reflect critically on the nature of language support. They were prompted to do this by the reducing size of NATO-led forces involved, which provided an opportunity to reduce the scale of language support and the costs incurred. The troop reductions were accompanied by reorganizations, which included the closure of some bases and the rationalization of operations in the remaining ones. There is also a suggestion that they were concerned about the adequacy of the services provided. In early 1998, it was decided to undertake a review of language services in the different NATO offices, and Ian Jones, a civilian who was the head linguist at NATO's SHAPE command centre in Belgium, was asked to undertake the review:

> *Ian Jones*: In 1998, I was requested to go to Bosnia-Herzegovina by the Chief of Staff of what had then become the Stabilization Force, SFOR, headquarters, in Sarajevo, because they had realised that the linguistic support was not perfect, shall we say, and they wanted to bring in somebody who had some greater expertise in that area to look at what they were doing.... I went down in June and August. I went down for a week and then two weeks, basically to carry out a kind of, it was a bit like calling in a management consultant, in a way, because they thought that things could be improved, so they asked me to go down there to look at what they were doing, to see how things were set up and organized and to come up with proposals for improving the organization.[23]

This intervention began from the principle of quality management that if the service was to be fit for its purpose it was essential to establish what the purpose was. It is an approach commonly followed in a language audit, which typically includes a needs assessment before proceeding to recommend on the language provision required (West 1994; Long 2005). The first visit of one week in June 1998 was aimed at identifying the needs that language support was required to meet, and comprised consultations with various offices based in Sarajevo. The second visit of two weeks in August aimed to assess how well the needs were being met. During this period, Jones also made visits to centres in Mostar, Ploče, Split, Slavonski Brod, Zagreb, Bijeljina, Pale, Banja Luka and Goražde. Following these visits, he made recommendations for change.

Jones considered that the operation in Bosnia-Herzegovina had moved from an adversarial environment to a more benign consensual environment, in which the language needs had substantially changed. The primary need for language support, he found, was to enable the forces to undertake a programme of work (from mine removal to building projects), to build support for NATO's aims, and to liaise with a broad spectrum of people from presidents and ministers through to the population at large.

Jones then evaluated how well the existing arrangements met the needs he had identified. His findings were that the arrangements fell a long way short of meeting the needs, on a number of measures. The first problem was that the services were unable to provide the levels of expertise required to carry out the very wide range of language tasks. Many of the interpreters and translators were not able to work at the appropriate level. Whereas high-level interpreting and translating would normally require expert skills at STANAG 6001 level 4,[24] most of those employed had lower levels of proficiency. Some had attained level 3 in English, which was barely adequate, and many had only level 2. He considered that they were not adequate to the tasks they were required to perform, and had been hired 'because we couldn't find anybody better than that'.[25] It was a particular concern that they were expected to carry out a lot of translation into English from Serbian or Croatian. The norm of professional translation and interpreting was that linguists translated into their native language, and none of those employed were English native speakers. The second problem Jones discovered was that there was a serious lack of continuity:

> *Ian Jones*: One of the first problems I found was just to do with the nature of the forces and the way the organization was mounted, was that the average length of stay of a military officer or NCO, the military supervisors, was about three months. They would go down to Bosnia, for three months, and then go back home again. So this caused, as you can imagine, enormous problems of first of all coming in from outside, having to learn their own job, learn the environment, and obviously problems of continuity. And very often the locally hired people knew more about what was going on than their

> so-called supervisors, they'd been there for a year, two years, or however long.[26]

The supervision of locally employed linguists was largely delegated to military personnel who did not have the knowledge or experience to carry it out effectively. His finding that they stayed in post on average for only three months appears surprising, since many contingents worked in tours of duty of between six and 12 months. The shorter postings arose from the frequency with which supervisors moved on to other duties in the course of a single deployment, reflecting the fact that language support was only one of their responsibilities, and possibly not their first priority. Where supervision was supplied by military linguists, they may also have been deployed at different dates from the contingent with whom they were working. The lack of continuity reinforced the third major problem, which was a lack of coordination:

> *Ian Jones*: There was also a huge problem in that there was no real Linguistic Service as such. They'd just hired a lot of people and scattered them around the organization and said, 'Right, you translate' or, 'You interpret', or whatever. There was no central control, there was no supervision, really, of their activities. And that led to various problems, not only of control of their activities, but of quality problems.[27]

The lack of coordination was a direct consequence of the highly delegated nature of the operation, where the organization of language support was left to the discretion of local commanders. It meant that there was no overall plan for providing a service and therefore, among other things, no ability to match the tasks with the people best fitted to do them, no consistency in the translations carried out, a great deal of duplication of effort, some offices overwhelmed with work while staff elsewhere were standing idle, and little or no mutual support between offices. He also found that in some cases the interpreters lacked basic tools, such as dictionaries, because their managers did not see a need to provide them. Jones was so struck by the lack of professional expertise that he organized a short training session to explain 'a few of the basics about what translators and interpreters are supposed to be doing'.[28]

As a result of his investigations, Jones prepared a set of recommendations to NATO. They did not touch on the large number of linguists employed by the contingents from contributing countries, and did not address the day-to-day work of patrols and low-level contact, but focused on the higher level work of the NATO offices. His main proposal was that 'that all the linguists be put into a single Linguistic Service under one Head',[29] so that the chief linguist would be functionally responsible for all the linguists directly employed at NATO offices. Jones recommended that a large proportion of the NATO linguists should be located centrally at the Sarajevo headquarters. This proposal followed a key tenet of quality management that the provision of high-quality services depends on effective leadership. Whereas the individual NATO offices had clear leadership according to the military chain of command, the language support services had no professional leadership. Jones also made a number of detailed organizational recommendations, which included introducing a structure of employment, comprising different levels of responsibility and seniority, up to and including senior revisers who would be able to supervise more junior colleagues and check the quality of work. He recommended that English native speakers should be recruited at a senior level, with security clearance to deal with classified material, which local interpreters could not handle. And he recommended that all media analysis work should be centralized to avoid duplication in monitoring and analysing press and broadcast material. All of these proposals were accepted by NATO planners, with the exception of centralization of media analysis.

Establishing the Linguistic Services Branch

The year after Ian Jones's report, it was agreed to advertise two posts as Head and Deputy Head of a new Linguistic Service, based in Sarajevo. These were duly filled and work began on reorganization in April 2000. The two-year period between the initial investigation and the implementation of changes reflects the complexity of the approval processes within the NATO structure. The operations continued to be scaled down, and by mid-2000 language support was based in Sarajevo and Banja Luka in Bosnia-Herzegovina and Zagreb, Ploče and Split in Croatia. The military bases at Mostar and Goražde were closed at around the same time. The position of Head of the service was taken by Louise Askew, who had previously worked for the International Criminal Tribunal for the Former Yugoslavia (ICTY) at The Hague. From her arrival in April 2000, she established the Linguistic Services Branch (LSB) along the lines that Jones had recommended, with direct assistance from him in the first few days. Her deputy was also an experienced native English-speaking linguist. Their task was to put the service on a professional basis, drawing in all of the translators and interpreters from the different NATO offices in the area. The first step was to establish the precise language needs and the work patterns that had developed, which was carried out through questionnaires and interviews. They discovered a wide spectrum of different situations, from very expert linguists to people who were unable to carry out the most basic work. The team gave detailed tests to more than 40 people who were eligible to join the new organization, and found that a quarter of them were not sufficiently proficient. Goran Šiljak, an interpreter with an Allied Military Intelligence Battalion since 1997, recalled that the tests were difficult:

> *Goran Šiljak*: And following the test, out of 54, I think more than 20 were let go, because they did not pass the test, which was extremely difficult, and later on when I discovered different, other tests that are out there to be taken, like TEFL or whatever, British Council test, I think that this one rates higher when it comes to difficulty level than most of those. Anyways, those who passed the test remained, and Mrs Askew decided to pull all of us, or most of us, into the central pool.[30]

The difficulty of the test is confirmed by other interpreters, including Edin Selimović, an interpreter who had worked in Tuzla since 1996, and who remembered that the tests took place over several days. Šiljak's memory of the numbers involved is rather higher than that of Louise Askew, who remembered 44 candidates, 10 of them unsuccessful. Askew also had the painful task of dismissing them:

> *Louise Askew*: And it was, I remember one afternoon, I was in my office and I had to give notice to these 9 or 10 people. And I had a German captain, no, major, was it captain or major, can't remember, B—, who was German, he was deputy DSO, and he was there just in case there was any trouble (laughs) and he sat on, in the corner, and he couldn't have done it, he said afterwards (laughs), 'I don't know how you did that'. And what was interesting was that there was only one out of however many it was who said, who reacted badly, and she did say, 'Have you any idea what it's like to be the only person in your family earning money?' and things like that. And of course, to which you say, 'No I do not have any idea, but I'm afraid this is what's happening, you know, and I'm afraid you know you didn't, you know, reach the standard and we can't keep you', you know, that sort of thing. No, but she was the only one who actually reacted sort of in that way, I expected a lot more sort of, you know, a lot more protests, let's say.

> The best one was a woman who had been working in the office that hadn't done anything. She was the last, and she came in and she said, 'Louise, I know exactly what you're going to say. It doesn't matter.' She started laughing (laughs), and then she went and said, 'I've had four great years', (laughs), 'maybe it's time that I've got to get serious, maybe it's time for me to get serious'. It was great. It was like well fab (laughs), job done (laughs). So ... yeah, that was that.[31]

Dismissing the 10 people was an unpleasant task, which Askew carried out with skill and humanity. The view of the deputy Director of Staff Operations (DSO), that he could not have done it, may also reveal a gender difference. All of the interpreters in question were women, and the task of giving notice to them may have appeared even more difficult to the male officer. No doubt the fact that Askew was female and a civilian enabled her to set a suitably professional tone in the interview. Her palpable relief at the good-humoured response of the final candidate reveals the stress she was nonetheless feeling. Following the reduction in staff numbers, the LSB was reorganized to allocate interpreters to duties that best fitted their capabilities. Askew reported that she encountered resistance to the changes in several units, where officers had developed a strong loyalty to their own interpreters, regardless of their competence.

Consistent working procedures were introduced in the LSB, including a strict system of revising, which ensured that every translation was closely checked and corrected before being issued. This proved a very effective way of improving the quality of work and Louise Askew judged that 'that was the principal method of training them, so S— [Deputy Head] who did most of the revision, he could work with them and get them up to standard'.[32] Discussion and collaboration between the interpreters was encouraged and explicit training sessions were introduced, as described by Edin Selimović:

> *Edin Selimović*: Yeah, we had language trainings. I think even, I think on, of course ... depending on our, on the workload, if we had time. I think, I think we even had weekly language trainings. We would just go in one room, all the interpreters, with the chief and deputy chief for an hour or two hours, and we would do translations or interpretations, and then we would all engage in discussing one or two things this way, the other would do it the other way, talking why, you know, pro and cons and everything. We just had a real good language training. Trainings.

Catherine Baker: And so can you remember a bit more about some of the exercises that you did in the training?

Edin Selimović: Yeah. For example, Louise Askew, Miss Askew, she would come, and she would take, let's say, article from British papers. Whatever British papers. And she would read out the article, and it would be our job to produce a translation. And then we would write our translation on a big whiteboard, for example, I would do that if I was assigned to do that, if I was told to do that. And then all interpreters would engage in a discussion, of what was wrong, what was good, what could have been done differently, you know, style-wise, terminology-wise, grammar-structure-wise. So it was good language training.[33]

The clear structure, standard operating procedures and continuous improvement, implemented by Askew and her team, were entirely consistent with the principles of quality management, although the terminology of business management was not used. Bringing together a scattered group of independent activities into a centralized service brought dramatic improvement in the language support offered to the SFOR forces. The changes reflected the transition of the Bosnian operations from crisis intervention to routine management, and a sharp reduction in the number of military bases. This enabled processes to be streamlined and put on a professional basis. However, the working environment placed limits on the process of standardization, as demonstrated by the attempt to introduce high-specification translation software:

Louise Askew: It's great if you're not in an operational HQ, if you're somewhere like NATO, if you have documents that are typed, that someone would come along with a disk or a memory stick and say, 'Ooh, it's a document', documents that look very similar, sort of sound very similar, fine. But in our service, where you'd get a document that was on a piece of paper that had been screwed up or something, that kind of thing (laughs), or, just documents, you couldn't get the electronic copy of, and then if you didn't have an electronic copy you then had to scan it, so you had to employ somebody to be the person doing the damn scanning, and then the scanner wouldn't work, or you couldn't get it on to the computer, or it would be in Cyrillic (laughs), which would just make it even worse... despite the training we had, nobody ever really took it on board, and I don't blame them, because it was too much like hard work, by the time

> you'd scanned a document, fiddled about with it and so on you could have translated the damn thing.[34]

The LSB's experience with corporate translation technology was no doubt frustrating. But it is similar to many other attempts to bring advanced technology to a relatively low-tech environment. It exemplifies the need to match technical solutions to the practical problems they are meant to solve, and suggests that the language services had reached the limits of radical restructuring.

Improving quality

The introduction of a coherent operation providing high quality language services was a significant advance for language support to the NATO headquarters. It was achieved in the more settled conditions of the early 2000s and replaced what by then appeared to be a haphazard set of arrangements that had grown up in response to the earlier crisis conditions. It is doubtful whether the LSB could have been established at an earlier stage in the conflict. Certainly, a centralized system would have been difficult to operate in the periods of high tension, when language needs varied greatly and different centres had different priorities. It may be that the transition from an ad hoc to a professional system could have been made at an earlier stage in Bosnia-Herzegovina. It would no doubt be useful for military planners to consider how to judge at which stage of a peace support operation it would be appropriate to conduct a review of the type that was undertaken in 1998.

The context of this conflict highlights the fact that a coherent service requires a certain level of stability and continuity of operations. In the relatively chaotic conditions of the earlier 1990s, it is likely that more could have been done to improve the quality of language support within the very distributed arrangements. Since NATO manages standards for language proficiency, and has established structures for cooperation in language training, it might have been a logical step for it to develop resources for language support. However, it is a complex matter to suggest where responsibility might lie for developing local quality management of this kind, and each NATO country has its own approach. In the case of the British armed forces, for example, a specialist unit was subsequently developed to improve language support: the Defence Operational Languages Support Unit (DOLSU) (Lewis 2012). This was designed to respond to more recent operations in Afghanistan and Iraq. Other countries have taken different steps, though in most cases their focus has been on developing the language capability of their own forces rather than the use of civilian linguists.

Based on the experience of Bosnia-Herzegovina, there are a number of quality management tools that could have been developed to improve the localized arrangements. For example, a standard written test for candidate interpreters was part of the UN procedures, and a similar arrangement could easily have been adopted by NATO. Differentiated roles could probably have been introduced in the bases with larger contingents of interpreters, with one or more skilled linguists working as revisers to ensure the quality of outputs and provide training for other staff. A more explicit framework could have been developed to guide evaluation and feedback to interpreters, even where their appraisal was carried out by non-linguists. Some of these resources were made available in individual contingents, and none of them would have been beyond the ability of NATO's combined expertise. Ultimately, the decisive question was whether the language issues had sufficient priority to merit concerted action across the different forces. Languages were some way down the order of priorities for the NATO forces, and it was only when other priorities became less pressing that language issues received high-level attention. The solutions that were adopted had the potential to be transferred to other operations, but in the event it was the pressure of later and more extensive conflicts that sparked further improvements in the provision of language support.

5
Foreign/Local Encounters in Interpreting

Even though they came late in the history of operational language support in Bosnia-Herzegovina, the improvements made at the Linguistic Services Branch of HQ SFOR were significant. However, the locally recruited civilian linguists who benefited from them were only a subset of the number of local interpreters involved in the peace operations. Many were employed by other parts of the multinational force instead, and so they remained employees of the particular foreign military on whose bases they worked or of the contractors to whom the US military had outsourced interpreter recruitment. The experiences of local interpreters therefore had potential to vary greatly depending on which military they had been working for and even – because interpreter management was not fully standardized – depending on which base they had worked at, at which time. Many commonalities in their experiences can still be perceived.

As permanent residents of former Yugoslav countries (mostly, but not always, Bosnia-Herzegovina), local interpreters were embedded in local systems of meaning in ways that foreign soldiers or civilians who visited and then left the country were not. They were native speakers of the languages used by the population whom the multinational force aimed to influence, rather than of the languages that troops used to communicate with each other. They also remained in post for far longer than any foreign soldier. Most troops and units served tours of duty of six months, then handed their duties over to replacements. Peace operations, for the soldiers who embodied them, were thus a constant process of relearning and renewal. Interpreters, however, typically witnessed several military rotations while staying in the same post. They observed the effects of intervention over a longer time scale and they also became repositories of knowledge on which troops newly entering the 'foreign field' would draw.

Peace operations, like other military deployments, represent a foreign/local encounter on a large scale (Footitt and Kelly (eds) 2012b). They are constituted by many such smaller-scale encounters which are mediated by language intermediaries or forces' own language-trained personnel. Since they depend so heavily on local interpreters, however, they are also shaped by the foreign/local encounters that take place in the background of the acts of interpreting and translation. These are relationships where the greater power, privilege and mobility of foreign troops in comparison to local people intersect with the troops' inability to act effectively without the agency and knowledge of local interpreters. These encounters had the potential to express warmth and comradeship or tension and resentment. A further aspect of the foreign/local encounter in interpreting, the flow of detailed local knowledge from interpreters to troops, resulted in interpreters providing a continuity of knowledge to a military presence as individual personnel and units came and went.

Employer/employee relations

Local interpreters' perspectives on the work they did, and their motivations to continue doing it or to seek other work inside or outside Bosnia-Herzegovina, were affected by a broader structure of employer/employee relations. It is clear that, as a result of gaps in policy, interpreters doing the same kind of work for the same national military contingent could have very different experiences depending on the bases at which they worked and the dates through which they worked there. Although NATO employed some interpreters directly to work at the Sarajevo headquarters and its branches, interpreter recruitment and management by the national contingents was highly decentralized. IFOR and SFOR did not prescribe how interpreters were to be hired, tested, managed or paid. Different contingents were at liberty to offer quite different pay scales, which might come as a shock to interpreters at a base if one high-paying contingent was replaced by another paying lower wages.

The form of interpreters' contracts and the nature of testing were determined by national contingents within their logistics chain of command. For British forces in IFOR and SFOR, for instance, this was the Pioneer Labour Support Unit, based at the divisional headquarters in Banja Luka. Other management matters were left to the discretion of individual units and supervisors, and base commanders could also issue or change procedures regarding interpreters' behaviour on base. Many day-to-day procedures would therefore vary as units came and went. However, there was potential to escalate management matters to divisional level, meaning that policy was made incrementally during the time that British forces were present in the Banja Luka area (1995–2007). It took several years for the headquarters to agree on maternity leave for interpreters, who until 1998 or 1999 had only been allowed the general amount of sick leave because no policy had been made (in practice, new mothers had often but not always given up their jobs). Base commanders were only prevented from imposing curfews on off-duty resident interpreters after a complaint by a group of interpreters was referred up to the headquarters level. The decentralized nature of personnel management meant that the same system could produce very different experiences for different interpreters. Accounts from the British-led division, Multi-National Division (South-West), vary dramatically in their presentation of the foreign/local encounter and of how well interpreters considered that foreign troops had fulfilled their responsibilities towards them.

The example of workplace relations in Šipovo, a small town in Republika Srpska that contained several British bases in the late 1990s, presents a case where the high degree of flexibility appears to have worked to the benefit of local interpreters and the town's wider population. The area including Šipovo, sometimes known as the 'Anvil', had been captured by the HVO in September 1995 but was assigned to the RS under the Dayton Peace Agreement in return for Serb concessions of territory elsewhere, meaning that it had to be reintegrated into the Bosnian Serb republic after heavy looting by the HVO. A programme of civilianization at the Šipovo bases, which began in 1998, aimed to open a number of posts to skilled civilian workers which would otherwise have been filled by British soldiers from the combat service support arms. This benefited British forces because it enabled them to reduce troop numbers and incur lower overall employment costs, with the potential to extend the programme elsewhere if the Šipovo pilot was successful. Simultaneously, it benefited the town by opening up skilled jobs that had been in short supply during and after the conflict. The commander of the Royal Electrical and Mechanical Engineers (REME) workshop in Šipovo viewed the programme as also bringing a more philosophical goal: transparency:

> *Mark Ferguson*: [W]e put out an advert (laughs) for these five people, and of course we got mobbed. And it wasn't unexpected, but literally, [we were]. I remember going downtown, and my liaison officer was bravely trying to sit with one of our poor interpreters, and there were

literally hundreds of men around the liaison officer. All good-natured, but they'd heard there were jobs. I then got pulled aside by the mayor, who'd been the [VRS] brigade commander [during the war]. And he said, 'I hear you're looking for men to work.' And I said, 'Yes, that's right.' And he said, 'Just speak to me, I'll give you good men.' But this came down to this whole business of patronage, and how a former socialist society operates in that way, or a totalitarian regime. His view was, 'I'll get you mechanics.' And he said, 'I'll get you,' I remember, it was *dobar čovek* he was talking about, 'a good man,' 'I'll give you a dobar čovek.' And I said, 'Yes.' 'Yes,' I said, 'a good man would have been a soldier during the war,' I said to him in Serbian. And he said, 'Oh, *naravno,* of course, you know. Why would he not be?' And you'd say, 'Yeah, OK.' Well, what he actually was going to do was give it to his cronies. He was going to give jobs to people who he regarded as good men. And I said, 'No, we're going to do it on merit.' And this, interviewing people on merit, was something that they just really found great difficulty with.[1]

Transparency, alongside democratization, privatization and the rule of law, was one of the major transformations that the intervention as a whole aimed to bring about in Bosnia-Herzegovina (Coles 2007: 91–2). Ferguson's part in the civilianization programme enabled him to translate the push for transparency into everyday base/town relations. From a local interpreter's point of view, however, the British bases in Šipovo were remembered primarily for a feeling of hospitality and mutuality that far exceeded that described in other towns in MND (SW). Jelena Vlahović had worked at the British field hospital until late 1998, when she became pregnant, and had returned to work for British forces as a finance clerk in 1999 during a further stage of the civilian employment programme.

Catherine Baker: So when was it they started to replace soldiers with civilians [in Šipovo]?

Jelena Vlahović: Oof. To replace soldiers with civilians? It started in 2000, I'd say. The great initiative to employ as many Šipovo civilians as possible started in '98, and then gradually got bigger and bigger. But it stopped with me as a finance officer, with a couple of people who were doing IT equipment provision, repair, stuff like that, servicing, and that's it. I think those were the most responsible jobs that were given to civilians. Of course, only because of the security issues....

> [MND (SW) had] decided that actually the threat probably wasn't that high that we were going to fight again against each other, so they decided that they could help communities by employing people. In Banja Luka they were employing people who used to work in the Unis factory to help them, so they were focused on them, while in Šipovo that was the whole community, because it's a small community. And the people were really poor. I mean, they came back to their houses, which were burned down. Of course there were organizations who were helping them to rebuild them, but still, you can't just live on a house. You needed to earn money to feed your family, to get clothes for your children to go to school. You know. Needs are different.... So it was in '98, and I think that was a good decision. Because, I think the most... the strongest bond between people in Šipovo and British people was created with that. Because local people were very grateful, and Brits really felt that they actually were able to help in one community.[2]

As a finance clerk, Vlahović had helped to set up a practice that was not replicated across all British bases as a matter of policy but that appeared to have a profound effect on foreign/local relationships in Šipovo: the establishment of a voluntary welfare fund to compensate for the post-war, post-socialist paucity of welfare benefits. This had originated from an existing practice of troops contributing to charity collections for townspeople in need of social care:

> *Catherine Baker*: Whose idea was it to start doing that?
>
> *Jelena Vlahović*: It was, actually, the initiative came from... we had, how's that called, a labour unit, with the clerks who were actually taking care of contracts, employment, discharge, et cetera. And the people – because Šipovo is a small town, people would come to the SFOR base asking for help if somebody was sick. And of course we would always collect money, we had charity boxes in bars and stuff like that, for people who need social care, where they needed, I don't know, a house, or furniture, or books for children for school, or clothes, or things like that. And the idea came from that, and one of the – I think he was a labourer, just a person who would clean the camp area – he became very ill, and I spoke to our clerk, and she said, if we did that for people who are not directly employed by SFOR, why wouldn't we do the same thing for him? And we started then. And then whether it was needed or not, we would do that every month. And then we created some sort of fund,... and then

> we would have immediately, I don't know, €1,000 or €2,000 to give straight away, and then on a regular basis until that person is recovered. That was a model of self-aid. And Brits, I mean, officers and soldiers, were even more generous. They were giving money regularly. Without need, I mean, they just said, 'OK, where's that charity [box]?' They would give, you know, €10, €20, every week. Whenever they got paid... they would straight away give some money for charity. And I really liked it.[3]

The impact of the British military on Šipovo as remembered by Vlahović and Ferguson appears as a remarkable example of cordiality – something that could only be achieved, in Ferguson's account, after bringing the town into modernity by facing down the local wartime power structures and replacing the practice of *veze* ('connections') with recruitment by merit. Vlahović's memories of working in the same town then and later suggest that employer–employee relations remained at a congenial pitch, where economic inequalities between soldiers and the local workforce were pushed into the background by generosity. Indeed, she remembered soldiers who had served in Šipovo and other Bosnian towns commenting on how unusual Šipovo had been and even saying: 'Šipovo will never happen again to any of us.'[4] Long after rotating out of Šipovo, certain soldiers were still connected to the town through leisure practices, property purchases and even family ties.

Šipovo, however, was remarkable. In other cases, the linkage between the employing contingent's welfare arrangements and interpreters' perception of the foreign force worked to the opposite effect: troops' disregard for the welfare of interpreters permeated the foreign/local encounter and led to resentment. This is illustrated well by the narrative of an interpreter from Bihać, Emina Zaimović, who had worked for UN Military Observers during the war and held several other interpreting jobs afterwards. Bihać belonged to a different political entity of Bosnia-Herzegovina than Šipovo, but it was part of the same Multi-National Division of IFOR/SFOR, albeit in the Canadian rather than British area of responsibility. Zaimović remembered working for the Canadian unit as the least satisfactory of her interpreting jobs because of soldiers' attitudes towards the interpreters and other local people:

> *Emina Zaimović*: There was a pool of interpreters, and we had shifts, and we wore uniforms, Canadian uniforms, they gave us uniforms, and they had these little cars that were... the cars were not made of solid material, but of plastic, and of some sort of metal and I don't

know what, but it was terribly cold in these cars, and they would go out and patrol all day long, or patrol three hours, and you would go out and freeze in these cars and it was terrible. And, yeah. They had no...how can I put it nicely? They did not treat interpreters with respect. Not only interpreters, others, as well. With the respect that every human being deserves, I think. Yeah.

Catherine Baker: And so people stopped working for them?

Emina Zaimović: No...well, people...I'm not saying that everybody shares my opinion, but I couldn't wait to stop working for them. I mean, I worked because I needed the job, and it wasn't a well-paid one, either. But I just couldn't wait to stop working with them.[5]

Zaimović, in common with many post-war interpreters, was particularly concerned about the poor driving of military vehicles, which put interpreters as well as soldiers at risk of injury. They interpreted this as recklessness and a lack of respect for the humanity of interpreters, which they felt was exacerbated when injured interpreters and soldiers were treated unequally. The incident that most upset Zaimović was an accident in 1996 after which Canadian soldiers and a local interpreter had been treated in different hospitals:

Emina Zaimović: Just to tell you an anecdote, it happened that they had a car crash, and there was this girl who was seriously, seriously wounded in the car crash. Her leg was broken. And...the Canadians that were wounded in the car crash were taken to Zagreb hospital, and she was taken to the local hospital. We had no social security, no medical coverage, nothing. I mean, it was clear to us, we were given a contract to sign like that, and we signed those contracts, and we knew that we would, you know, we would not get any compensation or any help from them. But just to think about a human gesture, if the two of us are wounded together in a car accident, and you're taken to Zagreb, to the best hospital ever, and I'm taken to the local hospital here. And they did not – we made fundraising for her because she had no medical coverage to cover for the hospital expenses and to cover for the surgery. And some of them contributed, because they were nice people. But generally, as a unit, as a structure, as a system, they did not feel any obligation towards her. And they fired her. Because she couldn't work. Yeah. She had I don't know how many days of leave, she took leave, and she was fired. With a broken leg. Well, things like this made me comment so badly

> about them. I mean, they're not all bad people, but...it's just the way they are....I mean, I worked with millions of people from many different countries, and I'm...as a human being, I hate generalizing, and I hate saying these [people] are like that and those are like that, but this was...this was very frustrating. Yeah.[6]

The accounts of Vlahović and Zaimović both recognize that medical costs had been met through informal aid societies to which locals and foreign soldiers all contributed, yet Zaimović narrated distance between employers and employees and Vlahović narrated the reverse. The single incidents in each narrative were embedded in wider memories of social relations on and around the military base, creating – or negating – a social contract.

For people who had grown up in Bosnia-Herzegovina and other parts of former Yugoslavia, extended welfare provisions such as maternity leave or fair compensation after industrial injury were taken-for-granted aspects of a standard of living which had been assured under Yugoslav socialism and had now disappeared (Baker 2012a). Interpreters' narratives about the risk of injury were thus also narratives of coming to terms with this deep social rupture. The system of short-term rolling contracts within which most interpreters worked did not accommodate sickness and maternity leave well, although the professionalization at HQ SFOR after 2000 greatly improved benefits as well as pay for the interpreters employed at LSB. Interpreters without contractual sickness and maternity leave, however, faced uncomfortable choices at times of personal difficulty. Women frequently gave up their jobs on maternity if they could afford it, though one interviewee from Banja Luka had kept on working throughout her child's infancy. Interpreters too sick to work faced dismissal after their maximum leave period had expired, even if the injury had occurred on the job – the fate of the protagonist in Veselin Gatalo's semi-autobiographical novel about an interpreter from Mostar injured in the crash of a SFOR armoured vehicle (Gatalo 2004), and of the unfortunate co-worker of Zaimović.

In critical narratives of these foreign/local encounters, the risks posed to interpreters by soldiers played a major role: in Banja Luka, for instance, one often heard of a certain woman who had been wounded during a weapons inspection by an accident with a confiscated firearm. Soldiers could also cause psychological rather than physical wounds. To treat interpreters as no more than interchangeable logistical items without agency was experienced as particularly dehumanizing by Jovana

Zorić, an interpreter for British forces at Mrkonjić Grad, who recalled one upsetting briefing:

> *Jovana Zorić*: How come that you are so protected, you know, how come that you take care of yourself, and you're just treating locals like kind of disposable tools? Like, 'Don't forget that,' that was our favourite briefing for soldiers when they were going on a patrol. Don't forget your kit. I don't know, helmets, body armours. Don't forget your satellite box, the orange box of the satellite phone. Don't forget your interpreter. And we were like, as if I am [a] tool, sorry, excuse me? (laughs) I'm human, you know, kind of thing. So that was it.[7]

Saša Novaković, who had worked for British troops until they pulled out of Banja Luka, expressed the most regret at the contractual conditions to which he had agreed:

> *Saša Novaković*: [W]hen they closed down the camps [during the consolidation] many interpreters were left without a job. And the SFOR camps closed down five years ago. There are a huge number of them still without jobs. Really, they are without jobs. So now, I really think that if I could turn back the time now, and with that knowledge, I would never have worked for them. At least not with that kind of contract.... But then, I told you, for the one position of interpreter there were a hundred others waiting.... We had a better standard [of living] at the time. That was the only privilege.[8]

Some interpreters took matters into their own hands by purchasing health insurance privately, and the LSB/HQ SFOR interpreters eventually had access to an official health insurance scheme. The LSB aside, aftercare following workplace injuries and other sickness depended on goodwill rather than policy. Military employers justified the nature of interpreters' contracts on the grounds that the force could not have committed to longer contracts when the very duration of their military presence was so unclear, and that interpreters had entered into the contracts freely. One might question, however, whether ethical relations are governed entirely by contract (Butler 2011). In discussing another injury that had taken place during the war (an objectively more dangerous period than after Dayton), Zaimović put the case that employers' ethical responsibilities were greater than strictly contractual:

Catherine Baker: I wonder, what would the UN have done if somebody had been injured at work?

Emina Zaimović: There *was* an injury at work. Well, I was injured myself. During the time of war…we also did not have social and medical coverage and, you know, pension funds and stuff, but we were in a way taken care of. For example, there was a girl who had a broken arm, and she was taken to Zagreb hospital, at the expense of the UN. It wasn't arranged as part of the contract, but they made sure to take care of people if something should happen to them.…As an employee it's important to feel that way. I mean, I know that it's not in my contract that you would save my life, but, if you show as a human being that you care, that's more important to me. Which is – that was like that in the war. And I think that was more important than just having it in a contract.[9]

Equality in welfare was thus a prerequisite for harmony in the foreign/local encounter between soldiers and interpreters. However, it was not sufficient. Interpreters asked also to be viewed as equally human and worthy from a cultural point of view. As representatives of a highly educated social stratum who had seen their personal trajectories damaged and constrained beyond any pre-war imagining, they objected to any foreign gaze that treated them as inhabitants of a backward conflict zone. Such a gaze on the Balkans as un-modern, irrational and prone to conflict had its origins in nineteenth-century fiction and travel writing (Goldsworthy 1998; Bracewell 2009), enabling contemporary Bosnia-Herzegovina to be similarly portrayed as a place for Westerners to test their 'heroism and endurance' (Hammond 2007: 267). This approach was inadequate and detrimental to the foreign/local encounters of interpreting and of peace operations themselves.

Although the worst effects of wartime economic devastation alleviated after the implementation of Dayton, many foreign soldiers still understood Bosnia as an alienating environment and expected even harsher conditions than they met. Zaimović's frustration with her Canadian employers was based not only on the accident but also on the perceptions of Bosnia-Herzegovina that they had expressed:

Emina Zaimović: [T]hey had this mentality of rude macho soldiers, and I did not like it at all. And they would not appreciate the people that worked with them, like, us locals, they felt that we were a lower race, so to say. I mean, I had some good contacts with some of them, and some of the things they told us about Bosnia and the Balkans

> and the time that they were preparing to come here, they expected to find savages here, I would say. They would – like, one girl, I'm still friends with her, she told me that they were told to bring lots of shampoo and toothpaste and hygienic items because you could not find it here. And it was after the war, it was like two or three years after the war, of course you could find it here. And they would make jokes like, 'Oh, you have electricity, and you have running water in the house.' Part of it was a joke, but part of it was really talking down to people and being rude, and I did not appreciate that experience at all. Not at all. And they had this conspiracy in their head, like everything is against them, they are like the super super troops... No. I did not like that.[10]

Such disappointment in, if not resentment of, foreign soldiers' ignorance was a frequent discourse in interviews with former field interpreters – the very people who accompanied them on patrols and witnessed their reactions to Bosnian villages first-hand. Just as one explanation for the failure of refugee return programmes in rural areas was that 'most people deeply resented being thrown back onto what they perceived as premodern peasanthood' (Jansen 2006: 193), Bosnians who came face to face with soldiers' poorly formed preconceptions were upset to discover foreigners conceiving of their society as endemically poor, backward and violent rather than the site of a systemic shock which fate might have inflicted on any other European country.

Zaimović's brief employment with Canadian troops came during a period of crisis for Canadian Forces, which were recovering from discipline failures among elite regiments in Somalia and Bosnia-Herzegovina in the earlier 1990s (Winslow 2004); even a British officer who had served alongside Canadians in IFOR alluded to 'friction' involving a French Canadian battalion that had been implicated in one scandal.[11] Canadians' violence in those incidents has been linked, by Sherene Razack (2004), to cultural narratives of a protective white masculine North that have something in common with the adventure stories studied by Hammond (2007). Yet Canadian soldiers were, needless to say, not the only troops who lacked knowledge about Bosnian society. Tarik Begović recalled encouraging a US soldier to visit Sarajevo – the capital of the country – only for his encouragement to be pushed aside because: 'He was like, "You know what? There's a war in Kosovo and I'm not going down there."'[12] Saša Novaković remarked that 'some of the [British] soldiers, even officers, couldn't even tell a mosque from a church. They didn't know. And actually this is a problem here!',[13] because it left the soldiers unable to draw inferences about how a settlement would be labelled ethnically (see Chapter 6). Jovana Zorić, like many of her colleagues working with British troops in the extended vicinity of Banja Luka, found insensitive comments about Bosnians' living conditions very hurtful:

> *Jovana Zorić*: [S]ome of them, seriously, they were surprised that we have – 'Oh, you have newspapers, you have TV!' And I'm like, 'Guys, we are in Europe. The civil war happened now, but we had education. Most interpreters have university degrees, while most of you left school at 16.' That was ... and they would go into houses, 'Wow, your houses are really nice! Oh, wooden floor!' And I'm like, 'Yeah, that's the standard. Wooden floor is the standard here.'[14]

Interpreters commonly attributed such attitudes to a lack of 'education' – this being a core value in Yugoslav society, the symbol of an upbringing worthy of respect, the fulfilment of a social norm, and the reason they themselves had been able to find personal agency while negotiating the consequences of their country's disintegration (Baker 2011b).

Economic impacts of the foreign/local interpreting encounter

Before the outbreak of the war, the people who became locally recruited interpreters for foreign military forces had not conceived that their own country would become a place where such a job would exist. Many had not even imagined that they would have a career in interpreting and translation: they had typically studied languages for other professional purposes, or had done their most relevant language learning outside school. Only two interviewees had intended to be professional linguists, and even they were applying their skills in a different way than they had expected. The foreign/local encounter expanded into interpreters' non-work lives because it altered their socio-economic positionality.

The economic privileges of working for international agencies, including foreign military forces, were seen most dramatically in the wartime siege economies such as Sarajevo, Goražde or Bihać. Within the logic of a siege, where the besieger attempts to force a town's residents into conditions of greater and greater scarcity, interpreters were in the rare position of access to food, communications and supplies as well as hard currency. Zaimović had become an interpreter at a time when Bihać was under siege, and recalled receiving US $600–700 per month:

Emina Zaimović: It was good. Well, it was good at a time that nobody else was receiving any pay. I remember once or twice we wanted to have our salaries increased, because at the time we heard that UN [staff] in Croatia...were receiving a much higher salary. But that was not possible for some reason, I don't know why. Basically, compared to other UN missions and UN engaged staff, we were not paid the best, but given the circumstances and the local surroundings and given the fact that no economy was existing and nobody was receiving a salary I think I earned lots of money (laughs). Well, it made my living, so – good.

Catherine Baker: What sort of living standard would an interpreter have had at that time?

Emina Zaimović: There was nothing to compare with, you know. If you had a job...in the UN, you could work, but there were no – nothing was working, no shops, no coffee bars, no factories, so nobody really got any money, except for the army. And they did not get a salary. And, I don't know, hospitals. So nobody really had money. We were the only ones to receive a salary, I guess. But, then again, you could not buy anything, because there was nothing to buy, so...I don't know. Fifty kilos of flour was a hundred dollars. So...measuring value and money was, you could not compare it to standards nowadays. There was no...no normal market, no normal economy, nothing was even normal, so, you could not speak about standards, I guess. Basically, we could afford a living.[15]

Under these conditions, working as an interpreter also brought informal benefits. Many interpreters were able to use troops' shopping facilities or to buy goods while accompanying their employers on visits to the rear, placing them partially outside the wartime shortage economy. Here arose a potential conflict with the ethic of shared suffering that leaders impressed on their communities (even when circumventing it themselves) and that neighbours reproduced through gossip (see Maček 2009). This placed interpreters under extra emotional pressure and compelled them to carry out a high degree of 'facework' (impression management) to resolve the contradictions. Thus Boba Vukojevic, who worked as an interpreter in Sarajevo between 1993 and 1995, expressed solidarity with her neighbours in practical ways (by bringing back food from visits outside Sarajevo and never accepting payment) and also through symbolic practices (choosing to sleep at her family's apartment rather than in the UN's accommodation; avoiding wearing personal protective equipment in town since fellow townspeople did not have it).

Entire groups of extended family and neighbours would benefit from interpreters' earnings, although the business of providing for one's family during the siege of Sarajevo had the unfortunate but inevitable consequence of sustaining the black market (Andreas 2007: 9).

In places cut off from telecommunications, another resource to which interpreters had greater access than ordinary civilians was information – the everyday variety one had taken for granted before the war began – and international media. Sinan Halilović, a self-taught interpreter working for British troops in besieged Goražde and urgently needing to improve his English, initially used the base's tabloid newspapers as primary materials:

> *Sinan Halilović*: To me, newspapers were the key, really. Because I find newspapers like everyday language. It was *The Sun, Daily Mirror, Daily Star.* Things like that. These common newspapers, English papers. They were helpful to me. I could – my interest was in sports. So reading these sports reports and events through the papers helped me to improve my English. I was really keen on finding out what is happening in sport. In England and the rest of the world. In 1994 it was the first time for me to hear about Michael Schumacher. It was the beginning of his career, when he was driving for Benetton. That was the first time ever, for example. Or that was the time when Eric Cantona made his famous kung fu kick, OK. I found out about that through the newspapers. Newcastle almost won the [Premier League] title, but they were unfortunate, in '95. Things like that. I wasn't interested about politics, or economy, because I had politics all around me, during the war.[16]

Interpreters' economic advantages continued after the war. The salaries of interpreters employed by British forces near Banja Luka were approximately 900–1000 German marks. This sum was preferable to local wages in three ways: it was higher than the monthly earnings even for established professional jobs, was paid in hard currency, and was reliably paid for as long as the job lasted. The key reservation here is 'as long as the job lasted'. Interpreting posts were fundamentally insecure because the duration of the peace operations was always unknown. Indeed, interpreters suffered not only from job insecurity – whether their jobs would continue to exist – but also work insecurity – whether their health and safety would be adequately protected while at work. These were the two main forms of risk they discussed in interviews. Other types of labour insecurity (see Standing 2011: 10) – such as 'skill reproduction security', the opportunity to continue gaining and making use of new skills, which was never guaranteed except in the professionalized LSB framework – were also visible in the nature of their posts.

The economy of 1990s Bosnia-Herzegovina faced not only the challenge of recovery from war but that of recovery from the collapse of communism, yet, as Stef Jansen (2006: 186; emphasis original) points out, 'while Bosnia-Herzegovina's post-*war* condition was continually evoked, its post-*socialist* transformations were rarely publicly debated'. With the institutions of socialist society destroyed (or sometimes repurposed to serve nationalist politics), old points of reference around which individuals had expected to orient their working lives no longer existed (Baker 2012a). Though some had lived or had seen family members live in capitalist economies such as West Germany as economic migrants, the economy that emerged in Bosnia-Herzegovina during and after the war resembled a combination of patronage-driven sinecures and insecure casual contracts which shifted the burden of risk on to the employee far more than they resembled the mid-20th-century industrial societies of which they might have had experience. Bosnians were therefore expected to predict, educate and prepare themselves for, seek out and direct their own trajectories of employment in an unfamiliar and often unwelcome milieu where the vision of a trade or profession leading to stability and security was difficult to contemplate for most.

The creation of employment by peacebuilders is an often-overlooked aspect of the economic impact of peace operations. Critical assessments of the effect of peacebuilding on local employment by Christopher Cramer (2008) and Michael Pugh (2002; 2008) surprisingly do not refer to it. Insights into interventions' effects on local economies can, however, be found in literature on the wider adverse consequences of peace operations, such as the impact of foreign troops' presence on public health in the host country, the opportunities for smuggling and human trafficking, or problems with civil–military relations in troop-contributing countries. These are often termed the 'unintended consequences' (Aoi, de Coning and Thakur 2007; Kudesia and Rubinstein 2009), framing them as anomalies or accidents within a benign model of intervention (Higate and Henry 2009: 157). Kathleen Jennings (2010: 231) thus recognizes the concept of a 'peacekeeping economy', which 'refers to the economic multiplier effect of peace operations via direct or indirect resource flows into the local economy, as well as to the construction or reconstruction of housing stock and other infrastructure, including "entertainment infrastructure"' – a euphemism for the infrastructure of sex work. Another of the adverse or unintended consequences of a peacekeeping economy is considered to be the impact of foreign agencies' and militaries' recruitment of a local workforce, which may be to the detriment of local civil society.

Research in Kosovo and Afghanistan by Katarina Ammitzboell found that many negative socio-economic transformations and distortions become understood in local discourses as 'unintentional policies' (Ammitzboell 2007: 75). The perception of these distortions as policy then causes frustration. They include promised initiatives that are then delayed or not implemented; failures to use local capacity and knowledge in projects; high turnovers and wages of foreign staff; wage, rent and price inflations; and brain drains caused when 'students leave university, in particular in Kosovo, to be drivers, guards or translators, and doctors and other professionals leave to work in admin roles in NGOs or other internationally supported programs' (Ammitzboell 2007: 76). Suprita Kudesia and Robert Rubinstein (2009: 433) thus talk of 'local hire syndrome', 'in which highly skilled professionals work in unskilled, often menial positions [...] because they can earn more in unskilled positions with the peace operation than they could practicing their profession on the open market'. Even when these economic consequences are not desired or foreseen, a lack of policy on behalf of the organizations that have produced them is still experienced as policy. Foreign military forces and civilian agencies are thus likely to be held responsible for them regardless of the intentions with which they have approached economic relations within sites of intervention.

Assessments of 'brain drains' or 'local hire syndromes' caused by peace operations regularly discuss interpreters only as another form of unskilled labour. Robert Barry, a former head of the OSCE mission to Bosnia-Herzegovina, wrote of 'people who should be the judges and editors becoming the drivers and interpreters at wages higher than cabinet ministers receive' (Barry 1999: 102). Even Steven Sampson, an anthropologist extremely concerned with local agency, writes of international agencies employing 'a support staff of drivers, secretaries, translators and security guards' (Sampson 2002: n.p.). However, it is possible to conceive of interpreting and translation in a far more skilled way than this. The liminal position of local linguists, who are uniquely implicated in foreign soldiers' and project workers' acquisition of knowledge and who come to represent those organizations' policies in local eyes, is thought furthest through in Andrew Gilbert's ethnography of the OSCE: in one case a local woman had accused an OSCE interpreter of unreliability and breach of confidentiality, and in many other cases the information fixed in English-language written documents was seen as a privileged and transparent form of knowledge by foreign OSCE officials (Gilbert 2008). This perspective recognizes the linguists' agency not just as economic actors but as translators and interpreters who shift knowledge between languages and must choose how to reconcile nuances and ambiguities.

The reform of the HQ SFOR language service after 2000 (Chapter 4) shows that, with a testing, training and feedback system grounded in the standards of the linguistic profession, locals who had initially been hired as untrained field interpreters could indeed reach advanced levels of performance. In such a structure, local linguists felt supported and appreciated for their linguistic skills rather than dehumanized as tools, machines or logistical units. Some other contingents, such as elements of the British forces around Banja Luka, did manage to produce strong personal emotional identification in their interpreters, in a context where the local employees felt detached from what they thought of as nationalistic intolerance in their own neighbourhoods and political systems (Baker 2012b). This was at its most successful where troops were seen to appreciate interpreters as differentiated individuals, to respect the society in which interpreters lived as a modern European country undergoing a temporary crisis and to treat sick or injured local employees on the same terms as themselves. Informal incidents of rudeness, ignorance or disrespect, which often occurred in unsupervised and unregulated settings, prevented this and produced a degree of distance even further than that to be expected between those who would leave the area in a few months' time and those who, while not holding the full power and privilege of the force itself, paradoxically ended up providing the operation's human continuity.

Local interpreters as continuity

The knowledge base of experienced local language intermediaries was recognized as an asset by sensitive supervisors and users of interpreters. The commanding officer of 1 COLDSTREAM, a battalion that conducted many crucial liaison visits in fraught conditions, considered that local interpreters had been especially useful as new liaison officers familiarized themselves with the personalities of their key contacts:

> *Coldstreamer*: [E]verybody had had – all the key people, all the liaison officers, working with the warring factions, and all the company commanders – everybody had had at least a week on the ground

> to...gather all the experience they could from their predecessors, and be ready to hit the ground running, as it were, as their predecessors left.
>
> *Catherine Baker*: And were any interpreters involved in that sort of handover period?
>
> *Coldstreamer*: Well, the interpreters were involved because every time anybody went to visit a local commander, at whatever level of command, you needed to take an interpreter with you. And so the interpreters in many ways provided the continuity from battalion to battalion. And had a great deal of experience to pass on to us, in terms of the personalities that we were visiting, and whether or not they were behaving in their normal difficult manner or whether this really was a problem that we were faced by or whether this was just synthetic anger or whatever, in the normal sort of way. So the interpreters were from day one absolutely essential to any understanding of the situation.[17]

Coldstreamer's recognition that interpreters 'provided the continuity' between one unit and the next exposes a wide gap between policy and practice. The period of rotation in and out or 'handover–takeover' was conceived as a transfer of control and knowledge from one unit to the next, maintaining a seamless impression of military presence. In practice, the carrying out of handover–takeover was composed of many encounters between new troops and their contacts in the area, facilitated by the interpersonal awareness of interpreters who might have spent several years working at the same base and already witnessed several changeovers. During handover–takeover, when departing troops took their experiences and memories out of theatre and relieving troops' understandings based on pre-deployment training were amplified or challenged during their first contact with the area of responsibility, interpreters' unwritten and unformalized knowledge of how to achieve objectives in the local area came to the fore. Interpreters became impromptu cultural and political advisers and were relied on as such, meaning that an interpreter could have a high level of power in establishing new troops' first impressions of a local contact. Soldiers nonetheless had the choice to accept or disregard interpreters' advice, and interpreters of course had the choice of how candidly to share their assessments with the troops. A knowledge base that was essential to peace operations because of the liaison-based nature of peacekeeping and peacebuilding therefore rested with interpreters rather than being held independently by the military. Recognizing and valuing this agency on the part of language intermediaries can be beneficial for the success of peace operations:

> [I]f they are properly engaged, members of the populations served by the mission can assist as cultural instructors who have real responsibilities, and can serve as primary liaisons between the mission and the population. (Rubinstein, Keller and Scherger 2008: 545)

Liaison and civil affairs officers and patrol commanders of course participated in official handover–takeover procedures. However, they would supplement the lessons from their departing counterparts through informal conversations with interpreters, often en route to a meeting or a patrol: what's the best way to negotiate with the mayor? why had a passer-by been shouting when troops went past? (to take two examples that appeared in interviews). Interpreters could also convey important cultural information at a level of detail beyond that imparted in pre-deployment briefing and training. Asmir Pašić, who worked for the Nordic–Polish Brigade in Doboj, remembered supplying recent military history on an extremely localized level and also providing essential cultural background (how to infer ethnicity from personal names) which every Bosnian took for granted but infantry soldiers on patrols did not know:

> *Asmir Pašić*: We interpreters were the ones to provide them with knowledge, with information. They didn't know anything about it. They knew, they were briefed back in their home countries about the people here. We ... people living in Bosnia-Herzegovina, we could tell by name which ethnicity you are. Our first names and family names tell us this. They didn't know. So, I had a hunch they were briefed on what each of us was, among interpreters. And they told us they were briefed about the military situation here, especially the liaison officers and the commanders. The soldiers, privates, they didn't know that much. So we were the ones who had to tell them. And they were very interested in war stories. When we would drive together, they would always ... they always wanted us to tell them how the war went on in this particular area and which troops clashed on military actions et cetera. Because everywhere we went we could see traces of the war. Like destroyed tanks, bunkers, trenches, minefields. You could easily see where the front line was. And we would always usually walk, drive, with our patrols along the front line.[18]

US troop newsletters from Bosnia-Herzegovina gave examples of interpreters telling troops about significant events in the local area, such as the ABiH's defence of a civilian corridor at Zvornik in spring 1992, or the Kapija massacre of 71 young people at Tuzla in 1995 at which a number of future interpreters had been present (*The Talon*, 27 June 1997: 4; *The Talon*, 5 February 1999: 8–9). The advisory/teaching role of interpreters was rarely formalized, except in some cases where base commanders or chaplains had organized 'evening class'-type initiatives to keep troops from boredom or drunkenness during leisure time.[19] These were not mandated at a level higher than the individual unit and would not necessarily be kept up when one unit handed over to another with a different culture.

Informal knowledge exchanges, when satisfactory to both foreigners and local employees, represented an important stage in building up loyalty and trust in soldier/interpreter teams (see Chapter 6). Armin Kosarević, an interpreter and rock musician from Tuzla, had found that 'every time you had to prove yourself from scratch' when a new rotation arrived, especially to US troops who had arrived with serious misperceptions about the beliefs of Muslims in Bosnia-Herzegovina. Describing himself as more extrovert than some interpreters (who therefore created trust in different ways), he believed that answering troops' questions while travelling had helped them to bond and made it far easier for both parties in the relationship to work together:

> *Armin Kosarević*: There were some interpreters who were not very – they didn't like to socialize. You know, some interpreters were like, they sit in a car, he will keep quiet, and... depending on where they're going, he will just do the job there, sit in a car, be quiet. I was always, I always talked to them [soldiers]. They always had a lot of questions, like 'Hey what's this?', 'What's that?', and 'How do you do this?' And I always thought that by talking the time goes faster (laughs), and that's the way, I mean, to create this communication, because they don't know anything, when they come to Bosnia. They have so many questions. Of course they have their worries, and they have... that's the way to create this bond.[20]

A much more critical perspective on the responsibilities that could be placed on interpreters as a result of military rotation was expressed by an interpreter who had worked for British forces in Republika Srpska in the late 1990s. Jovana Zorić worked for three years at bases around

Mrkonjić Grad, another small town in the 'Anvil', where several British infantry, cavalry and support units were based in multiple facilities including the shoe factory and bus depot. Her narrative was characterized by an increasing sense of boredom, repetitiveness, and disillusion at the dehumanizing treatment and dangerous behaviour she had experienced from several units. Her boredom with the commitments made by new units – exemplifying Ammitzboell's remarks about the effect of promises not implemented – materialized in a wider context of beginning to find interpreting work repetitive and uninteresting:

> *Jovana Zorić*: [R]egiment after regiment, after six months, the new regiment would come, and they would start from beginning. Like, 'OK, let's get to know the area. OK. Let's do patrols for soldiers to know the area,' and you go around. And you go around the same villages, same places, because they have reports from the previous regiment. And then you would talk to the same people, same questions, again, same answers, and after like three [times] the guy, I don't know, head of the village would say, 'Well, I spoke to you like four months ago and you're asking me the same question.' And I was like, 'Yeah, I know, it was us, but it wasn't him, it wasn't the same regiment, so can you please explain the same over over again.' And so it at some point became pointless. You know. And then they would promise the same stuff. They would ask, 'So what do you need?' For example, 'What do you need in this village?' And the headmaster would say, 'Well, OK, we need new desks, and equipment in, a blackboard in, the school.' 'OK, we'll see what can we do. I can't promise anything, but we'll see what can we do.' That was, those two sentences, 'We cannot promise anything, but we'll see.' And four months later, six months later, you come and they say, 'So what do you need?' And the headmaster is like, 'I've said this before, but I know you can't promise anything, but you'll do your best, I know, I know.' And, you know, after some time you start to become – I was in a few situations very embarrassed, because I felt it's my responsibility. It wasn't; I'm just a machine to translate to, you know, to transform from English to Serbian, Serbian to English, but I just felt: this is pointless. Because, in four or six months, another will come, and, 'What's your name, where did you learn English, what do you do,' the same questions for you as interpreter, and same questions for the meetings.[21]

This kind of small-scale civil affairs work in which many troops participated off duty as well as on, repairing town and village infrastructure or obtaining supplies for community facilities such as schools and health centres, was often one of the most rewarding aspects of a tour in Bosnia-Herzegovina for foreign soldiers (Baker 2011a). Even when dissatisfied or unsure about the impact their time had had on the 'big picture' level of the intervention, they were able to find satisfaction in facilitating or personally carrying out these cheap and easily accomplished projects. Spending only six months in the locality, however, they would not personally experience the longer-term effect of a powerful and well-resourced military force staying in the area for years yet funding only limited improvements (for instance, civil affairs officers had the power to award start-up funds for enterprises, but the project had to be achievable within six months so that the same unit could assess the success of the grant). Zorić however, having witnessed this cycle repeated over several rotations, came to think of the formula of 'We cannot promise anything, but we'll see' as an empty pledge.

The frustrating effect of these promises was intensified by Zorić having personally to speak them and to receive whatever indignant or disappointed response the interlocutor chose. A significant dimension of the foreign/local encounter in interpreting is thus illustrated here. Interpreters, presenting the force's statements to local people in their own language, embodied the force itself, the international community and the apparent broken promises of both. Often wearing the force's uniform and usually perceived as more loyal to the force than to the neighbourhood, interpreters took the brunt of local frustrations, not least when rotation after rotation of troops offered no more but the same small-scale projects. In Zorić's account, the interpreter and the school headmaster both came to understand the civil affairs visit as a ritualized performance that actually dramatized the limits of the military force's power or will. This context was unavailable to newly arrived troops, whose happiness at making a small difference in what they perceived as a war-torn society in need of help was genuine, yet who were unable to act on the structural precarity that characterized Bosnia-Herzegovina after the 1992–5 conflict, the Dayton Peace Agreement and the multinational intervention.

6
Nationality, Ethnicity and Trust

Trust is essential for the products of interpreting and translation to be reliable: yet the language intermediaries who are considered the most trustworthy may not be those whose language knowledge or translation and interpreting skills are greatest. This problem is at its toughest in military language encounters. The potential consequences of an unauthorized disclosure of information are so great that military organizations and personnel consider them to outweigh the consequences of a language encounter not being mediated by the person with the highest available skills. More precisely, the notion of trustworthiness was inherent in military conceptions of suitability for the task. It was determined with reference to collective categories and relied on an assumption that any person local to the conflict zone would be biased whereas any person foreign to the conflict zone would not. The foreign/international and local categories could be broken down into more specific categories that at times could also affect calculations about suitability. As seen in Chapters 2 and 3, certain work would be assigned only to a (foreign) linguist with military training and not to a civilian. Regarding local linguists, it was assumed that every Bosnian necessarily fell into one of three subcategories of localness – a Bosniak, a Croat or a Serb. Both these types of distinctions were important in how linguists and the reliability of their translations were viewed. The fundamental distinction for the multinational military force was still between a perception of automatic foreign objectivity leading to trustworthiness and a perception of automatic local subjectivity that would always contain the possibility of unreliability.

The force's trust in linguists and language intermediaries, however, is only one dimension of the significance of trust in language support for peace operations. Language and the agency of linguists also have an effect on the very quality of trust in the force's mission that must be maintained if an intervention is to achieve its objectives. This is because peace operations aim to bring about not only an end to observable violence but also a change in attitudes, relationships and behaviour among the inhabitants of a site of intervention. They are not conceived as, and those who carry them out would not accept their description as, a simple imposition of external power. Rather, they must realize their transformative ends through more complex processes of interaction and persuasion. The micro-encounters of peace operations at an extremely low and everyday level are a major determinant of whether or not a mission will succeed, as Béatrice Pouligny (2006: 252) notes: 'Much is played out in day-to-day life, in a work of proximity and small gestures, seemingly insignificant, which will none the less make it possible or not to build relations of confidence.' A peace operation must also help local populations understand why it has taken the actions it has taken (Kronsell 2012: 104). This is difficult to achieve if the force's official and unofficial communication does not operate 'in a way that allows people to understand themselves as valued and respected' (Rubinstein, Keller and Scherger 2008: 545), but it is also difficult to achieve if the force's communicators are not trusted. Accurate and reliable outcomes in language encounters are clearly a prerequisite for the communications of peace operations to succeed.

Following Onora O'Neill (2002), one may conceive of trust as a predictability of outcomes: to trust another is to have confidence that they will act within a known and agreed range of parameters. Mistrust manifests when that range of parameters cannot be known. In a military context, trustworthy language intermediaries can be expected to translate and interpret to the best of their ability and to keep confidentiality; when intermediaries are not trustworthy, it cannot be known whether they will remain within those parameters or whether they will take other actions, such as altering the translation to benefit a certain party to a conflict, or leaking information to a party to whom it is not to be revealed. They must therefore be treated as if they will.

The simplest hypothetical language encounter between a local person and a foreigner depends on two directions of trust: the foreigner's trust in the local and the local's trust in the foreigner. In practice, of course, both actors also exist in relation to other individuals, groups and entities, in the immediate vicinity or in the distance, whose trust they may be anxious to preserve, use, manipulate or gain; whose interest they may wish to attract or avoid. A paradigmatic language encounter in peace operations such as a conversation during a military liaison visit therefore involves at least a quadrilateral of trust: between the local and foreign interlocutors, between the local and other locals (who may be mutually mistrustful of each other) and, perhaps, between the foreigner and other foreigners (military superiors or subordinates; humanitarian workers; political advisers; journalists). And this supposes that the local and the foreign soldier are talking directly to each other. In practice, such language encounters in Bosnia-Herzegovina were usually conducted through a language intermediary – an individual in whom both interlocutors must trust in order for them to agree on the content of the translated message. This not only complicated the trust relationships of an encounter but mediated each interlocutor's capacity to trust the other, since they would form verbal impressions based on the speech produced by an interpreter, and their non-verbal impressions too could be affected by advice provided before or after (or even during) the encounter. Interlocutors also had to attempt to determine the backgrounds of their counterparts in order to decide whether, or how far, to trust. Great weight was placed in these calculations on discerning the nationality and ethnicity of language intermediaries.

Determining ethnicity in the field

The participants in peace operations and humanitarian missions typically seek quick and uncomplicated ways to determine ethnic and national identities (Malkki 1992; Ghosh 1994), and those who served in Bosnia-Herzegovina were no exception. Most foreigners in contact with Bosnia-Herzegovina viewed ethnicity as a clear and fixed attribute that governed every aspect of personal and public life, from people's voting intentions to their preferred residence to whether they would receive one with trust or mistrust. This representation also tended to interpret ethnicity 'as a destructive social force' that was sufficient to explain the outbreak and course of the Bosnian conflict (Banks and Wolfe Murray 1999: 157). An example is the introduction to the 'Culture and History' section of the *Bosnia Country Handbook* produced by the US Department of Defense for IFOR troops entering Bosnia-Herzegovina in December 1995:[1]

> KEY JUDGMENTS
>
> In the Balkans, past history is closely linked with perceptions of the present and future.
>
> Religious and cultural animosities have developed over centuries and are deeply ingrained among the various warring factions.

> Violence has been, and will likely continue to be, prevalent. (Department of Defense 1995: 2–1)

The 'warring factions' were synonymous with the three ethnic groups around which this picture of Bosnia-Herzegovina was organized. In this concept, every person in Bosnia-Herzegovina possessed a clearly-defined ethnic identity (Serb, Croat or Bosnian Muslim/Bosniak) which was manifested through their language variant (Serbian, Croatian or Bosnian), their religious belonging (Orthodox, Catholic or Muslim) and a set of associated customs (for instance, whether they celebrated holidays on 25 December, 6 January, or the shifting date of Islamic Bajram). Membership of one of these three ethnic groups would therefore in turn be the prime determinant of how other locals related to them, even if, as a foreigner, one attempted to embody an ethic of indifferent ethnicity-blindness or performative reconciliation. As Kujamäki (2012: 95) suggests, the structure of ethnic relations within a site of deployment is likely to complicate the foreign/local distinction in decisions about language support. An officer who demonstratively brought Serb interpreters on liaison missions to Bosniak forces and vice versa shortly after the Dayton Peace Agreement, during the fraught phase of implementing the transfer of territory and making the Inter-Entity Boundary Line material, would be operating within a performative-reconciliation mode and using the interpreter's ethnic identity as a resource just as it was possible to utilize the gender of the interpreter (Chapter 2). When working with troops who used their language intermediaries in this additional performative way, local interpreters found their daily routine became a time of resolving wartime myths and making ethical choices about how to present themselves to others.

This was the experience of Slađana Medić, a student of English from Banja Luka who began working as an interpreter for British forces in January 1996. She was offered a post at a base in Mrkonjić Grad, one of the towns that had been captured by the Croatian Army and HVO near the end of the war and was now to be incorporated into Republika Srpska. The job therefore touched her collective identity from the outset:

> *Slađana Medić*: [M]y first job was in Mrkonjić Grad, and that was under the Croatian Army at the time, and because I am a Serb, it was like a hostile army. And the town itself... well, was assigned to Republika Srpska by the Dayton Agreement. And they were supposed to withdraw from the town and leave it to Serbs. When we first arrived in

Mrkonjić Grad there was nobody there. There was only one granny. She was the only one that was living there, apart from the Croatian Army. And everything was burned down, pretty much. The British soldiers, they had removed corpses from the town. Human ones, but the animal ones were still there. And because I hadn't seen the war at all until that point it was a bit ... different. But I felt safe.[2]

On another assignment at this time, Medić was taken on a liaison visit to an ABiH headquarters. She managed an underlying anxiety about crossing this ethnicized boundary by placing her trust in the British troops' responsibilities towards their interpreter, but also by using common-sense South Slav understandings of the significance of naming in conveying ethnic identity to protect herself from possible intimidation:

Slađana Medić: Anyway, my first job was a visit to the 5th Corps (laughs) in Sanski Most. It was a Muslim army, and I can't say I was happy (laughs). It wasn't pleasant. But the British soldiers, they reassured me that they would protect me, because I'm wearing British uniform, and they would be eligible to shoot if somebody wanted to harm me. Because I'm wearing their uniform, and that would be an attack on Great Britain. So we went there, I introduced myself as Selma[3] (laughs)

Catherine Baker: (laughs)

Slađana Medić: Yeah, I didn't have the courage to say that my name was [Slađana] (laughs). And then, as it happens, I talked to one of the soldiers, and he said, 'Where are you from?' And I'm not a good liar, and I don't like to lie. And I said, 'Well, I'm from Banja Luka.' And I thought, like, my God, now he's going to shoot me immediately. And then he said, 'Really?' I said, 'Yeah.' But I wanted to avoid talking to him, but he was really persistent to talk to me. And then he said, 'Oh, right, well, I have a sister down there, she stayed.' And I said, 'Mm hmm, yeah, well, quite a few people stayed.' And then we parted. But I didn't have to translate anything at that meeting, because there was another interpreter. This was just, I was just there as a back-up (laughs) interpreter, I didn't interpret anything.[4]

Personal names in Bosnia-Herzegovina provided many clues to individuals' ethnic identity, and through the advice of linguists or native speakers many visitors to the country also became aware of this. Some names served as a positive identification so that a Turkish-sounding first name or a polysyllabic surname containing the particles *-beg-* or

Hadži- (originally Ottoman/Islamic honorifics) would code the bearer as a Bosniak; others offered negative identification, where a name was associated with two ethnicities, but not another. Certain names did not connote ethnicity at all, either because they derived from shared folk traditions or they were loaned from German, French or English; these were popular solutions for Bosnian parents who came from different ethnic backgrounds, shared the ruling party's ideological objections to nationalism and/or identified their families as Yugoslav (Bringa 1995: 19). Some foreigners would acquire sufficient knowledge to begin making name-based ethnic distinctions on their own, as in this account concerning Bugojno in 1994:

> *Louise Robbins*: I also deployed a Muslim interpreter, he was a volunteer. The CO wanted to get into Goražde, which was one of the enclaves, and he was smuggled in and then called forward a convoy. They needed an interpreter. So Dino, short for Sabahudin, how Muslim is that?, he got as far as a [Serb] checkpoint, where he showed his ID card... He was a Muslim. And they wouldn't let him through because he was a Muslim, and he was RTUd, returned to unit. So I had to find another volunteer to go, who was of the right ethnicity, right religion.[5]

Understanding ethnic naming conventions became yet more important once a foreigner had understood that, when it came to dialect, locality trumped ethnicity and complicated distinction between ethnicities: members of different ethnic groups in a particular area would speak similarly, to the frustration of nationalist language experts such as those in Republika Srpska who attempted to impose *ekavica* (as spoken in Serbia) rather than the *ijekavica* generally in use in northwest Bosnia (Greenberg 2000). Another British military interpreter who had served before Robbins remembered that his unit had often used its most experienced local interpreter, Dobrila Kalaba, on visits to the HVO and ABiH:

> *Nick Stansfield*: Dobrila was actually, although she was a Serb, she was obviously part of our negotiating team, and did an excellent job. Usually, because they were from the same area, this was her home area, there was no difference in accent. It would be the surname that would indicate which ethnic group they might belong to. But even that wasn't a hundred per cent. Sometimes it was, I mean, if it was Stanković, for example, it would probably be Serbian, almost

exclusively. But there were, you know. There are names which would not give that away.[6]

Locals as well as foreigners used personal names as a guide to interacting with others. At the time when the Factions Liaison Office at HQ SFOR operated a policy of adapting the language of letters and reports to the ethnicity of the recipient, documents addressed to an RS institution were clearly to be sent in Serbian but Federation institutions conceptually contained both Bosniak and Croat staff members. 'You know by the name of the person receiving the letter whether he was a Bosniak or a Croat,' remembered Edin Selimović, one interpreter who had been involved in translating these documents. 'And then you would say, "OK, this translation goes into Bosnian language." '[7] Temporarily renaming oneself into another ethnicity, as Medić did when apprehensively arriving at a meeting with the armed forces of a 'different' ethnic group, was a comfort strategy during superficial and unlikely-to-be-repeated social interactions, at the risk that the pretence might fall apart under further questioning and give rise to mistrust. Slađana's performance as the implicitly Bosniak 'Selma' was momentarily threatened when the interaction became conversational rather than professional, but recovered by the fact that, even during the war, life histories did not always correspond to nationalist boundaries. A non-Serb – like the soldier's sister in Medić's story – might have reconciled themselves to living under Serb nationalist authority in Banja Luka; many Serbs had remained in Sarajevo and contributed to defending the city against Bosnian Serb forces; Tuzla had become a 'paradox' where civic politics remained multiethnic although the city was defended by the increasingly nationalist ABiH (see Armakolas 2011). The identity she performed was striking enough to be remarkable, yet not entirely implausible.

However, this type of performance depended on keeping the local interlocutor's trust. In another account from the cluster of interpreters who began working for British forces near Banja Luka in 1996, a new interpreter (known by his British nickname of 'Mitch') faced the troubling ethical decision of whether or not to tell an inexperienced British officer that Croat forces were looting a village from which they were supposed to withdraw. Mitch's real personal name was a resource for identity management and performance since 'when you say it, you know, it is a common name used by Croatians and by the Serbs; but it's a Christian name'[8] – in other words, a name that is not evidently Muslim, thus marking its bearer within the system of three fixed ethnic identities as either Serb or Croat. At the climax of the confrontation, where Mitch had been visibly implicated in making the charge of looting against the Croatian unit, the Croatian officer in charge attempted to determine his ethnicity. Mitch understood that to present himself as a Serb at this point would escalate the Croatian's suspicion of him but to present himself as a Croat might enable him to make common ground and defuse the situation:

> *Mitch*: The next thing was the Croatian captain said 'OK, well, if you think that we are stealing, go to the truck and tell us what to take off. What do you think is not ours?' So we went there, and that lieutenant again said, 'OK,' he told me, 'tell me what to point out.' So I was again, you know...being placed in a very very difficult situation, where, I mean, nobody is that dumb not to know that I am the one who has orchestrated that. Or who is behind it, you know. So I would say to him, 'point to the yellow sofa.' So he's pointed, so they took it off from the truck. And that's how we did [it]. And at the end, that Croatian captain and some other Croatian officers were very very angry, obviously most of their troops were very angry. He said, 'OK'...he now addressed me. He said, 'OK, who are you?' you know. 'What is your name, where are you from?' you know. So then I was in a very very difficult situation, where I had to decide, or I decided, to lie. If I told them that I was a Serb, and that I am doing it all on purpose, it would even steer the situation even worse. So I said, I'm [real first name] and I'm from a town called Bugojno, which was, let's say, merely a majority of Croatian population, so they thought I'm a Croat. And then they said – I mean, obviously they couldn't do anything, or they weren't so stupid to do anything to me at that moment – but they said, 'Right, if you are ours...why are you doing it to us?' I said, 'Don't look at me, I've got nothing to do with it, mate, you know, it's all this stupid lieutenant who has organized it all and he thinks that you are stealing, I can't explain to him that it is all your stuff, so I had to go the easiest way and try to flatter them just in order to calm the situation down.'[9]

Complicating the concept of ethnicity in Bosnia-Herzegovina

In the course and aftermath of a war that was fought by armies representing ethno-nationalist ideologies and characterized by the strategy of eliminating all but the members of a certain ethnic group from claimed territory, reading the Bosnian conflict as a war between the armies of three distinguishable ethnic groups simplified the problem of absorbing complex information about the 'patchwork war' in a short time. Left unqualified, however, it inhibited a full understanding of how fundamentally the initiators and prosecutors of the conflict had altered the social fabric of pre-war Yugoslavia, where the discourse of the Yugoslav state had attempted to exclude ethnicity from public relevance.[10]

Ethnicity, or in local terms one's belonging to a certain *narod* (people), had not been made salient in most Yugoslav workplace situations because the language and discourse of the workplace did not address that aspect of an individual's self. It came to the fore instead in private, family and neighbourly life in such fields as wedding practices (religious ceremonies were discouraged but not banned under Yugoslav socialism), funerary customs, death notices and the dates of winter celebrations. The non-religious festivals and life-stage markers developed by the socialist regime (such as New Year's Day celebrations, children's gifts brought by Djed Mraz or Grandfather Frost or the civil marriage ceremony without which the state would not recognize a partnership) deliberately also incorporated Yugoslavs of all ethnic backgrounds into the same ceremonies. All Bosnian children learned both Latin and Cyrillic scripts until the war unambiguously associated Cyrillic with Serbian language and culture.

Yugoslavia's socialist leaders had optimistically hoped that younger generations, the great hope of socialism, would increasingly take up the census option to declare as Yugoslavs. 'Yugoslav' accompanied the form's ethnic categories and appealed to the children of mixed marriages and to those who ideologically aspired to a supranational identity; on the 1991 census, 242,682 of Bosnia-Herzegovina's 4,377,033 inhabitants (5.6 per cent) had chosen this option, the highest percentage of Yugoslavs in Yugoslavia (Markowitz 2007: 42). However, ethnicity was not erased from society in practice. Ethnic difference was noticed but managed and negotiated, and often affected interpersonal relations less than differences in economic status or urban/rural inequalities (Sorabji 1993). As the anthropologist Cornelia Sorabji found during fieldwork in mid-1980s Sarajevo: 'the *narods* were separate, but even their separate existence was predicated upon their interconnectedness; neighbours were warm, trusting and united, but at another level this unity was predicated upon difference' (Sorabji 1995: 90). Ethnicity had greater impact in everyday life in rural Bosnia-Herzegovina because churches played a greater role in the community and socialist state institutions were less present in daily life (Bringa 1995). The village institution of *komšiluk* ('neighbourhood'), trust relationships between neighbours that superseded religious or political differences, would be reinterpreted during and after the war as a model for non-nationalist ways of living (Maček 2009: 105–11).

The simple triadic framework for understanding ethnicity in Bosnia-Herzegovina was precisely what the conflict had in fact been designed to achieve. To manipulate Yugoslavia's systemic politico-economic crisis into violent fragmentation required elites in 1989–95 to undermine these relationships by creating and constructing antagonisms that played on myths of the Second World War and earlier historical crises when killing had been justified in terms that could be mapped on to contemporary ethnicity. Nationalist leaders depended on the individuals whom they targeted as the desired population of bounded areas identified as ethnic homelands to politically and financially support the war, to refrain from challenging their discursive hegemony by interpreting events through non-nationalist frames, and, in the case of men and a limited number of women, to fight and kill in service of strategic aims. Undesired populations became statistical problems and security threats to be removed, violently, from the map – the logic behind the wartime Serb, Croat and Bosniak nationalist ideas. Ethnic cleansing itself was often carried out by officially unaccountable paramilitary groups, while news and even entertainment media supported messages that the ethnic aggression of others had made separation inevitable.[11] The strategy is set out in V. P. Gagnon's analysis of the Serb–Croat dimension of the Yugoslav conflict:

> [P]eople identify in multiple, overlapping, porous, and contextually dependent ways that are not reducible to the narrow term 'ethnic'. These identifications are constructed socially in day-to-day interactions and social environments. The key in politics is to make certain identities more relevant than others, and others irrelevant to politics…
>
> This doesn't necessarily require changing people's self-perceived identifications. Rather, it means forcing them in particular contexts to act – or not act – within the narrow range of one 'identity' defined in a very specific and particular way. It may also mean constructing identities or meanings of identities that did not formerly exist. (Gagnon 2004: 26–7)

In neighbourhoods, workplaces, military units and in public, as imagined by Serb, Croat and Bosniak leaders, nothing mattered more than ethnicity; moreover, in the dominant discursive frame of the wartime societies, nothing *was allowed to* matter more. The same individuals who before the war had unreflectively spoken the linguistic and symbolic dialect of their current or previous home towns were compelled to make novel choices about how to speak (often responding to imported norms from Serbia or Croatia) and revise their understandings of what was suitable to speak about. Sociolinguistics recognizes the concept of a 'community of practice', where 'people come to develop and share ways of doing things, ways of talking, beliefs, values – in short, practices – as a function of their joint engagement in activity' (Eckert 2000: 35). In sociolinguistic terms, the ethnicizing logic of the Bosnian conflict was for individuals to be continuously situated within the imagined community of practice of their ethnic group – its common enterprise being the independence and consolidation of a nation-state – regardless of which actual community of practice they operated within at any given time. Far from being a simple quality that was easy to ascribe, a person's ethnic identity in 1990s Bosnia-Herzegovina had the significance it did as the result of a complex process, inseparable from the exercise of power and violence before, during and after 1992–5. Appreciating this background, and similar processes in other conflicts, may help participants in peace operations to individualize and thus develop more accurate evaluations of the trustworthiness of language intermediaries and others.

Ethnicity, essentialism and native/heritage speakers

Anthropological perspectives on ethnicity invite us to think of it as the continually evolving result of interaction between people and of symbolic boundary-making practices that construct membership in and exclusion from groups (Cohen 1985; Jenkins 1997). Applying this constructivist approach to another area (Greek Macedonia) where nation-states have used cultural policy, bureaucracy and violence to separate a complicated human landscape into discrete ethnic majority and minority populations, Anastasia Karakasidou argues that ethnicity has been a social tool which 'provides one of many possible symbolic media through which people may unite in the pursuit of their particular goals or interests' (Karakasidou 1997: 19). A coherently conceived ethnic group is a prerequisite for conceiving, implementing and maintaining the idea of a nation-state as a political entity expressing the group's right and will to self-determination (a goal of every nationalist elite in former Yugoslavia), although not every ethnic group will result in a nation-state.

Nationalism in the abstract imagines the population distribution of the ethnic group and the political borders of the nation-state will be congruent (Gellner 1983), yet such a result is impossible to achieve, particularly when nationalist movements attempt to create smaller states on the territory of multinational empires and federations. Publics and diplomats nonetheless continue to imagine international political space as divided into nation-states based on a majority ethnic group, producing a hegemonic discourse in which claims to independence can only be made 'in nationalist terms, most often defined as a particular, cultural – linguistic or ethnic – kind of difference' (Gagnon 2004: 21). The incentive to create this type of state, harnessed to a politics of fear and criminality, produced the violent results of the Bosnian war.

During and after the war, however, foreigners' search for quickly delivered and understood knowledge drove them towards a simplified essentialism as a way to make sense of what they considered the 'ethnic war'.[12] Sometimes, whether from exasperation or from an idealized ethic of impartiality, the three main groups of Serbs, Croats and Bosniaks were imagined as interchangeable *except for* differences in traditions and religious practices which were shared equally among all members of the group and had to be respected at all times. Another essentialist structure of understanding related to guilt and emplotment, identifying one set of villains (frequently Serbs) and another set of heroes, underdogs or victims. A third response was essentialized sympathy, transferring fondness for one group or organization (such as reading one particular armed force as competent soldiers) on to that people as a whole. All three of these modes produced distorted perceptions with unwelcome effects (Simms 2002: 175–85).

For practical purposes, even a Bosnian from a mixed background or who preferred not to identify as a member of an ethnic group would be classified by foreign soldiers as part of one group or another, the same process that was occurring much more coercively in the local world. The commander of 1 COLDSTREAM retold a conversation with one of the senior local interpreters at Vitez:

> *Coldstreamer*: 'Somebody has told me that I'm a Muslim,' he said, 'I've got no – not a Muslim at all – but because I'm not a Croat or a Serb I must therefore be a Muslim. And,' he said, 'some Croat has decided to live in my house and steal my car, my father's tractor works was bombed by the Serbs, my father has been forced out by the Croats to live the other end of Novi Travnik and lives in a sort of garden shed with my mother,' he said, 'the Croats decided my girlfriend was a

Serb, and she was shot dead by a sniper and died in my arms on the veranda of the officers' mess. So,' he said, 'the only thing I have left a year on is my guitar, so,' he said, 'if you think you're confused, join the club.'[13]

Supervisors' ascriptions of ethnicity sometimes (as in the team managed by Louise Robbins during the Bosniak–Croat conflict) determined the tasking of interpreters. However, this was not a fixed policy, and it became less and less likely as the war and its checkpoints grew more distant. In 1996, many supervisors were clearly prepared to take an interpreter they assigned to one group to visit representatives of another, even in situations where force might be threatened. Asmir Pašić, who worked for the Danish battalion in Eastern Bosnia, lived and worked in an area near Tuzla that had been left divided by the conflict. The 'four towns' of Doboj, Maglaj, Teslić and Tešanj had previously been interconnected, with residents travelling frequently between them. In 1992, the VRS took control of Doboj and Teslić and the ABiH took control of Maglaj and Tešanj. The violence of ethnic cleansing complemented and compounded the psychological work of breaking up residents' intercommunal networks in order to create monoethnic bounded territories where Serbs and non-Serbs would be permanently separated. Pašić, a Bosniak, accompanied Danish units on many visits to shut down military sites in 1996:

> *Asmir Pašić*: [T]he talks were also tense sometimes. Especially in the beginning, when there was, no army trusted IFOR, international troops, at the beginning. So you as an interpreter had to endure all these meetings, and... Especially in '96, you know, early after the war, me as a Bosniak would often go to the Serbian brigades. And you would know that it's not... it's a different army than [being]... in a town that was controlled by your own ethnicity['s] army. So you go to a different army. So this had an impact on all of us interpreters. We went different sides, so it was the first time for us to see the opposite army. For my Serb colleague to see the BiH army [ABiH] and for me to see the Serbian army. And we had to... they didn't select us as per nationality... so they used us for all three sides. So this had a psychological impact on you as well. When you first, in '96, met the opposite army that you experienced as the one shooting at you during the war time. So that's what we had to overcome as interpreters, as well.[14]

The heritage speaker Nikola Andrijašević had encountered various practical and philosophical approaches to the question of whether or not to match the ethnicity of interpreter and interlocutor:

> *Nikola Andrijašević*: Sometimes you would also select interpreters depending on their geographical and religious basis. Simply because you didn't want to bring an interpreter that could antagonize a meeting, so if you had an interpreter going into, let's say a Serbian interpreter going into a meeting you'd want to have with a number of Bosnian Muslims, you'd not necessarily bring your normal interpreter, you would adjust your choice of interpreters to prevent any potential clash of personalities. Because you don't want the interpreter to become an issue. He's just there as a tool, and if he's creating friction by his religion or his ethnic background, then that's subtracting from the task in hand.
>
> *Catherine Baker*: And was that actually a firm policy?
>
> *Nikola Andrijašević*: It was a policy, but it was not always possible to meet the policy, because of limited resources. And some officers felt that they wanted to ignore the question of ethnic background, because they felt that that was the whole principle of integration, and rebuilding the country. So they'd go in and if one of the chaps they went to meet raised the concern that the interpreter was of a different ethnic background, then we'd say, 'Well, he's one of our interpreters so that's all you need to worry about. He's an SFOR interpreter.' Almost forcing the issue of, you need to start accepting other ethnic groups, and working with them. So that the policy very much shifted from individual to individual depending on how he or she wanted to force an issue or avoid a potential conflict.
>
> *Catherine Baker*: And what about if you had an interpreter who had a mixed background?
>
> *Nikola Andrijašević*: Again, in some areas that was a plus point, in some other areas they would be viewed with caution, resistance... it was very much a hit-and-miss, really difficult to judge how they would be accepted or not by one of the other ethnic groups.[15]

Speaking from the perspective of 2009, a Bosnian interpreter who had been working for HQ SFOR since 1997 and belonged to the professionalized LSB did not find ethnic tasking appropriate but acknowledged it had worked to preserve trust immediately after the war:

> *Goran Šiljak*: The passions were still running high and some people simply resented the presence of people of a different ethnicity let alone them interpreting the meeting, they simply didn't trust them. But mainly, it has never been too much of a problem, and nowadays it's not a problem whatsoever.... I'm not sure that I would have a problem with it if I was asked on the basis of my ethnicity or background to go to a certain place and into a meeting with a certain person.... But then again, I'd have to admit that I would probably at least try to ... to make note that I think it's wrong to cater to such requests. Because I do think it's wrong, especially when it comes to my colleagues and myself, because if there is one thing that we are, that is that we are professionals, really. To the bone. And it's a little bit insulting, I mean ... it's always insulting when people judge you on the basis of your skin colour or your name or your religion or your ethnicity or whatever, but it's I believe even more insulting when they judge your professional performance on the same basis.[16]

During this research, the interviewer's questions about whether assignments would be determined by the ethnicity of a local interpreter elicited such varied responses relating to different times, places and units that, when compared to the strength of policies on operational security or force protection, the force as a whole could not be said to have had a policy either way. Policy guidance on balancing the different considerations might have benefited the units and troops on the ground to whom this important judgment was delegated.

Foreignness, localness and threat

Even though local interpreters were not necessarily tasked according to their ethnicity, a certain essentialism of loyalty nonetheless affected their management and use. This essentialism was located in assumptions that all members of a local ethnic group *would* share the aspirations of the leaders who spoke in their name and/or that all members *could* (voluntarily or under duress) be leaking information to security forces or investigation targets. The British military language trainer Gregory Cook summed this up in the concept of 'baggage', which stood for a collectivization of non-objectivity:

> *Gregory Cook*: I don't know if this is a terribly tactful way of saying it, but somebody who is not native English will normally bring some form of baggage, we call, that's how we'd refer to it, as baggage,

in terms of values, contacts. You've got to be aware that ... when, in becoming interpreters for the military they may have other objectives, which may differ from the military's. They may still have relatives in the conflict zone. They may be under blackmail pressures. They may for some reason or another want revenge, if they were expelled or ... And so there may be personal conflicts, there may be family matters, there may be matters of revenge, value system, all sorts of things. Which as an employer of a native interpreter you've got to be aware of.[17]

Heritage speakers, members of a foreign military who had grown up speaking the local language in the household without necessarily achieving any formal qualifications, themselves had to contend with a vestige of this essentialism even though they were ostensibly equal members of the armed force to which they belonged.

Both bureaucratically and practically, heritage speakers are conceived as first and foremost professionals from the states whose uniforms they wear, and as only tangentially part of the ethnic group whose language they speak. The citizenship requirements and vetting procedures necessary for them to be deployed and used as linguists are supposed to eliminate any risk from potential divided loyalties. Nikola Andrijašević exemplified the desired subjectivity of a military heritage speaker:

Catherine Baker: And how did your own family background affect the work you did?

Nikola Andrijašević: I had very little – it had very little effect. Short of giving me a firm understanding of the region. I never lived in former Yugoslavia. I'd done a few fleeting visits, so I wasn't personally involved, or I didn't feel like I was personally involved in the conflict, it was very much a professional challenge as a British officer.[18]

Andrijašević's presentation greatly emphasized his military identity, that which made him the same as his fellow soldiers, over his inherited Slovene and Serb ethnolinguistic identities, which would have made him separate. This was also evident in his presentation of his language learning background:

Nikola Andrijašević: I also learnt Serbo-Croat at home, and as the family language, and I was also exposed to Slovenian as my grandmother that was living with us at the time spoke it only and often spoke it with my mother, but I never had any formal training or understood it to a great extent.

Catherine Baker: Did you learn to read and write it, or just to speak it?

Nikola Andrijašević: I learned to speak it, I was reading some articles, I learnt Cyrillic but I didn't practice it often, but I never had any occasion to write it....

I was very well briefed into the happenings of former Yugoslavia, from my youth. My father followed the breakdown of Yugoslavia from the early nineties, I read and kept updated both on the English press, Italian press, and some of the foreign press, be it Serbian or be it Croatian press. So I had a very very good understanding of the issues and the problems of the former Yugoslavia.

Catherine Baker: What sort of opportunities had you had before this to visit former Yugoslavia?

Nikola Andrijašević: I visited former Yugoslavia as a child. The last visit there, I believe, was in the late eighties, as a teenager visiting Belgrade and Zagreb and Ljubljana. Before that I spent a number of summers in Slovenia, so I have some distant memories of visiting as a tourist.

Here, the Serbian and Croatian press are clearly 'the foreign press'; Slovenia and the rest of former Yugoslavia are places he visited only 'as a tourist' rather than sites producing sentiments of belonging. This subjectivity of distance is very different to the best-known account by a heritage speaker and British military linguist, Milos Stankovic's memoir, which provides a far more emotional and far less distant retelling. The circumstances of Andrijašević's and Stankovic's service were different, and Andrijašević did not experience the pressures of concealment that badly affected Stankovic and his two comrades with Anglo-Saxon pseudonyms (Chapter 1).

This type of cover is not an unusual thing to ask of heritage speakers in the military, and was required for instance of French-speaking agents in the Special Operations Executive who were required to pass as French nationals. The historian Juliette Pattinson has applied the concept of passing, 'whereby individuals of one race, gender, class, religion or sexuality attempt to appropriate the characteristics of the "Other" and desire not to be recognised as different,' to the SOE case, and recognizes the stress it caused (Pattinson 2007: 15). The dynamic of passing for concealed heritage speakers in Bosnia-Herzegovina was similar, but the nature of what was concealed was different. These soldiers were not aiming to pass as ordinary townspeople/villagers and display local nuances of habitus; rather, their passing performances aimed to mask identities they already possessed. Pattinson's observation that anxiety and apprehension of 'slippage' was an ongoing facet of agents' experience may nonetheless be transferred to heritage speakers who served in the war: 'To pass is to ward off failure, and yet passing is always haunted by and troubled by potential failure' (Pattinson 2007: 85). Stankovic's memoir is an account of dangerous and high-stakes conditions in which he was unable to mend the rupture inflicted by revealing his family origins in southern Serbia to Serb officers (Stankovic 2000: 35).

This level of threat must not be considered to apply to every place, time or environment in Bosnia-Herzegovina. Rather, it illustrates the extremes of deploying real or perceived ethnic identity as a resource, something that was also done in less extreme ways: Mitch and Slađana had both attempted to change local interlocutors' responses to them by speaking from the position of a different ethnic identity. Yet ethnicity could also be a positive resource. Asmir Pašić constructed his interpreting career as a model for reconciliation and the gradual reestablishment of trust between ethnicized communities who had been involved in recent communal violence: in his informal role as intermediary among former friends in opposing armies, his Bosniak ethnicity convinced a Bosniak officer to trust him, while his institutional affiliation empowered him to approach the Serb officer and indirectly initiate the conversation:[19]

> *Asmir Pašić*: So these joint meetings of the three different armies became more frequent. Because we interpreters had a big role in it, bringing them together. Because all these three military brigades, all these three sides' commanders would know us from the meetings that we held separately with them. So when we'd come to a military base they would recognize us, and they would have more trust. Like a Serbian brigade commander would talk easily to me, but he would not talk in the beginning with his counterpart BiH army commander that easily. So it was our role to link them somehow.... It was not that I was ordered, but I also felt the need somehow to bring them together, in order to make the meetings more relaxed and make the job for us interpreters more relaxed.[20]

His working responsibilities similarly empowered him to make private journeys between differently ethnicized towns that most private individuals in 1996–8 still thought of as unthinkable. Pašić and his colleagues were not de-ethnicized by their role and uniform. Rather, they occupied a position of 'ethnicity plus', which gave the interpreter a powerful agency as mediator.

Pašić's narrative above points to a gradual change in intra-Bosnian dimensions of trust that altered relationships between locals as people acquired greater confidence from working together. SFOR officers and local interpreters involved in the defence reform process both noted a decline in inter-ethnic or inter-entity suspicion in this particular context from approximately 2002, permitting the integration of the Bosnian armed forces in 2005. These impressions are in line with scholarly findings that, out of all social settings in post-Dayton Bosnia-Herzegovina, the workplace was where inter-ethnic trust was most successfully produced because this was where Bosnians of different ethnicities were most likely to interact at similar levels of status and power, giving them the opportunity to build up trusting relationships (Pickering 2006). This, too, can be explained by O'Neill's notion of trust. O'Neill (2002: 76) considers that the most satisfying emerges from 'active inquiry', where counterparts are able to talk, ask questions and monitor results over time. Shared linguistic understanding, if not a precondition for trust, must therefore be at least a facilitator for it.

Managing trust in language encounters

Decisions about whether and how much to trust an intermediary were based on a mixture of policy, accreditation and experience. Although other dimensions of identity such as age, gender or military training would also inflect trust during a particular encounter (Kronsell 2012: 104–5), the military policies that aimed to test trust or compensate for an institutionalized lack of trust revolved primarily around the dimension of nationality and citizenship, inflected secondarily by military or non-military status. The operational security regulations of each military force excluded local nationals, other foreign nationals and non-military citizens of the same state from access to restricted areas and sensitive information. Nationality trumped military status, not vice versa. The fact that some interpreters had military experience, for instance as male conscripts, did not make them more trustworthy in terms of operational security and confidentiality, although it did make them more reliable in the sense that they could be trusted to pull their weight on an overnight outdoor stay.

In local interpreters' working lives, operational security policies meant remaining on bounded areas of the base – an obvious spatial performance of security (see Higate and Henry 2009) – and often not finding out until the last minute the nature, time or location of an assignment. Locals could not be security-cleared on the same basis as foreign troops, since the very security services who would possess the information for a clearance were the force's intelligence adversaries. Headquarters still performed a lower level of clearance to ascertain, at a minimum, that an employee had not been indicted for war crimes and, ideally, was not connected to local security forces. In practice, interpreters not uncommonly proved to have local military commanders, police officers or municipal leaders among their close or extended families – a product of the militarization of Bosnian society but also a result of their socio-economic position, since the most likely people to have the language skills to become interpreters belonged to professional-stratum families.[21] The decision to use any non-military (local civilian) interpreter rather than a trained soldier with language skills demanded a degree of trust in the expected interlocutors and in the safety of the environment. In the words of one experienced British supervisor of local interpreter cells, a military interpreter was 'an armed person who could look after himself or herself' in a dangerous or unpredictable environment; a local civilian, in contrast, would need to be defended, influencing the risk assessment whenever soldiers planned to face hostility.[22]

Ascertaining loyalty, or rather limiting the impact of disloyalty, was nonetheless only one element in the trust relationship, albeit the easiest element to regulate through policy. Interlocutors also had to trust in an intermediary to render a reliable or (a telling figure of speech) a 'faithful' translation – presupposing that every translation could be entirely faithful, a notion that contemporary translation studies would question (Baker 2006). Some foreign soldiers had enough language knowledge to monitor interpreters' performance (Chapter 2). One Serbian-speaking British officer had been able to observe that a particular interpreter was distancing himself from the commanding officer's confrontations with the local mayor by refusing to interpret in the first person but instead turning the English sentences into reported speech by prefixing 'kaže da' ('he says that'). He had not initially disclosed his language knowledge but would reveal it during a conversation so that the interpreter would lose face:

> *Mark Ferguson*: [A]ny interpreter that did that to me, I would say in Serbian, so that the other person understood, I would say don't say kaže da, you interpret word for word, OK? And ... of course, bollocking them in their own language, in front of the other person, establishes,

from a psychological point of view, saying this guy now knows that I know ... [I]n that sort of dance of influence, you're sort of saying, 'No, you're only here because I can't do every word, because it's easier for me to do it this way.'[23]

The great majority of foreigners, with little or no local language proficiency, could not personally monitor interpreters' and translators' performance and were not trained to identify or observe the various skills required of linguists. They therefore had to delegate their evaluation of intermediaries' skill to an accrediting expert or organization and trust this to be authoritative. Trust, in practice, consisted of much more than formal accreditation or certification; it was built also through repeatedly being able to observe a linguist's reliability, and through satisfactory informal knowledge exchange (Chapter 5). It would be conveyed through personal experience of communicating through a particular interpreter or in personal recommendation from a colleague, often the interpreters' military supervisor or one's outgoing counterpart. Working as a local interpreter through several rotations or at varied locations thus entailed repeating the trust-building process, from a starting point of distance and strict adherence to policy to a potential – but not always realized – position of interpersonal trust and friendship where policy could be pushed into the background. Armin Kosarević had worked through half a dozen US troop rotations in the Tuzla area:

Armin Kosarević: [T]hat kind of job really creates a special bonding between people that work. So every time, from the beginning, you have to build this connection. And, I don't know, maybe after four or five months my experience was we became very close, and we became very good friends. And then they leave (laughs). So the next rotation, it's the same thing. They don't trust you in the beginning. They think they don't need you. They think they can do it without you. And they always, like, if there are some kind of papers – because we ride in the same vehicles – they always have to hide. When you ask them what time we leave tomorrow they don't want to tell you, [they say] 'just be here at eight o'clock,' even though you have to go at two o'clock, they don't want to tell you this information because they're always suspicious you will abuse them in some way. But after a month or two they realize it cannot work that way. They kinda ease, and we get this ... we start to build a different relationship.[24]

Interpreters for foreign military forces did not owe any contractual duty to the locals whose language they interpreted on behalf of their employers, but the success of a language encounter, and sometimes even the personal safety of an interpreter, would nonetheless also depend on how well the local interlocutor trusted them. Local interlocutors with knowledge of English could also monitor the performance of interpreters, potentially placing them under scrutiny from both sides:

> *Asmir Pasic*: I remember in '96, '97, as you were interpreting at the meetings with the military, they were distrustful of IFOR and distrustful of the other armies. And there was a great intelligence war going on in Bosnia. Each army was spying on each army and each army was spying on SFOR. And we interpreters, we would come to a military base, especially if we are Bosniak – if I'm a Bosniak, and if I come to a Serbian military brigade – they would always have someone to check on our interpretation and to check our movements with IFOR. And I remember that, because one guy, who was a Serbian soldier, admitted this to me, that he was in charge of tracking down my translations, whether I was going to say something wrong, and tracking down my movement through the military barracks as we collected weapons, as we checked for the – whether the numbers of all the weapons were correct, compared to the list that we had. And I believe that the same experience [was] had [by] Serbian interpreters visiting BiH army brigades, on the other side. So the armies were distrustful of each other and distrustful of interpreters with ... with different, with the wrong, ethnicities, so to call it. So they checked on us when we would come to translate for them.[25]

The relationship between interpreter and local interlocutors could rest on several bonds depending on their characters and positions, the setting, the time, and the situation: family- or neighbourhood-based ties of obligation; inequalities of status; threats of violence or intimidation; an interpreter's own ethic of translator neutrality. Ethnicity, or rather the interlocutor's reading of ethnicity, was one ascribed characteristic that would influence the decision to trust; another, especially in wartime, was gender. When movement around Bosnia-Herzegovina depended on successfully negotiating the checkpoints of mutually hostile forces, female interpreters embodied the immense advantage that they would not automatically be presumed to be opposition soldiers or deserters, unlike men of similar age (even though all three armies in wartime Bosnia-Herzegovina did contain female soldiers). In 1993,

Lejla Delibašić had travelled through a tense checkpoint with Canadian troops during the evacuation of Vareš:

> *Lejla Delibašić*: And when I went out with the commander and his 2IC [second-in-command] to talk to them to negotiate our safe passage through...it was better that I was a female, because if I was a male interpreter they would have asked questions whether – you know, am I really an interpreter, was I fighting on one side or another, and that's what I was referring to. If you understand my point.
>
> *Catherine Baker*: So the people at checkpoints were suspicious of male interpreters?
>
> *Lejla Delibašić*: Which is logical. At least, it all depends on the part of the country in which you were, but in our region there were some problems with people because they were accused of fighting on one side or another before they became interpreters. That was the reason why. And again, it was a war.[26]

The gendering of trust did not always, however, function to invest women with more trust than men. Male interpreters might be better trusted to fulfil pseudo-soldierly values of toughness (suffering hardship without complaining; living outdoors at observation posts without frivolously wasting time on their appearance) whereas women, in an echo of the problems female recruits face in military training,[27] would have to work harder to convince others of their endurance and stoicism. In certain neighbourhoods, meanwhile, female interpreters might be trusted even less than men: 'They will always have their own interpretation of what we do...you are either a slut or the enemy',[28] said Radojka Gavrilović, an interpreter since 1997, who had been living in a Serb neighbourhood where SFOR was unpopular. These neighbours had clearly not trusted women to behave chastely in the company of men. Within the employing force, meanwhile, commanders and supervisors too might distrust women and female sexuality as potential threats to discipline and even operational security. While some commanding officers placed the onus on male soldiers to control their behaviour, others accepted male sexual desire as natural and expected women to maintain standards of moral behaviour and modesty (Chapter 3).

Interference with any component of the trust relationship impeded working relationships and could result in deep suspicion. One British artillery officer serving shortly after Dayton had been convinced that most interpreters he knew were in fact passing information to the local authorities or even working directly for an intelligence service:

> *Tony French*: I have no doubt there was some kind of collusion between the interpreters and the local authorities, but I'm sure it wasn't on a massive strategic level. Not James-Bond-like, or anything. It was just, 'Can you tell me how many soldiers they have. Can you tell me what type of rotation they're in.' You know, things like that, which I would have wanted to have known, actually, if I was in their shoes.[29]

On one occasion, he had even feared that an apparent expression of hospitality might turn out to be a trap:

> *Tony French*: [T]here was this pizza place that sprung up near the end, that I wouldn't have known about if my interpreter hadn't told me. You know, the first time, this is how suspicious we were, I'm just remembering this now. She told me about this place, but I was so suspicious I just thought it was a trap, I thought we were going to turn up and we were going to get slotted (laughs), so I turned up in our tank, and (inaudible). But from then on we didn't really have to worry...you know, there was a bit more trust between the two of us.[30]

Intelligence services are indeed known to have attempted to recruit and intimidate interpreters both during and after the war. Emir Suljagić, who was able to leave Srebrenica before the massacre in 1995 because he worked as an interpreter for Dutchbat, was threatened by the ABiH commander Naser Orić in his second month of work because he had visited a friend whose cousin belonged to a rival group in Srebrenica's municipal power struggle (Suljagić 2005: 115–16). In a series of raids termed Operation Westar in October 1999, SFOR and IPTF (International Police Task Force) officers discovered four operations by SNS and HIS (the Bosnian Croat and Croatian intelligence services) against international organizations in Bosnia-Herzegovina, including one (Operation Grom or 'Thunder') targeting the organizations' Croat employees. An action plan included in the captured documentation released by SFOR two months later included the recommendation: 'Pay particular attention to the interpreters of international organisations' leading officials'.[31] Translators and other local employees were also to be a source of information in Operation Munja ('Lightning') which sought continuous monitoring of international agencies, foreign forces, NGOs, and the diplomats and charities of Islamic states and Operation Puma which monitored ICTY investigators in Livno. The Westar documentation suggests the operations had been in place for two to three weeks before the September raid. The translation of a SNS report on the preparation of Operation Puma suggests, meanwhile, that even in 1999 the security-cleared translators in Document Exploitation (DOCEX) were still struggling with the neologisms of official Croatian:

> and with that same individual go through the razdjelnik and medurazdjelnik (DOCEX comment: new Croatian word – not sure of meaning, not in dictionary)
>
> ... a safe was found in the medurazdjelnik (DOCEX comment: most likely hallway in this case)[32]

The foreign nationals who translated these documents were high in institutionalized trust, if not so high in quality.

Translating and transmitting information becomes less successful and efficient where trust levels are low, since even everyday communication – such as Kosarević's arrangements for starting work – becomes hedged with suspicion. The military rotation system meant that an interpreter staying in the same place had to rebuild trust every six months with new groups of soldiers who deployed fresh from their operational security briefings. As O'Neill argues, trust relations have traditionally been built up over time 'by ... seeing how well claims to know and undertakings to act held up'; when this is not possible, active trust must be replaced by impersonal procedure (O'Neill 2002: 76). Official mistrust enshrined in security policy exposed the limits of fellowship between interpreters and foreign soldiers and could produce seemingly ridiculous results when based on what interpreters felt was a lack of sensitivity or understanding to the locality; if the foreigners had understood Bosnia properly, interpreters' interviews implied, they would not have needed to mistrust the interpreter. A Bosnian interpreter using an English pseudonym had been offended by the US and Dutch officers who conducted a security interview when she worked for HQ SFOR:

> *'Sara Jones'*: And they interviewed me, and they asked – at that time I had a boyfriend who grew mushrooms. So when you grow mushrooms you work in a basement and you need special conditions, et cetera. So they asked me to fill in a form, something about what your mother does, what your father does, what your grandparents

> do, ... what your (laughs) first neighbour does, it was something like that. And do you have a boyfriend, or husband, or someone, you know, and I said, 'Yes, I have a boyfriend.' 'What does he do?' I said, 'He grows mushrooms.' And this American, I remember him saying to this other one, 'Huh, yeah, you know, "growing mushrooms".' I really don't know what kind of a comment that was. Because it was just a normal and proper job, and he still does it. I mean, he's not my boyfriend any more, but he still does it. So it's not something illegal, you know. If you are trying to do something normal in this country everyone thinks you are keeping drugs, or something.[33]

Trust in a language intermediary was a blend of many factors: credibility; confidence in the reliability and accuracy of the translation; personal experience of working with the person; perception of the intermediary's loyalty to one's own group rather than to the Other. In Bosnia-Herzegovina, this perception in the eyes of foreigners very often ran along ethnic 'rails' ('he or she is a Serb therefore ...'). Interpreters' identifications with the ethnic groups and institutions that claimed to represent them were typically more complex. Their urban, professional, education-centric subjectivities prescribed a certain distance from the folk-tinged populism of Bosnian (and Croatian or Serbian) nationalist leaders; some took explicitly anti-nationalist stances during or after interviews, while others rejected various symbolic markers of nationalist political culture, from patriotic pop-folk music to the rural and religious greeting forms introduced to city language by village refugees during and after the war.

These new and shifting identifications created by the collapse of socialist Yugoslavia and the effects of physical violence were not necessarily accounted for in cultural training for peace operations, which as Robert Rubinstein has found (2008: 12), struggles to show culture as emergent and contested rather than stable and homogenous. No amount of cultural knowledge, however, could have determined whether an individual employee was working for a local intelligence service. To the extent that military information needed to be kept classified, some measure of procedural- rather than human-based trust was therefore inevitable in foreign forces' employment practices.

Neutrality, loyalty and identification

In the prevailing paradigm of professional interpreting, a short-cut to establishing trust – when and only when this principle is recognized by all interacting parties – is a shared belief in the translator's or interpreter's commitment to neutrality. A paradigm of neutrality and impartiality meanwhile also applies to the very soldiers involved in peace operations, who are socialized into 'a myth of stability, continuity, joint action, and neutrality' as they train for and join missions (Rubinstein 2008: 85). The historian Brendan Simms's critique of British policy in Bosnia-Herzegovina accuses the British command between 1992 and 1995 of deriving so much impartiality from the UN mandate that it restricted soldiers from preventing violence. Especially after Croat and Bosniak ethnic cleansing campaigns reached the British area of responsibility in 1993, Simms (2002: 177–82) believes that this lack of guidance led particular soldiers towards despair, cynical equivalency or an 'instinctive professional fraternalism' with Serb forces – all of which impeded a complex understanding of the conflict. Simms thus suggests that impartiality could be taken to too great an extreme.

After Dayton, however, foreign troops had taken up a peace enforcement mandate designed to display the coalition's greater military power to local forces and were no longer personally implicated in failures to prevent ongoing violence. The expectation not to take sides was not put to so severe a test as it had been in 1992–5 and commanders identified boredom rather than trauma as the main psychological factor affecting troops. Impartiality by this point had become routinized, accounting for a decreasing sensitivity towards local dimensions of ethnicity.

The idea of neutrality has been problematized when applied to soldiers. It also breaks down in studies of conflict interpreting, which recognize the high stakes of the tasks interpreters perform in wartime and postwar settings (Tobia and Baker 2012). Zrinka Stahuljak's study of civilian linguists from Croatia who volunteered to work for the European Community Monitoring Mission in 1991–2 found that they rejected the impersonal idea of the interpreter as conduit, instead considering themselves as activists advocating a Croatian cause to an organization that positioned itself as politically neutral. Although not holding to the concept of the interpreter as emotionally uninvolved, on the microlevel of the language encounter itself they nonetheless respected the organization's norms of interpreting and refrained from intervening in the translation. They resolved this contradiction, in the interviews used by Stahuljak, by appealing to a standard of linguistic professionalism: 'Because they are "professionals", interpreters must accept a form of erasure, at least while interpreting' (Stahuljak 2010: 399).

Practitioners and users nevertheless expected a high standard of interpreter neutrality. The ethic appeared in many interviews, including that of the Danish linguist Martin Lund Pedersen. By insisting that locals framed answers to questions as a response to the patrol leader and not to him, he avoided becoming 'a gatherer of information', which he believed would have exceeded his role:

> *Martin Lund Pedersen*: The interpreter is neutral, and objective. The gatherer of information cannot be that, by definition. Because if you gather information... I believe that you cannot avoid to... influence which information you get and which you don't. So you could also say that the way that I chose to do it was a way that protected me, because then it would never be my responsibility what information was gathered, then it would always be the guy I was translating for.[34]

Mitch, in the confrontation during the Croatian Army withdrawal, had struggled even harder with what his role should be:

> *Mitch*: I said [to the British officer], 'Yeah, many people will come back home... much happier than they actually left.' He said, 'Yeah, yeah, they will be finally at home, they won't have to worry about the war, about anything.' I said, 'Yeah, and many people will come back with their hands full.' He said, 'What do you mean?' At that moment I thought to myself, 'Oh my God, what am I doing?'. It's not my job to, or – the way I see it sometimes, whether as the interpreter I should just translate whatever is being told, or should I take an active part in whatever is being done. I think that was the biggest confusion, or the biggest question, that I had to face throughout my work.[35]

The most microscopic level of language encounter, at which it is still possible to observe judgments about neutrality and trust, was the patrol. Carried out several times a day by squads or platoons, the smallest military unit with the lowest-ranking and least experienced commanders, patrols were routine activities which risked becoming ritualized and perfunctory. As the looting incident in Mitch's interview indicates, however, every patrol contained the potential to deviate from routine in unpredictable and dangerous ways. It indicates also that local interpreters, just like foreign soldiers, struggled to reconcile on-the-ground experience with ethical codes and professional mandates, to the extent they were aware of these.

In communities where soldiers rotated in and out, a long-standing patrol interpreter could become the face of the force, held accountable by local stakeholders who did not subscribe to or were not familiar with the norm of interpreter neutrality (consider Jovana Zorić's narrative of repeatedly visiting a school in Chapter 5). Mitch's dilemma in the village, however, turned not on repeated conversations but on a single incident where different ethical obligations prescribed divergent courses of action: while professional neutrality counselled him to stand by and let the junior officer make mistakes, according to another moral code he would have become complicit in the looting if he had not intervened with his knowledge and greater life experience to alter the officer's response.

So far this discussion of trust and neutrality has emphasized the user's trust in language intermediaries. However, in a successful language encounter, the language intermediary must also trust the user: this element of the trust relationship receives far less attention. In conflict and post-conflict situations, the greatest trust locally recruited interpreters had to place in their employers and supervisors related to their own welfare: when entering vehicles or travelling through wartime checkpoints, they temporarily entrusted their bodies and health to foreign military oversight. This trust could be supported by law and symbolism, as in Slađana Medić's remark that 'I'm wearing their uniform, and that [attacking me] would be an attack on Great Britain',[36] or by power and force, as in Asmir Pašić's narrative where the more powerful equipment of IFOR helped him overcome his fear of attack: although he was aware that lightly armoured military vehicles were vulnerable to RPG fire, 'they [people who did not trust IFOR] were afraid of, perhaps, the air force that IFOR had, so they were never up to any true attacks on IFOR'.[37] Breaches of this trust relationship, when foreign soldiers failed to protect an interpreter, caused an accident or treated wounded interpreters differently from their own troops, harmed some individuals and troubled others, as seen in the discussions of vehicle accidents in Chapter 5. Lejla Delibašić was still upset that one UNPROFOR officer had not intervened at a checkpoint when local soldiers had detained a female interpreter:

> *Lejla Delibašić*: [T]here was one girl, who was stopped at a checkpoint, and she was not of the same ethnic background as people who controlled the checkpoint, and then they said 'You are not supposed to be here, you need to get off the vehicle.' And her UNPROFOR officer said, 'You know, maybe you should get out of the car.' ... She was detained for about two weeks, until respective UNPROFOR officers did their share of the work and released her, and then she said,

> 'I'm not going to work for UN any more, thank you, goodbye,' and left the country.... [T]here was no organization, no standardization, and a lot depended on the individual for whom you were working. I had a similar situation at the checkpoint, but the liaison officer for whom I was working...he didn't actually say 'It's none of your business what's her ethnic background,' he said 'She works as an interpreter for UNPROFOR, she has a UN ID card, you can allow us safe passage or not. You cannot take people off our vehicles and cars.'... [I]t's not a good thing when you depend on the personality of your next superior. You hope, you want to have a system, you want to have a standardized system, in which you are working.[38]

Similar incidents made experienced interpreters less likely to stay in military jobs when other opportunities were available. An interpreter's loss of trust in their employer could have more serious consequences than simply the end of a working relationship if the person chose instead to cooperate with local security forces or use their position to harm the force's personnel or objectives, though no participant in the study had gone to that extreme.

The opposite pole to rupture was identification with the employing force (expressed in positive recollections of its approach to interpersonal relations and conflict resolution, in the influence of military abbreviations and slang on interpreters' spoken English, or most enduringly in a change of life course resulting in movement to the employer's country). Many years after interpreters had first formed these dual personas, the divided identities could still often be discerned in English-language interviews as former interpreters struggled to reconcile their position on the margins of a foreign military collective with their practical reservations about the force's mission, operations or welfare provision (Baker 2012b). Mitch's narrative showed a characteristic slippage of the first person plural: although he stated at one point that 'under "we" I would always consider the people who were working as the interpreters or the locally employed civilians', 'we' is also sometimes used to stand for the British Army and its objectives (for instance, in a statement that a certain town 'is where we had a camp, and we were encouraging the freedom of movement in that area') even as, in other situations such as the village looting incident, British troops – and local soldiers – become undoubtedly 'they'. The incidents which illustrated the ethical dilemmas of local interpreters predominantly came, for Mitch, from the immediate postwar moment when the shape of social relations between local militaries and civilians was still uncertain. Many other experiences of mistrust and danger in this chapter (from Slađana Medić's visit to the Bosnian army corps to the suspicions of Tony French) tellingly also belong to 1996, the first year after Dayton and the moment when trust was being reshaped into a new post-war reality. In foreign eyes, the dimension of foreign versus local structured trust far more than the intra-Bosnian dimension of nationality. On the local level of social interaction, however, agency was still constrained by the aftermath of violence when Bosnian interlocutors projected their own identifications, fear and myths on to what they read as other Bosnians' ethnicities: a complex backstage to foreign experiences of nationality and trust.

7
Peacebuilding in a Multilingual World

The UN and NATO peace operations in Bosnia-Herzegovina were multilingual from the beginning. The forces were multinational, composed of military units contributed by many countries, bringing different languages and cultures. In some respects this echoed the changes taking place in the globalized world of the late twentieth century, with large and diverse migrations of population, traversed by mobile individuals and groups (Collins, Slembrouck and Baynham 2009). The local population was affected to a lesser extent by migration and mobility but experienced increasingly diverse flows of information through different media. It was deeply riven by cultural and ethnic differences that worked to diversify their language practices. This chapter will focus on the multilingual nature of the military forces, where complexities operated at several different levels, from the headquarters through to individual multinational units.

On a day-to-day basis, the linguistic practices were what Blackledge and Creese (2009: 25) have called 'multiple, plural, shifting and eclectic'. In particular, the notional use of this or that official language was always accompanied in practice by an array of communicative strategies that drew on whatever language resources were available. Although NATO was officially bilingual in English and French, its operations were predominantly carried out through varieties of English. The French units were initially committed to using the French language wherever possible, but in view of the high cost of maintaining translation and interpreting they gradually increased their capability in English. Russian was widely used as a lingua franca among eastern European contingents. And, while English functioned as the common language of military communication, the wide range of accents and dialects among English speakers produced a shifting and eclectic range of language strategies. For the most part, the multiple and plural language practices enabled the forces to operate effectively, and some of the most serious challenges to communication sprang from cultural rather than linguistic differences.

Multilingual operations

Historically, conflict has almost always involved contact between people of different languages. With the general exception of civil war, the combatants in conflict are typically from different linguistic backgrounds. Participants in the conflict are then compelled to engage with the language of the other, in command centres, on the front line or in negotiations. Language is integral to intelligence gathering and to combat in the heat of battle. In some cases, language becomes part of the fog of war, offering opaque codes that impede understanding. In other cases, language becomes an asset, a weapon that can be deployed or denied. In the case of modern peace operations, language differences are both more complex and more crucial, since they require intense and sustained relationships between the different parties involved (Bellamy, Williams and Griffin 2004).

In the conflict that broke out in Bosnia-Herzegovina, language differences were not a major barrier to communication, since the local language was intelligible to all the opposed parties. However, they tended to define themselves primarily by their ethnic identity and used language as a symbolic means of displaying their differences (Lovrenović 2001; Malcolm 2002). As the conflict developed, the parties chose to emphasize their differences in written script (Latin or Cyrillic), in choice of words and in some grammatical constructions. Language then became a cultural barrier, used to express opposed identities. For the forces sent to build peace, on the other hand, the linguistic challenge was considerable, both in understanding the local population and in understanding each other.

Peace operations are linguistically more complex than armed conflict. They involve contact with two opposed sides, but almost by definition they also involve forces that are independent of the combatants and are thus able to act impartially. These forces are generally drawn from different countries, and it is often a specific expectation that the troops deployed should be of a different cultural origin from those to whom they are trying to bring peace. At the same time, peace operations have a higher dependence on languages because they are aimed at engaging in dialogue with the opposed parties, bringing the parties into contact with each other and fostering relationships within the wider civilian community. In the strategic environment that emerged after the end of the Cold War, UN and NATO interventions in particular have been aimed at reshaping the regions in conflict (Paris 2004; Frantzen 2005). As peace operations become more explicitly the pursuit of politics by other means, the importance of effective communication with the local population and with the wider world becomes correspondingly more important.

However, language differences are not only an issue between the parties to a conflict: they are also internal to many participating forces. Troops are frequently required to serve alongside others who do not share the same first language. While this is the norm in large-scale military alliances, it is also common in smaller military configurations, often down to the smallest unit of command. The entire spectrum of configurations was represented in the operations in Bosnia-Herzegovina.

At the largest scale, many different countries contributed to the UN and NATO actions.[1] The first intervention was undertaken mainly in Croatia and Bosnia-Herzegovina between 1992 and 1995 by the UN's UNPROFOR. Almost 39,000 military personnel were deployed, drawn from 41 countries. The force was led successively by Indian, Swedish and French generals. After the Dayton Peace Agreement, signed in Paris in December 1995, UNPROFOR's role was taken over by IFOR, a much larger intervention, led by NATO and involving some 80,000 troops from 31 countries over the year to December 1996. Its successor, SFOR, initially involved some 32,000 troops and was deployed from 1996 to 2004, with the participation of some 38 countries.

During the 12 years of these operations, troops were deployed from 53 countries, comprising Albania, Argentina, Australia, Austria, Bangladesh, Belgium, Brazil, Bulgaria, Canada, Chile, Colombia, Czech Republic, Denmark, Egypt, Estonia, Finland, France, Germany, Ghana, Greece, Hungary, Iceland, India, Indonesia, Ireland, Italy, Jordan, Kenya, Latvia, Lithuania, Luxembourg, Malaysia, Morocco, Nepal, Netherlands, New Zealand, Nigeria, Norway, Pakistan, Poland, Portugal, Romania, the Russian Federation, Slovakia, Slovenia, Spain, Sweden, Switzerland, Tunisia, Turkey, Ukraine, the United Kingdom and the United States. The EU-led force (EUFOR), which has served since 2004, has involved some 28 countries, with decreasing numbers of troops on the ground. The scale and diversity of these operations suggests that the linguistic and cultural challenges were considerable.

The complexity was reflected on the ground, as Tony French, an artillery officer, explained:

> *Tony French:* Because don't forget it was international, so it was lots of, you know, next door to me on my left I had the French Canadians, on my right I had Americans. Where I was was a Czech area, so, you know, it was very internationalized. So, and you had to get continuity across everyone.[2]

This officer was based in Prijedor in the northwestern part of Bosnia-Herzegovina in 1996, but his experience was not unusual. The multinational operation involved close cooperation between forces from countries with different languages. The challenge was to 'get continuity across everyone', which in military terms was expressed as the need for interoperability. Within the NATO decision-making structures, the response to this complexity was explained by Ian Jones, a senior linguist at Supreme Headquarters Allied Powers Europe (SHAPE) near Mons, Belgium:

> *Catherine Baker:* Is there any sort of difference between SHAPE language policy and NATO language policy, or how do those two levels of policymaking fit together?
>
> *Ian Jones*: The only difference I could say is with regard to the official languages. Because NATO is much more bilingual. I mean, all NATO committees, which mostly meet in Brussels, with representation of the member nations, operate in English and French, whereas within the military structure, although we recognize French as an official language of NATO, the working language of the military structure is English.[3]

NATO policy is officially that English and French are the two working languages, and it is clear that this practice is observed within the political structures of the organization. Jones's comments on the pragmatic approach to operations reflect the general concern for interoperability, that is, the ability of NATO forces to communicate effectively with one another (Crossey 2005). The use of English as a lingua franca was important for the command structure and the working practices of the military, but did not extend far into the social life of the forces. Within their own milieu, troops naturally spoke in the shared language of their own culture, and socialized most readily with their own group. Nikola Andrijašević, a British bomb disposal officer with a former Yugoslav family background, based at HQ SFOR, described a typical experience in the bar at the SFOR headquarters:

> *Nikola Andrijašević*: In the bar in HQ SFOR, you'd probably walk in and hear at least six, seven different languages at any one stage. Obviously English was the dominant language, but you would have Italians, Italian officers, in a corner, French officers, German officers, in either, we had some... Argentinean, Albanian, and... I think some African Union officers as well, so as was very much a multinational bar with a myriad of different languages being spoken. And often you could spot two uniforms of two different nations talking in a third language that's completely alien to both of them.[4]

No doubt the linguistic diversity was relatively more visible at the headquarters, where most of the different units would be represented at any one time, but it is noticeable that a large part of the social interaction was between members of the same language community. At the same time, some socializing was between different groups, and, although they would often use English, Andrijašević suggests that they might also use another second language which they found more convenient. This would correspond to the widespread practice in civilian life, where participants is a meeting intuitively select the language or languages which provide the best communication.

The challenge for French

The main context in which English was not used as the common language was where French forces were deployed. France was the largest single contributor to UNPROFOR with 4493 troops out of the total of 38,130,[5] and made similarly substantial contributions to IFOR and SFOR. French was used to some extent by the troops of other countries, particularly Belgium, Switzerland and Canada, which included a proportion of native French speakers, and there were fluent French speakers in the small units from Luxembourg, Morocco and Tunisia. The fact that France formally withdrew from NATO military command between 1966 and 2009 meant that the use of French was largely abandoned for communication between NATO contingents. Ian Jones considered that this had become a universal practice:

> *Catherine Baker:* So the French in IFOR and SFOR for instance?
> *Ian Jones*: There's basically no French.

> *Catherine Baker:* And there's no circumstances where an operation would have French as its working language?
>
> *Ian Jones*: The only possibility might be if, just to give you, there's no political undertones to this, as I just spent two weeks in Senegal on a private visit, well, they speak French there. And if for some reason NATO were to do something in Senegal, then we might decide to have French, because that's the language of the nation there. The only problem is that the vast majority of NATO military personnel, both officers and NCOs, speak English and not French. So they're used to working in English. So it's really a pragmatic thing, I think, rather than a policy thing. It's obviously much simpler just to work in one language.[6]

Jones did see that there might be circumstances in which French would have operational importance, but he did not consider that these circumstances were present in Bosnia-Herzegovina. He may, however, have been unaware of the more complex situation that prevailed in the earlier stages of the intervention. At that time, French forces had a strong commitment to the use of French as a working language wherever possible. However, they were relatively isolated in this decision, as suggested by Boba Vukojević, a locally employed media analyst and press officer in the Sarajevo HQ in 1993–5:

> *Catherine Baker*: Well I'm asking sort of in general, how much did the UN use the French language.
>
> *Boba Vukojević*: For UN, English was the first language.... [A]s French were in the sector of Sarajevo, mostly French soldiers, and commander of the sector of Sarajevo was French, so they needed staff talking French. And especially they needed somebody who was in the press office talking Bosnian and French, so I was working... but also I was doing all translations from English into French, and from French into English, because I was kind of using both French and English. But English was mostly spoken in the UN. And French if needed (laughs). And it was needed, because the French were there.[7]

In practical terms, the need for translation and interpreting services for French was largely confined to meeting the requirements of the French forces themselves. Other contingents had some need for language services to communicate with the French, but for the most part English was used as the common language for communication between contingents. From the French perspective, the use of their national language was a political decision, asserting France's role in international affairs and in particular the country's independence from the domination of the United States. It was also a product of military practice, reinforced by the withdrawal of France from the NATO command structure in 1966, which reduced the need for its forces to speak a language other than French on a regular basis. The intervention in Bosnia-Herzegovina marked the beginning of closer military cooperation with NATO. However, it was a campaign which posed significant challenges at an operational level for the policy of prioritizing the French language. One practical difficulty was the relative scarcity of local people with knowledge of the language, as Boba Vukojević suggested:

> *Catherine Baker*: How easy was it for them to find local staff who spoke French?
>
> *Boba Vukojević*: Not very easy, because there were not a lot of people speaking French. And French even now is really [a] deficit language. So it was not very easy. And especially with a good command of the language. I mean, you can find somebody who speaks some of the French, but they really needed somebody who could write, and speak, and write good French. So it was not really easy. And even now it's not easy to find somebody who has a good, I mean, there are more French translators and interpreters today, but not many. Not many. Spanish, the same situation with Spanish and Italian.... So not very easy for them to find people in French. And even for the media, I know many French, Italian and Spanish media, they couldn't find somebody who speaks their languages, so they were obliged to find somebody who speaks English, and if they spoke poor English then it could be a problem. But usually they'd speak some English, and many of them couldn't find people speaking their native languages, so they needed to find somebody who at least speak English.[8]

The Bosnians had some contact with France, but there were few people who spoke its language, and the same was apparently true for other European countries, including Italy, which was an important power in the region. On the other hand, they had considerable recent contact with the English language through popular culture, especially music and cinema, and through the arrival of increased numbers of tourists in the decade before the conflict. Tourism had also brought contact with German visitors, but few French. As a result, French units were often compelled to use English as a language of communication. In this situation, the French forces were confronted with a tension between their political and their operational priorities. Another issue the French military had to face was the increased need for staff with the requisite language proficiency. This was observed by the commander of 1 COLDSTREAM, deployed under UNPROFOR:

> *Coldstreamer*: There were three multinational divisional areas, an American one based in Tuzla, a British one based in Banja Luka, and a French one based in Mostar. The French attempted for quite a long time to run their multinational division with French as its operating language. And this led to the most extraordinary sort of bureaucratic superstructure whereby every staff position tended to have about three deputies, so there'd be a Frenchman, a Spaniard, a German and an Italian or someone, all doing the same job, effectively. The French would be running this thing down the chain of command in French and expecting the, the Germans to report to them in French and things.[9]

The same practices were observed in 1999 by Nikola Andrijašević:

> *Nikola Andrijašević*: The headquarters was very much bilingual, both German and French, even though the mission main language was English. Each one of the battle groups would speak the national language, so it was quite a complicated system, whereby an order might be issued in English, from the headquarters, translated in French for some of the headquarters staff to deal with in French, and then reissued in German to the troops that might be dealing with it at the bottom level.
>
> *Catherine Baker*: So from English, to French, to German.
>
> *Nikola Andrijašević*: Yeah, or indeed from English to German then French.
>
> *Catherine Baker*: So who would do those translations?
>
> *Nikola Andrijašević*: Some of the staff, who was bilingual, would be burdened with doing most of the translation. There would be translator pools, but these were never big enough, so actually a lot of the translation of staff work was left to the headquarters staff. So it was key that the key decision makers and the key producers of these documents were bilingual, as the absence of one of them could cause a, quite a long delay in the issue of orders, they needed translation and they needed actioning and then maybe translating into a third language for the final tasks to be conducted.[10]

In many cases the work of translation was carried out by officers with specific language proficiency rather than by civilian translators, who were in any case difficult to recruit. The officers would in turn receive responses from the units concerned and translate them into French for the divisional commanders. As Andrijašević notes, this created a number of additional steps in the chain of command, each one a risk point, at which the presence of a suitably proficient officer was needed for orders to be processed. The potential delays clearly impeded operations, and the French responded ultimately by making changes, as the Coldstream commander observed:

> *Coldstreamer*: The problem was that the French then had do all the work themselves in turning all the reports from French into English before they could be sent up to Headquarters SFOR, which was run by American and British generals and operated like the rest of NATO in English. And the French in a very quiet, rather subtle way transformed themselves, their staff and their senior officers from a rather aggressively Francophone military, in the proud tradition of whatever it did, slowly but surely transformed itself into a very capable Anglophone organization, and in a way that the Russians who I worked with later on, I mean, the Russians came away from Yugoslavia having learned nothing at all, including having no conception of why it would have been an advantage to have developed an Anglophone capability for their officer corps. The French, on the other hand, no-one dared notice, or point out that this was going on, but everyone else, with a great sense of satisfaction, noticed that the French had bitten the bullet and accepted that to be effective in a multinational coalition, unless they were going to lead that coalition, which they might do in Africa or somewhere, anywhere else, they were going to have to operate within an English-speaking environment.[11]

The strong cultural commitment of the French unit was not sufficient to overcome the operational cost of maintaining the use of French in a multilingual setting. The cost is visible in both the upwards and downwards direction of the chain of command. Looking upwards, communication with superiors in NATO would need to be carried out in both French and English. Looking downwards, when commands and other documents were issued in French, they would need to be translated into the various languages of the component units, in this case Spanish, German and Italian.

The costs of the initial French stance can be seen in terms of resources and structures. The resources required included both additional staff and additional time to make the necessary translations. The structural difficulty was perhaps even more serious, with the involvement of several staff replicating the same function. This would potentially pose problems of consistency, since there would be several different versions of the same command and several officers exercising similar responsibilities. The decision of the French divisional commanders to adopt English alleviated the additional complexity in the upwards direction, and would be expected to do so in the downwards direction where the different units under their command had sufficient competence in English.

Certainly the French forces were committed to achieving competence in English, and Gordon Schofield, a civilian affairs officer deployed with SFOR in 1999, commented that:

> *Gordon Schofield*: With the French footprint in NATO, they're moving towards English, and most of the French I know, most French bases I know have got a language lab, to learn English. So, I think they're embracing NATO, and English, quite well.[12]

At the same time, the Coldstream commander was sensitive to the political difficulty of this operational change and was at pains to emphasize the benefits to the French command in increasing their capability. As an example of the success of this approach, he cited the French general André Soubirou:

> *Coldstreamer*: There was a famous general called Soubirou, and General Soubirou, who'd been there at the beginning, in 1992, in Yugoslavia, and then was back again in 1995, and Soubirou was a sort of... Foreign Legion toughie. I don't know if he was in the Foreign Legion, but he was a tough man, and, you know, had sort of, like Dave Allen, the comedian, only had about three and a half fingers on one hand, and all this stuff, and he was coming for a briefing to the British headquarters in Gornji Vakuf, in late 1995, and I turned to the Canadian lieutenant-colonel there, and I said, 'Ah, Kevin,' I said, 'General Soubirou's coming today. Of course, as a Canadian officer, you're completely bilingual, or you wouldn't be a lieutenant-colonel, and so you'll be briefing him in French, won't you.' Anyway, at once Kevin went very pale and said, 'Do you think I'll have to?' And I said, 'Well, absolutely, he'll expect you to, of course, you know,

> you must be bilingual, you can't get, I know your national language policy, you can't be promoted to lieutenant-colonel unless you're completely bilingual.' And he said, 'Well, I did pass, you know.' So I said, 'Well, you'd better be ready, mate, you see.' Anyway, General Soubirou came in and sat down, and Kevin stood up to give him the operations brief, and he went, 'Bonjour, mon général', and Soubirou goes 'non, non, s'il vous plaît, en anglais'. And so there was a, you know, the French very early on realized that there was influence to be had, if you could hold your own in English, and that that was the only way that it was going to work for them.[13]

The decision of General Soubirou to use English in this situation appears as an assertive choice. He was in any case the ranking officer, since Coldstreamer and his Canadian colleague were both lieutenant-colonels. He also establishes his authority in the situation by his display of confidence in using English and by his implicit judgement that French is not the first language of the Canadian. Soubirou's dexterity with language is confirmed by a short video clip filmed before NATO and UN forces started action to lift the blockade of Sarajevo in summer 1995, where he deftly handles questions by English and American journalists.[14] He responds good-humouredly in English to questions about his tactics, dismisses a final more detailed question offered by a journalist in hesitant French and concludes with a few encouraging words in French to the group: 'J'étais content de vous dire bonjour. Bon courage, hein [I was happy to meet you. Good luck, then]'. In both instances, Soubirou demonstrates an eclectic multilingualism, switching between English and French as best suited his purpose at the time.

Competence in French was not entirely absent from the theatre of conflict, and in particular a number of former Yugoslavs, especially Serbs and Croats, had served in the French Foreign Legion (Simons 2005; Porch 2010). Many of them returned to join the forces of their particular faction, where their military experience was generally respected by their colleagues and superiors. This was the case of Ante Gotovina, a general in the Croatian Army, and Ante Roso, a general in the HVO. However, their knowledge of French was not always seen as an asset, as Coldstreamer suggested, based on an episode with General Roso.

> *Coldstreamer*: And Roso is typical of a number of Croat leaders in that he was a Foreign Legionnaire, and he'd come back from the diaspora to command, in his case he became the commander-in-chief of the Croat forces, the HVO. And I went to a meeting in December 1993

> between General Roso, General Delić, who was the commander-in-chief of the Army of the Republic of Bosnia-Herzegovina, the Bosniaks, and General Briquemont. General Briquemont was the Belgian commander of UNPROFOR. So below General Cot, but in charge of the UN forces in Bosnia. And the meeting was held in the Canadian headquarters, and was held in French and Serbo-Croat. Which was a challenge for all concerned. But my French was up to understanding what was being said in French, and I could understand thanks to Russian what was really being said in Serbo-Croat. But the chaos was caused by General Roso, who, faced by ... Actually, it may have been General Cot at the meeting. But faced by a Francophone general, this chap, who was now a general but had been a sergeant, or something, in the French Foreign Legion, kept smacking his leg, as Foreign Legionnaires do, and saying, 'oui, mon général', and speaking to him in French. And the rest of the Croat delegation kept pulling his arm and saying, no, you've got to speak Croat, you're on our side, and you've, you can't speak to him in French because we don't know what on earth you're talking about. So it was an interesting linguistic challenge that this Croat commander had better French than he did Croatian, and that his own delegation were having to rein him in because he couldn't cut the mustard in his own native language. So that was a challenge.[15]

In this case, Roso clearly regarded French as his professional language, having served in the French army. He may have been more comfortable using French to discuss military issues, if Coldstreamer is right in suggesting his Croatian was not adequate for the purpose. His choice of language clearly undermined the confidence of his own delegation, both by situating him too closely with the NATO leader and by excluding his own colleagues from the discussion, since it would be embarrassing for an interpreter to be required to translate the general's French into Serbo-Croat for the benefit of his own side. However, there is also a suggestion that Roso's behaviour might have been more appropriate for a sergeant, the rank he occupied in the Legion, rather than for a commander-in-chief of the Croat forces. This would not be entirely surprising since the use of a particular language is context-specific and often carries with it an echo of the personal and social contexts in which it was learned.

The Russian connection

When Coldstreamer observes that his knowledge of Russian enabled him to understand the discussions in Serbo-Croat, this is a reminder that many NATO personnel had learned Russian as an important part of their military training for conditions of the Cold War. We have already seen how this enabled some officers to make rapid progress in learning Serbo-Croat. The fact that the Russian contingent is depicted as having entirely rejected the opportunity to develop its capability in English may at least partly be ascribed to the fact that the Russians also had very recent memories of the tensions and hostilities of the Cold War. However, Russian itself remained useful in facilitating links with the forces contributed by the forces of former Eastern Bloc countries, including Bulgaria, Czech Republic, Estonia, Hungary, Latvia, Lithuania, Poland, Romania, the Russian Federation, Slovakia, Slovenia and Ukraine. This was particularly important where several forces were working closely together, and is exemplified by the experience of the Nordic–Polish (NORDPOL) Brigade that served in SFOR in 1997–8. Thomas Nielsen, the brigadier-general in command of the brigade, explained the complexity:

> *Thomas Nielsen*: The Nordic–Polish Brigade was composed by five battalions. There was a Swedish battalion, a Norwegian battalion, a Finnish battalion, which was; the two first battalions, the Swedes and the Norwegians, were infantry battalions. The Finns were more or less an engineer battalion. Then there was a Danish battalion, which was an armoured infantry, we had a tank company in the battalion, and the Polish battalion, which was also an armoured infantry. Then we had an American, or an American artillery unit was subordinated to the brigade. We had a headquarters company, which consisted of components from all the Nordic countries as well as the Poles. And the brigade staff was composed of officers and NCOs from all the countries participating in the brigade. I need to tell you that in the Danish battalion there was actually a company which consisted of three platoons from the Baltic countries. So we had actually quite a lot of different languages in the brigade.[16]

It is difficult to imagine a more multilingual combat unit, with participants from nine different countries, each with a different language. The Danish battalion was particularly diverse, including platoons from Estonia, Latvia and Lithuania. Communication was very complex, as Nielsen explained:

> *Catherine Baker*: So how did people in the brigade communicate with each other?

Thomas Nielsen: Well, every communication was in English. So when I was visiting the Norwegian battalion I could speak Danish, they could speak Norwegian, to a certain extent the same goes for the Swedish battalion. We understand each other. We have to be very careful because, especially, well, the Scandinavian languages, they are, these years they are dividing very much from each other. So it's not so easy, especially with the Swedes, to understand them any longer. Well, I think it's easier for the Danes to understand the Swedes than the other way round. And then there was the Finns, which is quite a different language, we simply had to communicate in English. The Poles, I communicated with the Poles mostly in English, because it was very important that the Poles, it was also a training period for them, in order to join NATO. So they tried to learn English, military English. So we tried to commun…, but sometimes I had to communicate with them in Russian.

Catherine Baker: Why did you have to use Russian sometimes?

Thomas Nielsen: Because some of the Polish officers, and especially some of the elder ones, simply didn't understand a word of Russian, and if I gave an operational order, I had to be sure that the order was understood the right way. I could be quite sure that the other battalion commanders understood the order but not all the Polish officers, and especially the battalion commander at that time, he really did not understand, unless I gave the order to him in Engl, in Russian.[17]

Although Nielsen begins by saying that every communication was in English, his description makes it clear that the reality was much more complex. The Danes, Norwegians and Swedes would typically speak their own languages when meeting together, with the expectation of being understood, even though this might not always be the case. Communication with the Finns would generally be in English, though the Finnish forces would no doubt also include troops from the Swedish-speaking minority in Finland, and most of the officers would have a working knowledge of Swedish. Communication with the Polish officers was clearly the most difficult, since their English proficiency was at that stage more limited. When Nielsen says that older Polish officers 'simply didn't understand a word of Russian', it is clear from his subsequent remarks that he meant they did not understand English. For them, Russian served as a more reliable vehicle. His description matches the experience of Martin Lund Pedersen, a civilian Serbo-Croat interpreter in the same brigade.

Martin Lund Pedersen: There was one more infantry company which consisted of Baltic soldiers, there was a Danish commander of that company, but there were three platoons, one from each of the three Baltic countries.

Catherine Baker: So Estonia, Latvia, Lithuania.

Martin Lund Pedersen: Yes. Yes.

Catherine Baker: What language did they communicate in?

Martin Lund Pedersen: That's a good question. Their platoon leaders spoke English. And most of the privates and the other younger officers and NCOs, they knew Russian at that time. So they could communicate internally in Russian, the three Baltic countries. And then, it was only their leaders who knew how to communicate upwards, so to speak.[18]

Since the three Baltic countries had very recently emerged from the Soviet Union, Russian was still a *lingua franca* between them, and each had a significant minority of native Russian speakers in the population. All three states had moved to the teaching of English as the first foreign language in school, but the impact of this was only beginning to be felt in the armed forces at this period. The platoon leaders might be expected to have undergone intensive training in English to enable them to connect effectively to the command structure, communicating upwards, as Pedersen puts it. In the case of the Baltic countries and Poland, the fact that they were new entrants into NATO operations gave them a desire to adapt to the requirements, including using English as an operational language. However, their history and culture still carried a different set of linguistic practices, including the general use of Russian.

In the case of the Russian units deployed in Bosnia, the new cooperation with NATO did not carry the same political commitment to abandon former practices, and as Coldstreamer observed they were highly resistant to adapting their operational practices. The ensuing linguistic difficulties were in fact attenuated by the widespread knowledge of Russian among NATO officers, who had learned it as the language of the enemy in a Cold War context. And, in the spirit of that 'looking-glass war', it is likely that a number of senior Russians had acquired a knowledge of English for similar reasons. However, in the post-1989 climate, Coldstreamer considered that they had 'no conception of why it would have been an advantage to have developed an Anglophone capability for their officer corps'. This suggests that issues of language were symptomatic of a wider cultural divergence. The forces of the former Warsaw Pact countries largely shared a common culture, which was only partly rooted in a common language. Whereas they might adapt to a new language regime, it was much more difficult to adapt to a new culture. This was suggested by Thomas Nielsen who observed that the most significant issue in working with Polish units was their very different military culture:

> *Thomas Nielsen*: ... inside the brigade I knew from some of my successors that they still had quite a lot of difficulties in communicating with the Poles. The Poles were a problem in a way. They were very good soldiers, I can tell you, but they were ... First of all, there was the language barrier. And secondly there were the cultural differences. They had quite another military culture than the military culture of the Scandinavian countries. And that made it extremely difficult from time to time. (coughs) In the Scandinavian armed forces, you are supposed to act very independently. Of course you get an order, but you get, not necessarily a very detailed order, but you get an order and you are supposed to solve the problem. As a commander I give the battalion commander an order, a framework, and the means to do the job, and then I expect that he will do the details. That's not the case in, that was not the case in the Polish armed forces, because they were so dominated by the Russian tradition that the commander had to give the order in details to his subordinates. And the Poles expected to get that kind of order. And I had once again the advantage of knowing the Russian way of commanding troops, in the fields, so I actually had to make two orders. I had one order for one part of the brigade, and a special order for the Poles. Because if they didn't get it, they simply couldn't understand. And they didn't do anything unless they were specifically ordered to do it. And initiative was not supposed to be an important part of exercising.[19]

In this case the language barrier was only one part of the communication problem, and the cultural barrier was regarded as more intractable. The NATO culture was to issue 'framework' orders and to give broad discretion to local commanders who devised ways of implementing the order. This clashed with the Warsaw Pact culture of issuing detailed orders without delegated discretion. A similar clash of culture was reported by Ian Jones:

> *Ian Jones*: And, I remember, we have a glossary of NATO military terms which was actually started back in the 1950s, which is known as AAP 6, which is Allied Administrative Publication 6. You can actually find it on the NATO website, you may have seen it there. But we had to translate, we didn't translate the complete book for them,

but we had to translate certain key terms, representing key concepts. One of them being the distinction that we make in NATO between command and control, which ... they had no notion of. To them it was all the same thing. I don't know if you understand the difference between them.

Catherine Baker: For the tape, could you possibly explain it?

Ian Jones: Yes, certainly. Command is basically the authority that national military authorities have over the military personnel and, or units, or organizations, which are working for them. In other words it's complete control. I shouldn't use the word control, it's complete authority. It means that, for example, they can decide on promotions, and pay, or conditions of service, all sorts of things like that, which NATO has no authority. When military forces are made available to NATO, although we say that they are under NATO command, they really still belong to the nations that contribute them. And ... so NATO really controls what those forces do, but the Supreme Allied Commander Europe, who is my boss here, in SHAPE, cannot say to the Dutch army 'Oh I think that guy is very good, I'd like him to be promoted.' He has no authority whatsoever to do things like that. It also affects other areas, discipline, pay, all sorts of things like that, which are purely the responsibility of the nations contributing the forces. Now when the Russians arrived here, they didn't understand this distinction at all. And there were other terms, I forget what they all were, this was ten years ago. But we had to, in some cases, actually invent new terminology in Russian, to allow them to understand the distinction. Because when they arrived ... they had been given political direction, obviously, that they were to negotiate how Russia was to participate in the operation, but they could not accept that Russian forces, I mean they were just coming out of the Cold War, could be placed under NATO command. And we said, 'No no, you don't have to be under NATO command, it's under NATO control.' They said, 'What do you mean, NATO control?' They didn't understand.[20]

The non-specialist may have some sympathy with the difficulties experienced by the Russian officers in grasping this distinction, since Jones is compelled to use the term control to define command, and explains that 'NATO command' really means control. The distinction is not fully resolved in the NATO–Russian Glossary, to which he refers, which defines command partly in terms of control as 'the authority and responsibility vested in a member of the military forces for the purpose of using available resources, planning their employment, organizing, directing, coordinating and controlling military forces' (NATO/RUSSIA Joint Editorial Working Group 2002: 50). More recent versions of the NATO Glossary still retain the same definition of command in terms of control, as 'the authority vested in an individual of the armed forces for the direction, coordination, and control of military forces' (NATO Standardization Agency 2008: 2-C-9).[21] The difficulty is increased by the available Russian terms used to translate control: 'управления', which has a strong meaning of 'management', and 'подчинение', which has a first meaning of 'submission'. A further ambiguity is no doubt introduced by the French term 'contrôler', which has a strong meaning of 'monitor' or 'inspect'. The complexity of the ensuing NATO-Russian agreement is reflected in the arrangement which accompanied it, involving a Russian deputy to the Supreme Allied Commander, with responsibility for Russian forces in Bosnia.[22] Jones's illustration using the Dutch army as an example makes it clear what the terms mean in practice. Given the difficulty of providing a clear verbal definition, it appears that the distinction between command and control is cultural rather than linguistic. The case also confirms that meanings are conditioned by the context in which they occur, and that word-for-word equivalences are elusive, often in the most crucial instances.

Varieties of English

The general adoption of English as an operational language was an important factor in achieving coherent communication between participating forces. The broad ability of the forces to communicate in English was noted by Edin Selimović, a locally employed interpreter working for NATO since 1996:

> *Edin Selimović*: The official language of IFOR mission, SFOR mission, EUFOR mission and now NATO mission is English. So doesn't matter which country soldiers or a soldier came from, he or she spoke English. That was the official language of the mission.
>
> *Catherine Baker*: And were they all able to do that in practice?
>
> *Edin Selimović*: Oh, yes. Yes. Of course, they were not all fluent, but yes, they had to have some knowledge of English in order to do their jobs.
>
> *Catherine Baker*: And so, whenever you were interpreting, wherever they came from, they would always be speaking in English.
>
> *Edin Selimović*: Yes, yes. Or there would be no meeting (laughs).[23]

Selimović's experience was principally with officers of sufficient seniority to attend meetings, and it was generally expected that non-commissioned officers and more senior ranks would need to have a sufficient competence in English to function in their role. This was frequently seen as a challenge in the earlier stages of the Bosnian intervention, but it may well be that the passage of time enabled non-native speakers to practice and improve their proficiency in English. This was certainly the experience of Martin Lund Pedersen:

> *Martin Lund Pedersen*: But actually I think my English was more fluent then, because I used it every day, talking to... I befriended some, the Lithuanian officer, and we talked a lot, and that was in English, and some of the American officers I also talked a lot to, so I think my English was a bit more fluent, and I felt very much at home in the situation, as opposed to now.[24]

It is striking that he was particularly helped by his friendship with the Lithuanian officer, who clearly would not have been a native speaker of English. In view of the multinational composition of the forces, the most widely spoken form of English must have been between non-native speakers. Elvir Ćerić, a Sarajevan interpreter for the UN and NATO, felt that this experience had a negative impact on his own proficiency:

> *Elvir Ćerić*: How did this affect my English? How did I perceive this, working for international community organizations, had affected my English? It affected it a lot (laughs). Especially working for the UN, because... there is nothing, I mean, this UN English, which is very simple... and where you have to be careful not to use the English words that are not commonly used in an everyday communication, and therefore everything had to be simplified, because of the fact that UN involves people from all over the world, whose knowledge of English is not so good, and as an interpreter you had to adjust to that.[25]

No doubt Ćerić felt the impact because he had studied English language and literature at university, and had worked for 10 years as a professional interpreter at the time of the interview. He applied very high standards to his own work but also recognized the need for a simplified English, which was a particularly acute requirement with the UN, but also a factor in the other international organizations for which he later worked. Nataša Šimić, an interpreter for SFOR in Banja Luka, had similar reflections on her experience with a unit of Nepalese Gurkhas, whose English she found particularly difficult to understand, unlike the well-educated Household Cavalry officers who succeeded them.[26] The requirements of military communication meant that the varieties of English language became an important consideration. For most purposes, the English used needed to be readily understood by people of different language backgrounds. The variable levels and varieties of English meant that its adoption as a common working language was by no means a perfect solution, as Tony French observed:

> *Tony French*: But within the British division you would have all these brigades, which are the next level down...which was a complete mishmash of different nationalities.
>
> *Catherine Baker*: But everyone would be communicating in English.
>
> *Tony French*: Everyone. NATO's language is, yes, English, so everybody had to.
>
> *Catherine Baker*: How well did that work in practice?
>
> *Tony French*: (laughs) If we had had to fight, I think it would have been a bit of a nightmare. Because I would have been taking command from a Czech colonel, who would have got his orders from a French Canadian general...who would have got his orders from a British major-general. So...Jesus Christ. I would have no bloody idea.[27]

The chain of command was multilingual, with each step being conveyed in the variety of English used by the superior officer and being understood according to the variety used by the recipient. The scope for misunderstanding was substantial. The linguistic difficulty was compounded by the nature of the command culture, which in NATO took the form of broad indications of intent, delegating the operational detail to the level below. As Tony French summarized it: 'I can give you the intention of what I'm trying to achieve, and then it's really down to the sub-unit guys to make up their mind on what they do.'[28] In this case, the officers were expected to have sufficient competence in English and communicated directly with each other, without the use of interpreters. In practice, the arrangement does appear to have worked, though less smoothly than if all concerned were native speakers of the same language.

The use of English was reinforced by the widespread knowledge of the language among the local population in Bosnia-Herzegovina. Steve Morley, a military colloquial speaker in the Queen's Royal Hussars, based at Mrkonjić Grad, recounts an experience in 1999:

> *Steve Morley*: But I went to a little village to buy a load of flour and oil, for an old woman, and I went to the shop, and I said 'koliko kosta olje' [how much does oil cost?]. What's flour now? I can't even remember what flour is. Or whatever. And some bloke tapped me on the shoulder and he says, and I'd said to the lady behind, 'I speak like a child, I speak bad Serbian.' And the bloke behind me says in English, he says, 'You speak really, really good Serbian.' And I said, 'Well, you speak really good English.' I said, 'Where'd you learn to speak that?' And he said, 'I worked in a hotel in London for a couple of years.' And then, you know, again, it breaks the ice. And I had a couple of slivoviches with him, done my shopping and see you later. Yeah. Mainly the young people spoke English.[29]

The local population were internationally mobile and many had links with England through family migration. In addition, the influence of British and US popular culture was considerable, and served to motivate young people in particular to learn English. The prevalent variety of English was therefore a combination of standard Anglo-American popular usage and simplified English for international communication. This appears to have served adequately for operational purposes. The most frequently cited difficulties were encountered in communicating with native speakers who used strongly regional varieties of English. Sinan Halilović, an interpreter from Sarajevo, reported that he had particular difficulties with Welsh and Northern English troops:

> *Sinan Halilović*: The first regiment that I was employed with was RGB, ah, no, it was Duke of Wellington's Regiment. But they had people coming all over. Wales, north of England, south of England, east of England, Norwich, that part, all corners of England, really. Not, no particular. But Welsh was particularly difficult, really. I was encouraged by some soldiers who I could understand at that time, and they said, 'Don't worry, son, we don't even understand him.' It was a Welsh driver at that time, he was a driver to the CO, commanding officer, the colonel. He was that big fellow, really. And he was Welsh. Never I understood him, really. And the soldiers would just say 'No, don't worry, we don't understand him.' He would be talking something

> but everyone would be, 'Ugh, what is he on about.' Things like that. Really. He was difficult. So Welsh was particularly difficult, and northern England. Northern parts of England, Newcastle, Liverpool, like that belt. All the way, from Newcastle down to Liverpool, was difficult. Especially Liverpool. It was, even today I don't think that I would manage.[30]

Several of the locally employed interpreters have detailed their problems in understanding regional British accents, quoting Scottish (especially Glasgow), Welsh, Northern English and Cockney in particular. They also identify difficulties with understanding the varieties of English spoken by Indian and Nepali troops. Jovana Zorić, an interpreter for SFOR in Mrkonjić Grad, recalled having to interpret between two English-speaking soldiers:

> *Jovana Zorić*: Ah, officer from our camp was there, local police, like head of police, and the guy from international police, IPTF, International Police Task Force. And, 'What's going on? Quick, there.' And once I'm there, there is three of them, and it's just, around police, local police and stuff. And it's like arguing, or, I can tell it's like what the hell, like temperature raising, boiling blood. And interpreter standing, girl standing completely like pale, frozen. And I'm like, 'What's going on?' And I realized one, our officer, British soldier, was Scottish, with his strong accent. And he was shouting, and, to the IPTF guy who was Indian or something, so his English was good enough for normal accent but he couldn't understand a word of this. The guy was Scottish Highlanders, like from Inverness or something, and the interpreter, almost in tears, because, you know, they're going to, the big incident is maybe going to happen. And I'm like, 'OK,' so I was like, 'Calm down, everybody, calm down. What happened?' And the guy started, Scottish guy started talking, Scottish sergeant, 'Raargh!' It's like, 'OK, OK, whatever, you know. They don't understand what I'm talking about!' And I started translating, you know, interpreting, and the girl went, interpreter, she went – 'You understand?! Do you understand what he's talking about?!' So I was like, 'Yeah, yeah, yeah, just, you know, calm down.' So I ended up, it was the, kind of almost an incident because nobody, even an Indian guy who speaks English, but, you know, it was like one of those scenes that you actually translate between, interpret between two people, they speak English, but because British person, for any reason, it's

either from East End and his accent is so strong that another person can't understand, especially from IPTF, you would just repeat the same sentence in English, just this way, because they couldn't understand each other.[31]

Zorić's narrative gives a sense of the incoherence that the participants in this episode experienced. The tension is all the more acute because they feel that they should understand someone whom they recognize as speaking English but whose English is not intelligible to them. In fact, as Zorić's actions show, she had learned to understand the Scottish sergeant's way of speaking and was able to act as his interpreter. Other interpreters report similar experiences of being able to understand difficult forms of English after a period of familiarization. Tarik Begović, an interpreter from Tuzla, recounts his work with a US infantry unit from Arkansas:

> *Tarik Begović*: All of them, the whole unit I worked with, was black. They were all black people. Young people who spoke street English, full of slang. I was almost embarrassed for the first month working with them, because I could barely understand what they were saying. Especially when they were talking to each other, not to me. Because they were trying to be careful when talking to me, so they were, you know, speaking slowly without so much slang. It took me a month to get used to this. And, I don't even know if I wanted this, I don't remember if I wanted to, or it just happened, but day by day I started speaking like them. Which wasn't the most proper English in the world, but at the same time, I think it was professional for me to adjust to them, to make sure they understand what I'm saying. It was easier for me to make them feel me as a part of the team, which is exactly how I felt a couple of months later, as one of them. As part of this team. Not a Bosnian guy who's here to help them, but as one of them. As one of the team. It was a great experience. It was the best rotation I ever worked with. And, six months later, when they were leaving Bosnia, it was a really sad moment for me. And I recall the next rotation coming from New York. The people who spoke different English, without so much slang. And they were looking at me like I'm from a different planet. Because if they see a black person from Arkansas who speaks Ebonics, it's a normal thing. But if you see a Bosnian white person who speaks Ebonics, then it feels like something's wrong with this guy. But it just happened, you know.[32]

Tarik Begović's account shows that the language issue is not simply a matter of intelligibility. It is also a matter of identity. Where Zorić learned to understand her Scottish unit, Begović takes a step further to speak like his Arkansas unit. His reason is articulated as the need to integrate and become 'one of the team', and he finds himself in difficulty at the end of the six-month rotation, partly through losing people he has come to see as his friends, but partly because he has assumed an identity which is not sustainable. He is not a continuing part of the team, and the cultural identity he has assumed is in conflict with his social identity as a white Bosnian.

Although regional accent is frequently identified as a challenge to understanding, less dramatic difficulties were also experienced. An occasional concern is the use of slang words. Jovana Zoric recounts her bewilderment on encountering words like 'brew' for 'cup of tea' and 'scoff' for 'food', though these are lexical items that she soon learned and even recalled with some relish. Similarly, with abbreviations, which Nataša Šimić recalls as almost a different language:

> *Nataša Šimić*: You think you speak English, and you go into the Army, and I remember my first patrol or second patrol. We are on the top of the hill, collecting some weapons, and the sergeant-major says, somebody asks, a journalist came to interview the sergeant-major, and they asked so many questions. One of the questions was, 'When you collect the weapons, where are you going to store the weapons?' And he said, 'Oh, we will store the weapons in MG.' MG, good God! MG. MG. Sounds like nothing. It's just the abbreviation of Mrkonjić Grad. It's a small town outside Banja Luka. And so many things like that. And after a while you start speaking in abbreviations. Army, CO, OC, officer in command, CO, commanding officer, sergeant-major, CSM. They use so many abbreviations. And then you go for a meeting in the hospital and then you forget the words you have to use. You start speaking in abbreviations. So it's a different language when you get into the Army.[33]

Like many professions, the military have developed an extensive lexicon of standard abbreviations for their different functions, which will need to be learned by people dealing regularly with them. But they also generate specific abbreviations for particular situations. The abbreviating of Mrkonjić Grad to MG is a striking example, which is characteristic of the ways in which armies incorporate elements of their theatre of operations within their own military discourse. Nataša Šimić's reaction shows that she experiences it at least as a defamiliarizing gesture, and perhaps as a kind of expropriation.

Conclusion

The multilingual nature of the peace operations in Bosnia-Herzegovina presented a high level of complexity. At the level of day-to-day contacts, the troops continued to use the same approach that civilians typically use in multilingual contexts. So, they typically socialized in groups of their own culture, and when in mixed groups they instinctively used whatever languages they knew that would achieve the most effective communication. The main problems they encountered were in the formal command structure and in relations between units of different nationalities. In these cases the interaction between different languages required an apparatus of interpreting and translation, which placed a high cost on the forces, in terms of time and resources. It also undermined coherence, and it was no doubt fortunate that the cumbersome systems set in place were not placed under the pressure of cooperation in intensive combat.

The NATO forces largely adopted the policy of using English as the language of military communication. French forces, who had not previously operated within NATO command, initially maintained the use of French, but over three or four years they developed their capability in English, which enabled them to provide more effective leadership in the multilingual NATO operations. French remained a lingua franca among several contingents, as did Russian among the eastern European contingents. And officers from many countries had a knowledge of French or Russian from their education or military training.

The use of English certainly increased the effectiveness of military cooperation, though competence in the use of the language was very unevenly distributed. There were cultural and historical reasons for this, but as the campaign developed, the level of English proficiency developed considerably, especially among officers, who were mainly responsible for communications between units and with the outside world. It then emerged that the language differences concealed other differences, particularly in the military culture of particular countries. For example, the concepts of command and control could not easily be translated between English, French and Russian.

Paradoxically, it was the English-speaking units that experienced some of the most intractable difficulties with English as a language of general communication. Ordinary soldiers and non-commissioned officers from many countries and regions spoke strong local or regional varieties of English and used the idioms and jargon of their own group. These were often difficult for non-English speakers to understand, and sometimes unintelligible to other Anglophones. In this respect, even the English-speaking forces were multilingual.

The multilingual forces were in many respects a microcosm of the changing pattern of contact between languages in the wider world under conditions of globalization. The concept of globalization, though coined during the 1960s, became a key concept during the 1990s. As Manfred Steger (2009: 1; emphasis original) suggests, '"[g]lobalization" surfaced as *the* buzzword of the "Roaring Nineties" because it best captured the increasingly interdependent nature of social life on our planet'. The interdependence of military life is clearly demonstrated in the experience of multinational peace operations in Bosnia-Herzegovina, and it may be that, as some commentators have suggested, the operations in Yugoslavia paved the way to a more global role for NATO itself (Kitchen 2010; Nazemroaya 2012). Certainly, the involvement of more than 50 countries in the peace operations created a globalized environment in which many languages came into contact. The rich multilingual landscape that resulted was a learning experience for the forces involved as well as for the people in the area. It may still hold lessons that remain to be learned.

8
Lessons Identified

This study has investigated a broad range of issues related to language during a decade of peace operations in Bosnia-Herzegovina. It has examined a sample of the people involved at different levels, the practices in which they engaged and the patterns which have emerged. Successive chapters have drawn on the narrated experience of a spectrum of military personnel, mostly serving with the British forces, and of a range of civilian linguists, mostly employed from the area. They have examined the systems and structures that were set in place at various times and have also analysed the roles and relationships that emerged. To do this, we have used a number of analytical approaches, drawn from the study of oral history and language policy. This chapter now seeks to identify lessons that may be drawn from them to inform the future practice of those who have responsibilities in respect of languages in conflict and peacemaking and to inform the future research of scholars studying similar issues. Following the insights that we have gained, we present these as 'lessons identified' rather than presuming that they are 'lessons learned'.

Language capability in the military

The NATO forces took seriously their language capability and were well equipped to meet the language needs of the Cold War, which continued to set the strategic framework for some months after the dissolution of the Soviet Union in 1991. They were caught unawares by the sudden requirement for Serbo-Croat (as the language was then called) when they entered the UN operation in Bosnia-Herzegovina during 1992, and scrambled to respond. One response was to deploy personnel who were heritage speakers of the language. This met with mixed success since the individual's personal connection with the area presented complexities which in some cases offset their ability to communicate. In any event, the number of such people in the forces was very small. Even combined with a handful of soldiers that had studied the language at university, they did not provide a response on the scale that was needed, which was typically characterized as being at least one military interpreter with each company of around a hundred troops. It may be concluded that, for a language not widely spoken within the forces, high-level capability could only be generated through intensive training.

Instruction in Serbo-Croat for general military purposes was set up during the early months of the operation. Short courses of around 15 days gave volunteers some language awareness and a small repertoire of greetings, but experience revealed that it was difficult to achieve useful proficiency within a short period of training, even where learners had some previous experience of language learning. For troops compelled to attend such courses, the results were sometimes counterproductive, especially if they were not equipped with an understanding of language. A metalinguistic approach proved more effective, training troops to communicate by using available language resources. These included signs, gestures, body language, vocabulary cards and whatever knowledge of different languages they or their interlocutors might possess. This seems to be the best use of a short course, though not to the exclusion of some familiarization with the language.

Courses of around three months usually achieved a 'colloquial' level of language proficiency. Bosnian/Croatian/Serbian was difficult for English-speakers to learn, though it was more accessible when learners already had a knowledge of Russian, which had frequently been taught during the Cold War. Knowledge of a cognate language was a significant advantage, but literate knowledge of any other language was also beneficial. Colloquial linguists found, however, that commanders in the field generally expected a much higher level of expertise than was actually achievable. This led to serious frustrations and many colloquial linguists were then deployed on tasks which made no use of their level of language knowledge. In this respect their linguistic capital was less valued in the field of service that their broader cultural capital. The deployment of people with modest levels of proficiency carries benefits, but a stronger management of expectations seems desirable, perhaps through the adoption of more explicit titles, referring to assistant, apprentice or novice status.

Training for specialist linguists was put in place, with a programme of longer courses, typically lasting up to one year. However, in the early part of the operation 'military interpreters' were deployed with shorter periods of training. The term 'interpreter' is misleading since it was used in a very broad sense and could designate a range of roles and levels of language attainment. They were not necessarily trained in formal interpreting skills, and while these officers were able to meet routine needs, they often fell short of fully professional capabilities. In many cases, commanders also had an unrealistic expectation of what they could do. When their expectations were not met, they typically turned to the locally employed interpreters who tended to assume the technical language roles of formal interpreting and translating as well as the routine work of accompanying patrols. This was particularly apparent once the level of violence had reduced and civilian linguists were able to work safely. As with colloquial linguists, a clearer title would be an advantage. It would also be preferable to give trainees a longer exposure to language training and to introduce new teaching, perhaps developing the method of teaching through scenarios into teaching of other military disciplines through the language concerned (content and language integrated teaching).

Recent research suggests that civilian translators and interpreters have a wider cultural role than their linguistic duties might suggest (Venuti 1995; Torikai 2009). This applies to a much greater extent to the military linguists in Bosnia-Herzegovina, at whatever level of language proficiency. They were fully trained military personnel, often commissioned officers, with a portfolio of military capabilities. They frequently assumed a wider range of military roles, providing various forms of problem solving and support, to the point of acting as a 'fixer' in some cases (Stankovic 2000). In many cases, the broader role was more personally satisfying and they found that it was more likely to bring them recognition and promotion than their specifically linguistic expertise. It is clear that the military and civilian interpreters are related but not identical professions, and it may be that the designation 'interpreter' retains too much ambiguity in the military context.

NATO forces from non-English-speaking countries had a strong requirement for language support in using English, which emerged as the common language of military communication. This was recognized by the French forces, which developed their capability in English over three or four years. Where officers would not or could not operate in English they encountered difficulties in the formal command structure and in relations between units of different nationalities, requiring a costly and cumbersome apparatus of interpreting and translation. Competence in the use of the language was very unevenly distributed, but as the campaign developed, the level of English proficiency developed considerably, especially among officers, who were mainly responsible for communications between units and with the outside world. On the other hand, language differences often concealed other differences, particularly in the military culture of participating countries. It may be concluded that the use of English as a vehicular language was the most effective approach, but that its use should not be assumed to carry a uniform set of cultural understandings.

In their everyday operations, the forces were conspicuously multilingual. They operated and socialized mainly in groups of their own culture, and when in mixed groups, they instinctively used whatever languages they knew that would achieve the most effective communication. Although English was most commonly used for communication between units, French remained a *lingua franca* among several contingents, as did Russian among the eastern European contingents. And many officers had some knowledge of other languages from their education or military training. The use of English as a *lingua franca* posed particular challenges for English-speaking units, particularly for ordinary soldiers and non-commissioned officers who spoke strong local or regional varieties of English. They had difficulties in making themselves understood by non-English-speakers and in some cases by English-speakers from other regions. Since the pattern of multilingualism is tending to increase in other sectors, it seems appropriate to encourage military personnel to widen their repertoire of other languages they can use to communicate. This applies equally to English native speakers, who would also benefit from training in the use of English for international communication.

The language support operations in Bosnia-Herzegovina were largely developed under delegated authority by local commanders, often in challenging conditions. Once the operation moved into calmer conditions, with reducing troop numbers, the highly diverse and uncoordinated arrangements that had developed were recognized as a problem. When NATO asked its civilian chief linguist to review the provision of language support in NATO offices, he found that the patchwork of improvised services failed to meet almost every criterion of quality management and was not fit for purpose. He proposed that the scattered arrangements should be brought together in a single unified service centred in Sarajevo. This resulted in the establishment of an effective Linguistic Services Branch, which provided a model of good practice for the military language support services run by contributing countries, and for other international organizations in the region. Although these changes could possibly have been introduced earlier, they could not have been envisaged in the very volatile conditions of the early part of the operation. It is clear that it would have been beneficial if more support had been provided to improve the quality of the distributed arrangements, but in order to ensure this is available in future, senior officers would need to give sufficient priority to language issues to spark remedial action at an earlier stage in operations.

Civilian language intermediaries

The category of civilian language intermediaries in the context of a military deployment includes two distinct groups, which are also internally diverse: one is the category of civilian nationals of the troop-contributing states who are recruited at home by military contractors, and the other is the category of 'locally-employed' civilians who are recruited at the site of intervention, by contractors or the armed forces themselves. The practice of providing language support through foreign civilian contractors had not reached the height in Bosnia-Herzegovina that it would reach during the coalition operations in Iraq and Afghanistan. The lessons identified by this study relate primarily to the recruitment and management of locally employed civilians, who are likely to stay in interpreting posts for longer and who are embedded in local society in a way that visiting foreign civilian contractors are not.

The trajectories of the longest-serving civilian interpreters and translators in Bosnia-Herzegovina show that, with appropriate testing, training and feedback, it is possible to develop untrained field interpreters into linguists capable of operating at a high professional level, including simultaneous interpretation. Not every person will have the aptitude or desire to take this path, but the successes recorded at the Linguistic Services Branch of HQ SFOR demonstrate rewards to the employing organization and to the linguists themselves. The LSB model of language service management offered a higher level of job security and skill reproduction security than other models observed during the peace operations in the 1990s, and the level of professional development that interpreters in this model could reach would also improve personal prospects for international mobility, which has become a widespread goal in post-war Bosnia-Herzegovina. Interpreting and translation should be recognized not as an unskilled stopgap but as highly skilled work. The attitude that further training is not necessary for interpreters who have passed entry tests is not conducive to professional development. Military organizations that are able to provide training for civilians in other occupations such as financial administration should also be capable of providing it for civilian language intermediaries.

A conflict zone field guide for translators/interpreters (T/Is) and users of their services produced in 2012 by the International Federation of Translators (FIT-IFT), the International Association of Conference Interpreters (AIIC) and The Red T recommends a number of rights and responsibilities for both parties that are borne out by the experiences contained in this study. Civilians are made aware that they should 'have a right to protection both during and after the assignment', should receive security and emergency training before deployment, and should have 'medical and psychological assistance' made available to them if necessary. The guide also states that they 'have a right to pay and other contractual provisions that reflect the hazardous conditions', with reasonable working hours and periodic breaks that will improve concentration and therefore quality. Civilian linguists should moreover 'have the right to refuse a task that compromises your professional or personal standards and ethics and/or unduly endangers your safety' (FIT-IFT, AIIC and Red T 2012: 1). The users of civilian linguists are reminded that 'T/Is may be at risk by working for you. Whether or not you are contractually responsible, protect them and, if necessary, their family both during the assignment and afterward' (FIT-IFT, AIIC and Red T 2012: 2). These recommendations echo issues raised in this study. More detailed recommendations can be made on the basis of former interpreters' narratives. Civilians who have been injured as a result of their work for the military should receive the same treatment as soldiers themselves, and the risks to civilians of vehicle accidents should be taken seriously, meaning that leaders down to section level must emphasize the need for driving with due care and attention. It is important also to ensure that explicit and implicit promises of protection and security are met. This obligation will vary with the degree of risk to civilian language intermediaries, which in recent coalition operations has greatly exceeded the risk level of the later operations in Bosnia-Herzegovina.

Civilian language intermediaries also have responsibilities. Writing as professional linguists, the authors of the FIT-IFT/AIIC/Red T field guide recommend that language intermediaries, '[r]egardless of who engages you, serve all parties equally, without expressing your opinions or sympathies' (FIT-IFT, AIIC and Red T 2012: 1). This diverges from the prevailing military concept in which civilian language intermediaries are seen as working for the force. Reconceptualizing their role around a greater degree of independence could improve the safety of locally recruited linguists if local audiences also accept this reconceptualization. The more that translation and interpreting are perceived as highly skilled professions, the more successful such a reconceptualization is likely to be. The suggestion by the chair of the Red T organization that linguists in conflict zones should be able to display a symbol akin to those displayed by medics and journalists (Clark 2012) represents one of many means to raise awareness of the specialized and professional role of linguists in conflict zones. Some interviewees in this study made other recommendations based on their own experience, for instance, that forces' publicity campaigns and psychological operations should make clear to the local public that language intermediaries are not to blame for what is said by representatives of the force.

In return for this recognition, it is essential for language intermediaries to maintain high standards of accuracy and confidentiality (FIT-IFT, AIIC and Red T 2012). This becomes all the more important in light of the power that the intermediaries hold in how the aims of a peace operation are presented to the local population at sites of intervention. The declared aims and objectives of peace operations produce expectations and thus have a performative dimension (Higate and Henry 2009: 103). They constitute the benchmark against which troops, contingents and the operation itself will be judged. The responsibility for translating these aims and objectives into a given interaction falls to the member of the military who is speaking or writing, but the responsibility for giving this meaning in the eyes and ears of local audiences is that of the language intermediary. Frequently this person is not a member of the military. The final step of this production of meaning is therefore outside the military's total control and, whenever a language encounter requires translation or interpreting, rests ultimately within the agency of the linguist.

Research using narrative interviews

The broad discipline of cultural history seeks to understand events through the symbols and interpretations that surround them (Burke 2004). It provides some tools that are most effective in achieving understanding when they are used at some distance in time or space from the here and now. Things done in the heat of battle need to be examined in the cold light of day, and a dispassionate approach may cast valuable sidelights which can illuminate the present. However, cultural history also needs to engage with matters that are close in time and meaning if the more evanescent areas of symbolization and interpretation are to be captured. Things done in heat may appear merely puzzling to the dispassionate gaze, and the voice of passion may both bring alive the past and resonate more deeply with the concerns of the present. The practice of oral history is particularly well suited to manage the difficult interfaces between present and past, memory and history, witness and analysis.

Oral history invites the participants in an interview to reproduce – literally to produce anew – narratives and memories of everyday experiences and extraordinary circumstances that can offer historians and linguists unique insights as long as they also recognize its limitations. In the cultural history of war developed in Penny Summerfield's history of women workers during the Second World War (Summerfield 1998), or Alistair Thomson's accounts of Anzac veterans (Thomson 1994), the testimony of lived experience, delivered through language, is necessarily embedded in the cultural contexts in which protagonists have been implicated during and after the events they remember. As Summerfield (1998: 11) points out, 'experience cannot exist outside discourse, agency cannot exist independently of language'. The observation reminds one that even the most routine translating or interpreting encounter is alive with conscious and unconscious choices whether or not to amplify, silence or explain language and experience. It must equally be borne in mind when dealing with oral research data, not least since responding to an interview involves multiple acts of translation, whether cultural (military-to-civilian) or linguistic (native-language-to-English), on the interviewee's part.

Among the advantages of oral history, for one of its early champions, Paul Thompson, is how it enables researchers to pinpoint exactly the topics they are looking for. Relevant autobiographies, he writes, may be few and far between, and even then may well overlook the area of one's own research. This is confirmed in many memoirs of officers who served in Bosnia. They relate encounters with people, and only a throwaway comment at the end of the anecdote reveals that an interpreter had been present all the time. Oral history, by contrast, empowers researchers to 'think…as if they themselves were publishers: imagine what evidence is needed, seek it out and capture it' (Thompson 2000: 6). To an extent, the observation rang true for our research: how else could we find out about scarcely documented topics such as the evolution of management structures for local linguists, or translation practices in military liaison offices, if not by asking the people who took part in them?

However, oral history is not solely a way of collecting data that would be inaccessible by other means – the reason why the technique has appealed to social historians since the 1970s – but is also an exploration of how memory is subject to change. The forms of Alistair Thomson's Anzac interviews, collected more than 60 years after the speakers fought in the Great War, were the result of decades of social and personal transformation in the veterans' lives:

> How we make sense of experience, and what memories we choose to recall and relate (and thus remember), changes over time.... our remembering changes in relation to shifts in the particular publics in which we live, and as the general public field of representations alters. (Thomson 1994: 9)

Although the conflict in Bosnia-Herzegovina is fresher in memory – 10 to 20 years ago, with some narratives by currently employed interpreters running up until the present day – one or two decades are more than enough time for fields to begin to shift. Global contexts, such as the increased awareness of Islamic fundamentalism after 9/11 and the course of coalition military operations in Iraq and Afghanistan, alter perceptions of the significance of an event, as do narrower collective contexts (such as the outcome of Bosnian politics 15 years after Dayton) and the circumstances of an individual's own life: parenthood, retirement, grief, marriage, redundancy, emigration.

Every interview narrative draws on 'pre-existing story-lines and ways of telling stories' (Passerini 1987: 8), which may come from widespread public discourses, popular culture, local oral cultures to which the narrator belongs, the 'particular publics' (Thomson 1994: 9) to which the narrator contributes and answers, and/or the narrator's earlier retellings of the same events. At the same time, the narrator's agency in selecting resources from this repertoire and the interviewer's changing concerns during the life cycle of a project produce a contingent encounter that would not take the same shape at a different time or even in a different space (compare the varying levels of privacy and intimacy that might weigh on an interview in a home, a workplace, a university interview room or a neighbourhood café), let alone between the same narrator and a different interviewer. The researcher's direct participation in producing evidence through questioning may open spaces that have not yet been filled by widespread popular memories. Public memories of any conflict follow certain tropes and themes, leaving other aspects – usually including the crucial role of language, translation and interpreting – much less visible. The less dangerous, more predictable yet still unsettling state of military operations and civilian life in a post-conflict society is not so often memorialized at all.

Conducting interviews over 15 months gave our understanding of the project itself an iterative nature as successive narratives extended our preliminary expectations of the project's scope. The expansive format of the interview, its open questions and the decision not to interrupt an interviewee opened up a space for the interviewer to defer to her participants, although a repertoire of silent facial expressions from the interviewer did permit some conversational back-channelling. The participants' narratives enabled us to come to terms with the environments in which the project's 'language encounters' were embedded: their housing, their equipment, their leisure time and the shelters they used. They drew us into a strong sense of empathy and provided an insight into the simultaneously exciting and sobering narratives of violence and force. For example, we were struck when an Army officer responsible for language support described this side of war to the project team as 'non-kinetic': a memorable term for the researchers, yet a routine component of military discourse.

Our dispositions as interviewers were greatly influenced by conversations with the sound archive staff of the Imperial War Museum (IWM), the third partner in the Languages at War project. Since the project was designed to offer interview participants the opportunity to contribute their interviews to the IWM sound archive if they so wished, we had taken care to obtain the archivists' advice on questioning and recording. We sceptically asked ourselves in the first months of the research how many participants would really want their full interviews made public. We were surprised then to find out that almost all of them did. 'Daddy's going to be famous,' one participant told the interviewer that he had joked to his son as he left the house that morning. 'The Imperial War Museum is interested in his story.' Without the candidness, generosity and hospitality of our participants, this book would never have come about.

Equally surprising and invigorating was the extent to which our participants were willing to share not only their experiences but also their reflections on how they fitted into a larger picture. In many cases, this was a pondered assessment of events. It was also one of the mechanisms through which they were able to achieve a necessary distance from the emotional heat of those events. Their reflections provided new ways of thinking about the issues which often sat uncomfortably with the presuppositions of the research project. In particular, they challenged us to rethink the questions with which we had begun, and led us to develop new and better questions, which could have implications for other areas of research.

The decision to publish our findings in book form came easily as we reviewed the interview material. But decisions about its content and its structure were more difficult, as we sought to incorporate both an analytical treatment of the 'research data' and the engaging multiplicity of voices that had inspired us to write the book in the first place. The competing bottom-up and top-down perspectives have been reconciled by organizing the book into a series of thematic studies which combine the analysis of particular issues with extensive quotations from our informants, which often convey the emotion and texture of their voice. It also reflects our developing understanding of the ways in which 'policies' or patterns of behaviour are embodied in individuals and groups, and expressed in their interactions. Policy analysis and oral history may be two different genres with their own conventions, but we hope that this book demonstrates how both approaches can productively combine.

Language policy

The area of language policy studies, within the broad discipline of applied linguistics, provided tools for understanding the patterns and structures behind the language practices. It offered an important perspective from which to understand the language issues in the Bosnian operation. In particular, it prompted an investigation of the overall patterns of organization in the provision of language support services and an inquiry into the institutional frameworks within which it was developed. Overwhelmingly, the language policy perspective is connected with the efforts of states, political parties and lobby groups to shape the language practices of a country in response to social changes or political objectives (Cooper 1990; Schiffman 1998). Applying this approach to institutions has proved difficult. Only quite recently has attention begun to shift to the 'micropolitics' of language policy within particular institutions (Alderson 2009).

On the one hand, the practice of institutions is in part determined by the broader political and social environment, but on the other hand, each institution has its own purposes and procedures which may require a particular stance on language issues. Quite often, the stance is not expressed in explicit policies, even in a large institution. As an international institution, NATO did have an official policy on languages, which was to recognize two operational languages, English and French. However, its management of language use and language capability was not the subject of any more detailed policy. The implications of NATO's operational language policy are explored in our examination of peace operations in a multilingual world, where it is discovered that English became the pragmatic choice as the language of military communication for many purposes, but that the forces involved used a plurality of eclectic language strategies, including many varieties of English, in their day-to-day operations. And both French and Russian remained *linguas francas* among several contingents. This chimes well with recent research on English as a *lingua franca* and suggests that researchers in that area could profitably turn more attention to the military context.

NATO had various forms of collaboration which were not recognized as policy, but which contributed to shaping practice. This mainly concerned work to develop practice in language training and testing formalized in the STANAG 6001 table levels of proficiency. The impact of the STANAG levels was felt particularly in the provision of language training for military personnel, which was often, but not always, calibrated to produce outcomes of training courses. These issues are examined in the chapter on serving in a foreign field, particularly in the context of short courses of language awareness, lasting around a fortnight, and longer courses of around three months, designed to produce 'colloquial' speakers. Though not seen as policy, these structures were influential and gave rise to patterns of practice. In the period since the 1990s, they have continued to develop and provide an important focus for the work of decision-makers in the area of military language training. These arrangements behaved in many respects as policy by providing guidelines for future practice, and it would be useful for future research to examine the ways in which these and other assessment structures shape practice and how suited they are for the purposes to which they are put.

A terminological difficulty in applying the perspectives of language policy is that 'policy' is viewed by the military as a civilian activity, which is primarily the responsibility of governments. The military equivalent in NATO is the concept of 'doctrine', which sets out high-level principles and general guidance. At the time of the Bosnian intervention, NATO did not have a doctrine in the area of language, but has subsequently produced a Doctrine Note on the significance of culture to the military, which includes a brief discussion of the relationship between language and culture, and the role of language in communication (Development Concepts and Doctrine Centre 2009). At the time of writing, a more extensive note on language was being prepared. It would be useful for researchers in language policy to engage more fully with these processes of shaping practice, which are equivalent to policy formation.

The forces deployed in Bosnia-Herzegovina were governed by the policies of their own governments and military structures, but largely adopted the NATO approach to doctrine. They all had their own handbooks and regulations which guided practice on such matters as how language support should be organized. There were marked differences across the forces, and in many cases commanders of units were given delegated authority to make arrangements as they saw fit. This corresponds closely to Michael Hill's concept of 'discretion', used to account for the importance of delegated decision making (Hill 2009: 225). A high level of discretion was clearly necessary for commanders in the volatile conditions of the early part of the operation, which provides confirmation that higher-level policies, doctrines or guidelines are typically articulated in distinctive ways on the ground. The patterns of practice that emerged were produced by a combination of frameworks and decisions at different levels. This is a productive approach which could usefully be more widely noticed by researchers and practitioners.

In a similar way, the participants interviewed were more comfortable with describing their practice than analysing the reasons behind it. They rarely raised policy as an issue, except when prompted by an explicit question. In most cases the closest thing to policy that they described was the culture of a specific military unit or the approach adopted by a specific superior officer. Those of our informants who were most closely concerned with decision making at national or international level were similarly inclined to view their own activities as enabling rather than prescriptive. They presented their role as largely about solving problems which had arisen, such as setting up language learning programmes or improving language support services. From this perspective, policy appears largely as a formalization of practices and intentions, and for this reason we consider that a conceptual shift is required, which focuses on institutional language practices. Explicit policies, doctrines or guidelines may be a component in shaping practice, but may be less important than systems, customs or other established patterns in giving structure to practices.

As the patterns of language practice emerged, it became clear that issues encountered by our informants were rarely confined to language questions. Certainly, there were instances where the wrong word caused a problem or the right choice of words smoothed over difficulties. But in most cases the issues were as much social and cultural as linguistic. Military and civilians alike struggled with complex issues of identity and relationship. The linguistic capacities they brought were always bound up with their cultural experience and intercultural sensitivity.

To a large extent, therefore, the information we have gathered enables us to identify what the operational issues were in relation to language. It has also obliged us to regard language issues as intricately connected with a much wider range of social, cultural and military issues, and confirms the importance that the main theorists of language policy assign to wider social contexts.

The question of how the forces involved in peace operations modified their policies in the light of experience thus needs to be reframed in terms of how their experience shaped the patterns of practice. This approach sits well with the established practice of military commanders, who routinely draw up a formal account of lessons learned at the end of their deployment. The intention is that officers of the unit which replaces them will read the document and learn from their experience. The same principle applies at both the higher and lower levels of command. At the higher levels, decision makers and trainers may introduce new systems to overcome difficulties encountered in theatre. And at the lower level, individuals may learn from their own experience and that of others to avoid repeating mistakes and to operate more effectively. In principle, this reframing of policy changes as lessons learned in shaping practice could usefully be applied to areas currently considered under the heading of institutional language policy.

There are limitations to the process of lesson learning, however. The value of the lesson depends heavily on the willingness and ability of the learner to learn from the 'lessons identified' and on situations arising in which the lesson is relevant. In the case of Bosnia-Herzegovina, lesson learning was also limited by the regular rotation of military units, at intervals varying from three to 12 months. This resulted in regular transitions in which important information could be lost in the hiatus between two military units. For this reason, we discovered that some of the most sustained lesson learning in the theatre of operations is found among the locally employed civilian interpreters and translators. They mainly stayed in post over a period of years and often provided valuable continuity for successive military units. Away from theatre, educators are also repositories of lessons learned, as they develop the content of their training programmes in response to feedback from operations. It is an important function of policy in other domains to provide guidance for future actions, and to enable principles to be transferred across a number of comparable activities.

The lessons identified in one situation can only provide guidance for the future if they are passed on to others who can learn from them. This function can take many forms, including explicit policies, but reformulating it as 'shaping future practice' has the advantage of making clear that the production of policy is not a sufficient end in itself, but is only worth pursuing if it serves to inflect the actions of people in the future. However, there are many obstacles to learning lessons, and there is a need for mechanisms to be established within institutions to secure the transfer for lessons from one context to another.

Much academic discussion of language policy has focused on civilian life, and on policies which were enunciated by government agencies and by educational institutions. This has proved helpful in relation to stable long-term social structures. However, it does not help to understand what happens in the fog of war or in the first steps towards peace and reconstruction. This is a life of short-term engagements, where split-second decisions may mean life or death, where the tides of war move in days and weeks, and where rotations of a few months provide the underlying rhythm of operations. In these circumstances, a discussion of policies is more helpfully replaced by attention to patterns of behaviour, which are embodied in individuals and in units. The patterns come from many sources, including training, individual experience and possibly from the experience of others.

Towards new paradigms

These approaches may not only help to achieve a better understanding of the issues of language and culture in conflict and in peacemaking but may also offer lessons which could be applied to the issues of language in other institutions, in commercial enterprises, in education and in the wider areas of social life. Our subject has some very specific features, which are not readily transferrable to many other situations. But at the same time it offers some patterns of organization and action that may be traced across a range of contexts. A conceptual framework that combines these two characteristics in their complexity is suggested by the work of the Italian philosopher Giorgio Agamben, who offers a notion of the 'paradigm' that may be helpful.

Developing Thomas Kuhn's well-known concept of the paradigm as a general theoretical framework for scientific enquiry, Agamben argues that the concept needs to be more directly linked to particular phenomena if it is to enable us to move beyond the natural sciences and understand the broader social and cultural realms. He therefore suggests that a paradigm should be understood as a form of knowledge based on analogy, in which one case is exemplary of a group of phenomena, while retaining its own singularity (Agamben 2009: 31). This approach suggests a reciprocal relationship between the particular case and the general principles which it exemplifies.

In the case of the military intervention in Bosnia-Herzegovina, it enables some general principles to be derived without reducing the particular uniqueness of the events. This is especially helpful in responding to the challenge of identifying more general lessons that might be drawn from the particular experience. As we have examined the accounts of a range of participants in the events of the 1990s, we have been attentive to the ways in which their particular experience may be of value in understanding wider issues. But, at the same time, the accounts we have studied give a very strong sense of the unique and special nature of the experiences recounted. While often they were carrying out tasks for which they had been well trained, our interviewees were also often required to exercise a high degree of creativity and ingenuity. This combination suggests that our subject may well be paradigmatic in the sense of a singular experience which is also exemplary.

A very general lesson may be drawn from way in which responses to language issues changed over the period of the operation. In the early stages, military responses came in the shape of a scramble. Responding rapidly to events, the forces were poorly prepared for the language needs they encountered, and responded on the ground with a process of 'bricolage', improvising language support solutions with whatever means came to hand. Given ingenuity and good will most of the solutions worked well enough and usually continued for some time, taken over by different units with minor changes as they came and went. The provisional arrangements gradually became less effective, but in the case of NATO offices they were only changed as the result of a major review, which considered the distributed arrangements as whole, and reorganized them as a coherent system.

The durability of improvised arrangements was considerable, reflecting practical ingenuity, and the transition from bricolage to system was only achieved by rational review and upheaval. On the one hand, this is a pattern that characterizes response to crisis in many contexts. But on the other hand, the military could draw the lesson that crisis-response may be a more regular feature of operations in the twenty-first century and consider how to provide more elements that could be used to assist the necessary improvisation. Conversely, the need to bring more coherence to the language services was only recognized as a result of expert review, and it might have been useful to consider the need for coherence at an earlier stage in the operation. This would have needed senior commanders to attach greater importance to effective language support and identify it as an area in need of coordination. There is evidence that NATO has subsequently paid more attention to this area (Lewis 2012), but as a result of the more large-scale operations in Iraq and Afghanistan rather than as a lesson learned from the experience in former Yugoslavia. It would be fruitful to examine the ways in which the forces involved in these later conflicts addressed the issues that confronted their predecessors in the 1990s.

It would be valuable to compare the experience of NATO with other international organizations. An obvious point of departure might be the international institutions that were involved in the interventions in Bosnia-Herzegovina, including the United Nations and its agencies (UNICEF, UNHCR), the ICTY and the Office of the High Representative. A large number of non-governmental organizations, news media, contractors and other bodies might share similar characteristics. It would be useful to compare the military context with language support services to other institutions and organizations acting within states. At the time of writing there are major debates across Europe on the provision of translating and interpreting services across the public sector (Viezzi 2012). These include language services for the courts, the police, the health service, border agencies and other institutions. There are also regular enquiries into the language policies and practices of public and private organizations, including businesses, educational institutions, local government and voluntary bodies. The insights the current study has produced might productively be tested against these examples of institutions.

An issue that is threaded through our study is the impact of international intervention on the people of Bosnia-Herzegovina. This has been viewed mainly through the life experiences of the civilian interpreters who agreed to be interviewed. However, they rarely explore the ways in which the intervention has affected their relationship with language. And more broadly, it would be valuable to examine the linguistic impact of the intervention on the social, political and cultural environment of the country.

The archive of interviews we have compiled remains a rich resource, from which we have drawn a limited cross section of extracts to inform the arguments we have developed. Other researchers with a different agenda would find much that could enrich their own researches. Our interviewees ranged broadly across their experience and there is material there to inform studies in the military and political history of the Bosnian crisis, the living and working conditions of military personnel, the culture of the international forces, and the personal and professional itinerary of civilian linguists.

As with any enquiry, we are conscious of questions that we have not been able to answer. In some cases, these are questions that lie outside the scope we set ourselves. For example, we limited the scope of interviews to a small number of countries that sent forces to participate in the operations, and did not attempt to achieve a representative sample of the 53 participating countries. We cannot answer in detail how for example the French forces or the US forces viewed their participation and how they met their language needs. We have seen their experience through the eyes of others, but it would surely be interesting to capture the views of people who served in those forces.

In other cases, the questions we have not been able to answer have arisen in the course of our enquiries. For example, we established that a substantial proportion of the most expert linguists were deployed in intelligence roles. We were not able to examine these in detail, mainly because we were not able to interview any intelligence officers who served in Bosnia-Herzegovina. We were able to interview one intelligence officer who worked in the United Kingdom and language teachers who taught intelligence officers. They provided some insights, but we are aware that the confidential nature of the work means that much of it could not as yet be put in the public domain.

A third area of unanswered questions arises from the nature of oral history. Interviewees often speculate about an event. This raises a question which can often not readily be investigated. For example, several interviewees offered speculations about the number of interpreters employed by international forces in their particular area. The estimates varied very widely, and there was no way to adjudicate between them. There was also no way of gaining a plausible estimate of the number of interpreters employed overall for most of the period. One estimate was that Tuzla Air Base alone had perhaps 200 in 1997, while other estimates had 44–54 serving the NATO headquarters offices in 2000. No documentary evidence is available to confirm any of the figures, since official records are not in the public domain. For the operation as a whole, records were not collected centrally, and some records were not kept locally, especially in the early part of the operation.

The final area of unanswered questions, and perhaps the most intriguing, is how far the military learned lessons about language support from the experience of Bosnia. Most of the advice we have received is that the experience did not significantly inform later conflicts. This is plausible for a number of reasons. First, military commentators repeatedly emphasize that each conflict is specific and that the experience of peace operations in Bosnia does not easily transfer to the occupation and nation building in Afghanistan and Iraq. Similarly, British soldiers rarely compared their experience to other conflicts, although one did say, for example, that Bosnia was quite different from Northern Ireland, where he had served, and another that it was quite different from Rwanda, where she later served. Second, the process of learning lessons is highly uncertain. The formal process involves preparing reports which are then read, or not read, by others, who may or may not choose to take account of them. It is difficult to know whether any such reports paid attention to language support issues since such reports would be classified documents, which are not open to public scrutiny. Third, lessons may not have been learned from Bosnia because there was no obvious institutional mechanism to carry forward any learning points. NATO's potential mechanism was the Bureau for International Language Cooperation, but its remit was language training and testing, and it had no specific responsibility for language support more broadly. The NATO headquarters at SHAPE might also be thought of as a possible mechanism, but when it was involved in 2000, it saw its role as a kind of 'management consultant' and had no direct responsibility for the continuing scrutiny or management of services.

At the level of individual countries, the process of lesson learning was very varied, and our information in this area is confined to the British forces, which had no specific mechanism until the establishment of the Defence Operational Language Support Unit in 2007. Even then, the unit's main focus is to generate high-level language capability within the forces rather than to address the management of language support on the ground (Lewis 2012).

Some of the experience of the operation was fed back into the training programmes, as we have described. It is possible that some of the experience of language support may have carried over into training for other missions. Yet even here, the barriers to transfer were considerable. Experience incorporated in one language programme might well transfer to another programme in the same language, but it is less likely that it would transfer to another language. In most cases the tutors would be civilians, often native speakers of the language taught, and therefore engaged only in teaching one language, or two cognate languages, such as Russian and Serbian. A small number of military linguists might be in a position to link between languages, but the issue of language support in the field would not be a particular concern, since their role was to teach languages. Civilian language services, by contrast, would appear as an alternative, if not as competition, to the military specialist.

It is clear that many lessons were 'identified' in the course of the operations in Bosnia-Herzegovina, and that some of them were even 'learned'. This study has sought to identify a wide array of lessons that may be added in retrospect, with the benefit of the research tools of oral history and language policy analysis. One of the most significant insights to emerge in this has been the gap between identifying and learning lessons. A.E. Housman is frequently quoted as commenting:

> A moment's thought would have shown him. But a moment is a long time, and thought is a painful process. (Flew 1975: 5)

If learning from experience is difficult for individuals, the difficulties are much greater for institutions. The process of retrieving the lessons of the past may be a long one, typically fraught with obstacles. And the process of applying them to present circumstances is inherently painful. In this respect, the military are not different in kind from many other major institutions, and they have at least recognized that that the process of learning from the past is a challenge constantly renewed. We cannot expect to make the process of learning and implementation any less painful, but we hope that the lessons this study has identified will at least help to make the moment of retrieval a little less long.

Appendix
Note on the Language Variants in Bosnia-Herzegovina

The urgency of language planning debates in Bosnia-Herzegovina since the Dayton Agreement stems from interlinked anxieties that derive from the logic of destroying cultural ambiguity for the sake of making ethnopolitically based claims to territory and resources. The movement among Bosniaks to define and standardize a 'Bosnian' language has its roots in the fear that the Bosniak ethnic group could be at risk of assimilation by Croats and/or Serbs if its apparent lack of a national language put it on an unequal footing. The fear that the country would be partitioned between Croatia and Serbia – a war aim of Milošević and Tuđman between 1991 and 1995 – has left its legacy in an imperative to place Bosnia-Herzegovina ethnoculturally, as well as politically, on equal sovereign terms with both neighbouring states and thereby to protect the country from encroachment. Simultaneously, Bosnian Serb and Bosnian Croat elites – not to mention their counterparts in the neighbouring kin-states – fear that the propagation of a standard Bosnian language might provide a rationale for transforming their groups into minorities rather than constituent peoples of the post-Dayton state under some future revision of the constitution.

Within the complex of language variants formerly known as 'Serbo-Croatian', or in some cases Croato-Serbian, literary standards have been grounded in the most widely spoken dialect, štokavian. Two sets of language reformers in the nineteenth century, Vuk Karadžić in Serbia and the Illyrian movement in the Habsburg South Slav lands, settled on štokavian because it was spoken in Serbia, Montenegro, Bosnia-Herzegovina and much of Croatia. The čakavian and kajkavian dialects (all three dialects are named after their word for 'what') were spoken on the Dalmatian coast and in northwestern Croatia respectively. Within štokavian, four types of difference constitute the variants:[1]

- the transformation of the old Slavic vowel *jat* into the vowels 'e' (eastern variant) or 'ije' (western variant); hence the variants' alternative names ekavian (*ekavica*) and ijekavian (*ijekavica*)[2]
- differences in lexical items: the eastern variant word for 'bread' is *hleb* whereas the western variant has *kruh*
- whether or not the infinitive in modal verbs is replaced with *da* + present tense (characteristic of the eastern variant)
- whether or not Cyrillic script is used (since the break-up of Yugoslavia, a strong symbolic association has been formed between Cyrillic script and Serb identity)

The differences between these variants represent a continuum of gradations rather than an absolute binary. In ijekavian-speaking parts of Bosnia-Herzegovina, for instance, one finds *hljeb* for bread, that is, the eastern word *hleb* modified by the western transformation of *jat*. Moreover, linguistic features' symbolic connotations are also subject to change.

The symbolic association between Cyrillic script and Serb identity is now widely established throughout the Yugoslav successor states, yet the use of Cyrillic in Bosnia-Herzegovina during federal Yugoslavia did not necessarily carry an ethnonational subtext. The Bosnian newspaper *Oslobođenje*, which was to become the symbol of defiant journalism in besieged Sarajevo, had alternated between Latin and Cyrillic script in Titoist times as an implicit daily signal of the language's two centres and Yugoslavia's own self-image between east and west (Pupavac 2006: 122).

An overview of language planning in Yugoslavia and Bosnia-Herzegovina reveals a consistent history of language being planned in such a way as to facilitate political claims – whether that be a claim to as wide a community as possible in the case of pre-1918 Yugoslavism, or the claims to fragment a community that have been made from the late 1980s (if not the late 1960s) onwards. Vuk Karadžić and the Illyrianist Ljudevit Gaj had developed their language reforms separately, with Gaj choosing štokavian because it was the variant spoken by most Croats and Karadžić describing all štokavian speakers as Serbs. As part of the project to create a South Slav union, the two movements' representatives agreed in Vienna in 1850 to treat the tongue as one language with two scripts, Latin and Cyrillic. The name of the language nonetheless caused arguments between Yugoslavists and Croat particularists in the South Slav parts of Austria–Hungary during the nineteenth century; once Austria–Hungary began to administer Bosnia-Herzegovina in 1878, its longest-serving governor Benjamin von Kállay in fact attempted to promote a 'Bosnian language' himself as part of a territorially based identity (*bošnjaštvo*) that would counterbalance Serb and Croat nationalist movements (Okey 2004). The Kingdom of the Serbs, Croats and Slovenes, as the first Yugoslavia was officially known, made a short-lived attempt to conceive of the whole country as having one 'Serbian–Croatian–Slovenian' language, but the language would lack an official name until 1954 when the linguists of socialist Yugoslavia made the Novi Sad Agreement. This policy adopted both scripts and two names, Serbo-Croatian and Croato-Serbian.

The attempt to devise a 'unified (*jedinstven*) language' and balance Serb and Croat linguistic claims, in line with the Titoist strategy of preventing either group or republic from becoming more influential and threatening the delicate balance of the federation, was undermined by a declaration of a separate Croatian language in 1967, an early step in the mass movement that became known as the 'Croatian Spring'. The federal government's clampdown on the Croatian Spring in December 1971 led to the proscription of the Croatian cultural institution, Matica Hrvatska, which had supported the linguistic declaration.[3] A new Yugoslav language policy introduced in the hyper-devolved 1974 constitution allowed each republic to determine one or more 'standard linguistic expression' (*standardnojezički izraz*) as its official language(s). The republic of Bosnia-Herzegovina's choice of ijekavian Serbo-Croatian/Croato-Serbian and a 'Bosno-Herzegovinan standard linguistic expression' was originally intended to strengthen the 'unified language' in the country by promoting linguistic identification with a territory rather than with ethnic groups. Retrospectively, it became available to be interpreted as the first introduction of a separate Bosnian standard into Yugoslavia's language politics.

The Croat nationalist movement that came to power in the republic of Croatia's first multiparty elections in 1990 and proceeded to turn that republic into a sovereign state followed the Croatian Spring discourse of doubting there had ever been a 'unified language' and dismissing it as a political imposition. The work of the linguist Dalibor Brozović, whose *Deset teza o hrvatskome jeziku* (*Ten Theses on the Croatian Language*) had been among the most polemical texts of the Croatian Spring, could now be implemented as state language policy (Greenberg 2005). Brozović's argument that Croatian had developed in isolation from Serbian and followed Italian, German and Czech models justified a policy of linguistic pluralism (to the extent of introducing neologisms and medievalisms to replace Serb lexis) that ran in parallel with official attempts to separate Croatia from Yugoslavia, Serbness and socialism in all areas of public life. The disintegration of Serbo-Croatian thus began in newly sovereign Croatia and attempted to force both insiders and outsiders to reinterpret the linguistic past. Croatian state language policy also had a direct impact on language use in Bosnia-Herzegovina. Areas of Bosnia-Herzegovina under HVO control were administered as if they were extensions of the state in Croatia, and Croat-run schools continued to use Croatian educational resources (including language textbooks) after the war. Post-war Croat elites used the Dayton discourse of minority rights to oppose educational integration on the grounds that Croat culture could only be maintained by transmitting the Croatian language to new generations through school (Hromadžić 2008: 556). In Republika Srpska, meanwhile, language policy between September 1993 and February 1998 took on the thankless and extremely unpopular task of introducing ekavian (as spoken in Serbia) to ijekavian-speaking regions while accelerating the uptake of Cyrillic. Cyrillic was spread more successfully than Ekavian, though certain obstacles remained: the RS's own public institutions, for instance, often had to communicate in Latin script because their typewriters did not have Cyrillic keyboards (Pupavac 2006: 124).

For the Bosniak language planners, the question of whether a Bosnian standard ought to balance eastern/Serbian and western/Croatian variants permitting a maximum of options or whether it should accentuate its difference from both the Serbian and Croatian standards nonetheless remained unresolved. A symposium of linguists in Bihać in 1998, which has since been seen as the '"first congress" for a Bosnian standard language' (Ford 2002: 350), dramatized the divergent strands in the corpus planning of Bosnian. While Dževad Jahić and Senahid Halilović emphasized the amount of Turkisms and the prevalent phoneme /x/ (which would produce the Bosnian word *kahva* for 'coffee' rather than Serbian *kafa* or Croatian *kava*) as evidence of a distinctive Bosnian linguistic identity, Josip Baotić argued for a Bosnian standard that would 'deepen the awareness of linguistic unity' among the peoples of Bosnia-Herzegovina and cater for all the country's ethnic groups rather than acting to make communication more difficult.

Notes

Introduction

1. According to Bartelby.com, the remarks were made at a White House luncheon on 26 June 1954. The exact words are not known, but were quoted as 'It is "better to jaw-jaw than to war-war,"' in the sub-heading on the front page of *The New York Times,* 27 June 1954. http://www.bartleby.com/73/1914.html (accessed 1 June 2012)
2. Language is frequently discussed as a component of conflict resolution, but normally in terms of communication in a common language, usually English. The limitations of this approach have been pointed out by Ray Cohen (2001), who compared conflict resolution in three different languages.
3. The broader conclusions, drawing on comparisons with other conflicts, are presented in Footitt and Kelly (ed.) 2012b.
4. The following account draws on numerous sources. Succinct accounts of the 1992–5 period are provided by Lovrenović (2001), Malcolm (2002), Kalyvas and Sambanis (2005) and Hoare (2007). The following period is discussed in detail by Bose (2002).
5. Two autonomous provinces of Serbia, Vojvodina and Kosovo, also contributed a member to the presidency.
6. The historian Marko Attila Hoare argues that SDA's public conciliatory stance and its status as a Bosniak nationalist party with Islamicist undertones left it unable to prepare the Bosnian population for war. As a result, '[t]he success or failure of resistance to Serbian aggression would depend wholly on the competence of the PL [Patriotic League], SDA or other bodies at the local level' (Hoare 2004: 44) – partially accounting, if so, for the war's 'patchwork' character.
7. The reference is to the singer and songwriter who during the 1990s changed his name to 'the Artist Formerly Known as Prince'.
8. Since Stankovic (2000) has chosen in his writing to present his name without diacritical marks, the authors have followed this preference.
9. The website of *Soldier* is available at http://www.soldiermagazine.co.uk/ (accessed 2 October 2010). It carries a small number of extracts from the Bosnian conflict in its 'Flashback' section.
10. The website of *SFOR Informer* for 1996–2005 is archived at http://www.nato.int/SFOR/ (accessed 2 October 2010).
11. The oral historian Alistair Thomson uses the idea of 'composure' to describe his concept of the memory-making process: 'We compose our memories to make sense of our past and present lives. ... In one sense we compose or construct memories using the public languages and meanings of our culture. In another sense we compose memories that help us to feel relatively comfortable with our lives and identities, that give us a feeling of composure' (Thomson 1994: 8).

1 Serving in a Foreign Field

1. Interview, 24 July 2009.
2. Interview, 12 June 2009.
3. Interview, 12 June 2009.
4. Interview, 12 June 2009.
5. Interview, 18 May 2009.
6. Interview, 17 September 2009.
7. Interview, 18 May 2009.
8. Interview, 7 January 2010.
9. Interview, 7 January 2010.
10. Interview, 6 May 2009.
11. Interview, 18 May 2009.
12. The figure is taken from the UN website, which gives the numbers of troops deployed by different countries: http://www.un.org/en/peacekeeping/missions/past/unprof_b.htm (accessed 23 June 2012). It should be regarded as an approximate figure only.
13. The process of establishing training for the British Army is discussed in Kelly (2012).
14. Interview, 2 March 2009.
15. See http://www.dliflc.edu/index.html (accessed 7 May 2012).
16. See http://www.defense.gouv.fr/portail-defense/actualites/cfiar-le-centre-interarmees-qui-apprend-a-renseigner (accessed 7 May 2012).
17. See http://forsvaret.dk/fak/eng/Pages/default.aspx (accessed 7 May 2012).
18. Interview, 17 September 2009.
19. See http://www.bilc.forces.gc.ca/conf/index-eng.asp (accessed 7 May 2012).
20. See the circular on 'Certificats militaires de langue', issued in 2011 by the Association Nationale des Officiers de Liaison et des Interprètes de Réserve (ANOLIR): http://spip.anolir.org/IMG/pdf/Certificats_Militaires_de_Langue.pdf (accessed 7 May 2012).
21. Interview, 2 March 2009.
22. Interview, 2 March 2009.
23. Interview, 17 April 2009.
24. Interview, 24 July 2009.
25. Interview, 24 July 2009.
26. Interview, 17 April 2009.
27. Interview 17 April 2009.
28. Interview, 5 May 2009.
29. Interview, 12 June 2009.
30. Interview, 17 April 2009.
31. Interview, 17 April 2009.
32. Interview, 17 April 2009.
33. Interview, 24 July 2009.
34. Interview, 7 January 2010.
35. Interview, 27 July 2009.
36. Interview, 17 April 2009.

2 The Multiple Roles of Military Interpreters

1. This is clarified on the websites of the two directorates: http://ec.europa.eu/dgs/scic/index_en.htm and http://ec.europa.eu/dgs/translation/index_en.htm (accessed 23 June 2012).
2. Interview, 26 February 2009.
3. Interview, 17 September 2009.
4. Interview, 4 May 2009.
5. Interview, 17 September 2009.
6. Interview, 26 February 2009.
7. Interview, 17 April 2009.
8. Interview, 26 February 2009.
9. Interview, 5 June 2009.
10. Interview, 17 September 2009.
11. Interview, 26 February 2009.
12. Interview, 2 March 2009.
13. Interview, 2 March 2009.
14. Interview, 2 March 2009.
15. Interview, 2 March 2009.
16. Interview, 26 February 2009.
17. Interview, 2 March 2012.
18. Interview, 26 February 2009.
19. Interview, 26 February 2009.
20. Interview, 5 June 2009.
21. Interview, 5 June 2009.
22. Interview, 17 April 2009.
23. Interview, 17 September 2009.
24. Interview, 26 February 2009.
25. Interview, 26 February 2009.
26. Interview, 26 February 2009.
27. Interview, 17 September 2009.

3 Language Support on the Ground under UNPROFOR

1. http://daccess-ods.un.org/access.nsf/Get?Open&DS=S/RES/770%20(1992)&Lang=E&Area=UNDOC [accessed 11 November 2009].
2. Interview, 17 September 2009.
3. Interview, 17 September 2009.
4. The military's ideas about what tasks did and did not require a person with military training and/or one of their own citizens are discussed further in Chapter 6.
5. Interview, 17 September 2009.
6. Interview, 17 September 2009.
7. Interview, 17 September 2009.
8. Interview, 24 July 2009.
9. Interview, 24 July 2009.
10. Interview, 26 February 2009.

11. Interview, 26 February 2009.
12. Interview, 26 February 2009.
13. Even a blond ethnic Dane who had learned the language by working with Bosnian refugees in his home town remembered that locals had often thought he was Slovenian (and therefore likely to speak 'Serbo-Croat') 'because there are more Slovenians with blond hair, and my physiognomy is maybe closer to Slovenian than it is to Bosnian... and then, because my name is Martin, that could also be ...'. Interview, 4 May 2009.
14. Interview, 24 July 2009.
15. Interview, 24 July 2009.
16. Interview, 24 July 2009.
17. Interview, 17 September 2009.
18. Interview, 29 October 2009. A plate of cake was in front of the interviewer and the speaker at the time.
19. Interview, 27 October 2009.
20. Interview, 26 February 2009.
21. Interview, 18 May 2009.
22. Interview, 18 May 2009.
23. Interview, 24 July 2009.
24. Interview, 26 February 2009.
25. See, for instance, Summerfield and Crockett 1992: 437–8.
26. Interview, 17 May 2010.
27. Interview, 18 May 2009.
28. Interview, 17 September 2009.

4 Improving Language Support

1. Interview, 12 June 2009.
2. Interview, 12 June 2009.
3. Interview, 12 June 2009.
4. Interview, 19 May 2010.
5. Interview, 17 May 2010.
6. Details of troop numbers and other organizational matters are provided on the NATO website documenting the SFOR operation, http://www.nato.int/sfor/docu/d981116a.htm (accessed 25 May 2012).
7. Interview, 16 May 2010.
8. Interview, 26 October 2009.
9. Interview, 16 May 2010.
10. Interview, 16 May 2010.
11. Interview, 26 June 2009.
12. Interview, 12 June 2009.
13. Interview, 12 June 2009.
14. Interview, 26 June 2009.
15. Interview, 12 June 2009.
16. Interview, 12 June 2009.
17. Interview, 17 May 2010.
18. Interview, 16 May 2010.
19. Interview, 14 May 2010.
20. Interview, 4 May 2010.

21. Interview, 12 May 2010.
22. Interview, 17 May 2010.
23. Interview, 31 March 2009.
24. The STANAG levels of language capability are explained in Chapter 1.
25. Interview, 31 March 2009.
26. Interview, 31 March 2009.
27. Interview, 31 March 2009.
28. Interview, 31 March 2009.
29. Interview, 31 March 2009.
30. Interview, 26 October 2009
31. Interview, 25 February 2009.
32. Interview, 25 February 2009.
33. Interview, 26 October 2009.
34. Interview, 25 February 2009.

5 Foreign/Local Encounters in Interpreting

1. Interview, 3 November 2009.
2. Interview, 14 May 2010.
3. Interview, 14 May 2010.
4. Interview, 6 May 2010.
5. Interview, 6 May 2010.
6. Interview, 6 May 2010.
7. Interview, 18 November 2009.
8. Interview, 13 May 2010.
9. Interview, May 2010.
10. Interview, 6 May 2010.
11. Interview, 12 June 2009.
12. Interview, 16 May 2010.
13. Interview, 13 May 2010.
14. Interview, 18 November 2009.
15. Interview, 6 May 2009.
16. Interview, 29 October 2009.
17. Interview, 18 May 2009.
18. Interview, 13 May 2010.
19. The US troop newsletters give an example of one such class organized at one of the US bases, Camp Bedrock. Hour-long classes were held twice a week in the library tent at the initiative of one local interpreter and the camp's Morale, Welfare and Recreation coordinator and between three and nine troops attended per week (Fischer 1999). The article begins with a specimen sentence in Bosnian and English, though the sentence in Bosnian appears to have been badly garbled from Yugoslav cursive handwriting: 'Ja sam Sabina prevodibc Poducovcm Bosanki jezik Americke vojnike u Bosni. [Ja sam Sabina prevodilac. Podučavam bosanski jezik američke vojnike u Bosni]. Interpretation: I am Sabina, interpreter. I am teaching the Bosnian language to American soldiers in Bosnia' (Fischer 1999).
20. Interview, 19 May 2010.
21. Interview, 18 November 2009.

6 Nationality, Ethnicity and Trust

1. The handbook contained 10 pages of 'Culture and History' as opposed to 49 pages on the military strategy, tactics and command structures of the 'factions' and another 22 on their weapons and equipment. More than half the handbook was devoted to the insignia and equipment of IFOR members.
2. Interview, 4 May 2010.
3. A common Bosniak name.
4. Interview, 4 May 2009.
5. Interview, 26 February 2009.
6. Interview, 17 September 2009.
7. Interview, 26 October 2009.
8. Interview, 5 May 2010.
9. Interview, 5 May 2010.
10. See Bringa 1995; Sorabji 1995.
11. On these strategies merging violence and communication, see Gordy 1999; Carmichael 2002; Žarkov 2007; Baker 2010b.
12. Similar dynamics have been noted with regard to Rwanda (McNulty 1999) and to foreign actors' normalization of violence in the Democratic Republic of the Congo (Autesserre 2010).
13. Interview, May 2009.
14. Interview, 13 May 2010.
15. Interview, 12 June 2009.
16. Interview, 26 October 2009.
17. Interview, 2 March 2009.
18. Interview, June 2009.
19. Although Serbian and Bosnian were constituted as separate languages by 1996, they remained mutually intelligible and no interpreter would have been necessary for a Serb and Bosniak officer to converse.
20. Interview, May 2010.
21. The security risks of family ties could however be managed as long as they were known: thus Louise Robbins at Bugojno, aware that one interpreter was married to a Serb army commander, made tasking decisions accordingly and stayed apprised of her off-duty behaviour.
22. Interview, 24 July 2009.
23. Interview, 3 November 2009.
24. Interview, May 2010.
25. Interview, 13 May 2010.
26. Interview, 27 October 2009.
27. See Woodward and Winter 2007: 66–7; Kronsell 2012: 54.
28. Interview, 27 October 2009.
29. Interview, 12 June 2009.
30. Interview, 12 June 2009.
31. http://www.nato.int/sfor/sfor-at-work/opwestar/grom/grom3-sc.pdf (accessed 2 March 2011).
32. http://www.nato.int/sfor/sfor-at-work/opwestar/puma/puma2-en.pdf (accessed 2 March 2011). 'Razdjelnik': (lit.) 'divider'.
33. Interview, 10 May 2010.

34. Interview, 10 May 2009.
35. Interview, 5 May 2009.
36. Interview, 4 May 2009.
37. Interview, 13 May 2009.
38. Interview, 27 October 2009.

7 Peacebuilding in a Multilingual World

1. This information is taken from the UN and NATO websites on their missions at http://www.un.org/en/peacekeeping/missions/past/unprof_b.htm (accessed 17 April 2012); http://www.nato.int/ifor/ifor.htm (accessed 17 April 2012); http://www.nato.int/sfor/ (accessed 17 April 2012).
2. Interview, 12 June 2009.
3. Interview, 31 March 2009.
4. Interview, 12 June 2009.
5. See the UN website on the peacekeeping missions at http://www.un.org/en/peacekeeping/missions/past/unprof_b.htm (accessed 17 April 2012).
6. Interview, 31 March 2009.
7. Interview, 28 October 2009.
8. Interview, 28 October 2009.
9. Interview, 18 May 2009.
10. Interview, 12 June 2009.
11. Interview, 18 May 2009.
12. Interview, 26 June 2009.
13. Interview, 18 May 2009.
14. 'French General Soubirou in the Bosnia', http://www.youtube.com/watch?v=1fcWvyakBrw (accessed 17 April 2012).
15. Interview, 18 May 2009.
16. Interview, 5 May 2009.
17. Interview, 5 May 2009.
18. Interview, 4 May 2009.
19. Interview, 5 May 2009.
20. Interview, 31 March 2009.
21. The 2008 version quoted is publicly available. The date of the entry shows that the last revision of the glossary item was in 2002, at the same time as the second edition of the NATO-Russian Glossary.
22. Interview, 31 March 2009.
23. Interview, 26 October 2009.
24. Interview, 4 May 2009.
25. Interview, 26 October 2009.
26. Interview, 14 May 2010.
27. Interview, 12 June 2009.
28. Interview, 12 June 2009.
29. Interview, 27 July 2009.
30. Interview, 29 October 2009.
31. Interview, 18 November 2009.
32. Interview, 16 May 2010.
33. Interview, 14 May 2010.

Appendix: Note on the Language Variants in Bosnia-Herzegovina

1. For a more detailed explanation of the variants, see Alexander 2006: 391–8.
2. A third variant, where *jat* transforms into 'i', appears in štokavian in western Bosnia-Herzegovina and parts of Slavonia and Vojvodina and also appears in čakavian. It was not chosen as a standard in the nineteenth-century language reforms.
3. It was reconstituted in December 1990 under Croatia's post-socialist government.

References

Agamben, Giorgio. 2009. *The Signature of All Things: On Method*. New York: Zone Books.

Alderson, J. Charles. 2009. *The Politics of Language Education: Individuals and Institutions*. Clevedon: Multilingual Matters.

Alexander, Ronelle. 2006. *Bosnian, Croatian, Serbian: a Grammar with Sociolinguistic Commentary*. Madison, WI: University of Wisconsin Press.

Ammitzboell, Katarina. 2007. 'Unintended Consequences of Peace Operations on the Host Economy from a People's Perspective'. In *Unintended Consequences of Peacekeeping Operations*, edited by Chiyuki Aoi, Cedric de Coning and Ramesh Thakur, 69–89. Tokyo: United Nations University Press.

Andreas, Peter. 2007. *Blue Helmets and Black Markets: the Business of Survival in the Siege of Sarajevo*. Ithaca, NY: Cornell University Press.

Aoi, Chiyuki, Cedric de Coning and Ramesh Thakur (eds). 2007. *Unintended Consequences of Peacekeeping Operations*. Tokyo and New York: United Nations University Press.

Armakolas, Ioannis. 2011. 'The "Paradox" of Tuzla City: Explaining Non-Nationalist Local Politics during the Bosnian War'. *Europe–Asia Studies* 63 (2): 229–61.

Askew, Louise. 2010. 'Clinging to a Barbed Wire Fence: the Language Policy of the International Community in Bosnia-Herzegovina since 1995'. PhD thesis, University of Nottingham.

Autesserre, Séverine. 2010. *The Trouble with the Congo: Local Violence and the Failure of International Peacebuilding*. Oxford: Oxford University Press.

Baker, Catherine. 2010a. '"It's Not Their Job to Soldier": Distinguishing Civilian and Military in Soldiers' and Interpreters' Accounts of Peacekeeping in 1990s Bosnia-Herzegovina'. *Journal of War and Culture Studies* 3 (1): 137–50.

——. 2010b. *Sounds of the Borderland: Popular Music, War and Nationalism in Croatia since 1991*. Farnham: Ashgate.

——. 2011a. 'Have You Ever Been in Bosnia?: British Military Travelers in the Balkans since 1992'. *Journeys: International Journal of Travel and Travel Writing* 12 (1): 63–92.

——. 2011b. 'Tito's Children?: Language Learning, Educational Resources, and Cultural Capital in the Life Histories of Interpreters Working in Bosnia-Herzegovina'. *Südosteuropa* 59 (4): 478–502.

——. 2012a. 'Prosperity Without Security: the Precarity of Interpreters in Postsocialist, Post-Conflict Bosnia-Herzegovina'. *Slavic Review* 71 (4). In press.

——. 2012b. 'When Bosnia was a Commonwealth Country: British Forces and their Interpreters in Republika Srpska, 1995–2007.' In *Languages and the Military: Alliances, Occupation and Peace-Building*, edited by Hilary Footitt and Michael Kelly, 100–14. Basingstoke: Palgrave Macmillan.

Baker, Mona. 2006. *Translation and Conflict: a Narrative Account*. London and New York: Routledge.

Banks, Marcus, and Monica Wolfe Murray. 1999. 'Ethnicity and Reports of the 1992–95 Bosnian Conflict'. In *The Media of Conflict: War Reporting and Representations of Ethnic Violence*, edited by Tim Allen and Jean Seaton, 146–61. London: Zed.

Barry, Ben. 2008. *A Cold War: Front-Line Operations in Bosnia 1995–1996*. Stroud: Spellmount.

Barry, Robert L. 1999. 'Lessons Learned from Bosnia'. *Helsinki Monitor* 3: 100–2.

Bellamy, Alex J., Paul Williams, and Stuart Griffin. 2004. *Understanding Peacekeeping*. Hoboken, NJ: Wiley-Blackwell.

Blackledge, Adrian, and Angela Creese. 2009. *Multilingualism: a Critical Perspective*. London: Continuum.

Bose, Sumantra. 2002. *Bosnia after Dayton: Nationalist Partition and International Intervention*. London: Hurst.

Bourdieu, Pierre. 1986. *The Forms of Capital: Handbook of Theory and Research for the Sociology of Education*: 241–58. Translated by J. G. Richardson. London: Greenwood Press.

——. 1991. *Language and Symbolic Power*. Cambridge: Polity.

Bracewell, Wendy. 2009. 'Balkan Travel Writing: Points of Departure'. In *Balkan Departures: Travel Writing from South-Eastern Europe*, edited by Wendy Bracewell and Alex Drace-Francis, 1–24. New York and Oxford: Berghahn.

Bringa, Tone. 1995. *Being Muslim the Bosnian Way: Identity and Community in a Central Bosnian Village*. Princeton, NJ: Princeton University Press.

Brumfit, Christopher J., and Keith Johnson. 1979. *The Communicative Approach to Language Teaching*. Oxford: Oxford University Press.

Burg, Steven L., and Paul Shoup. 1999. *The War in Bosnia-Herzegovina: Ethnic Conflict and International Intervention*. London: M. E. Sharpe.

Burke, Peter. 2004. *What is Cultural History?* Cambridge: Polity.

Butler, Judith. 2011. 'Precarious Life: the Obligations of Proximity'. Annual Neale Wheeler Watson Lecture, Nobel Museum, Stockholm. http://www.nobelmuseum.se/sites/nobelmuseet.se/files/page_file/Judith_Butler_NWW2011.pdf (accessed 12 June 2012).

Carmichael, Cathie. 2002. *Ethnic Cleansing in the Balkans: Nationalism and the Destruction of Tradition*. London and New York: Routledge.

Clark, Ken. 2012. 'A Paradigm Shift in Perception'. *Red T Blog*. http://red-t.org/news-paradigm.html (accessed 15 June 2012).

Cohen, Anthony P. 1985. *The Symbolic Construction of Community*. London and New York: Routledge.

Cohen, Raymond. 2001. 'Language and Conflict Resolution: the Limits of English'. *International Studies Review* 3 (1): 25–51.

Coles, Kimberley. 2007. *Democratic Designs: International Intervention and Electoral Practices in Postwar Bosnia-Herzegovina*. Ann Arbor, MI: University of Michigan Press.

Collins, James, Stef Slembrouck, and Mike Baynham. 2009. *Globalization and Language in Contact: Scale, Migration and Communicative Practices*. London: Continuum.

Comaroff, Jean, and John Comaroff. 1991. *Of Revelation and Revolution*. Vol. 1: *Christianity, Colonialism and Consciousness in South Africa*. Chicago: University of Chicago Press.

——. 1997. *Of Revelation and Revolution*. Vol. 2: *The Dialectics of Modernity on a South African Frontier*. Chicago: University of Chicago Press.

Cooper, Robert L. 1990. *Language Planning and Social Change*. Cambridge: Cambridge University Press.

Council of Europe (2001). *Common European Framework of Reference for Languages: Learning, Teaching, Assessment*. Cambridge, Cambridge University Press.

Cramer, Christopher. 2008. 'From Waging War to Peace Work: Labour and Labour Markets'. In *Whose Peace?: Critical Perspectives on the Political Economy of Peacebuilding*, edited by Michael Pugh, Neil Cooper and Mandy Turner, 123–40. Basingstoke: Palgrave Macmillan.

Cronin, Michael. 2002. 'The Empire Talks Back: Orality, Heteronomy and the Cultural Turn in Interpreting Studies'. In *The Interpreting Studies Reader*, edited by Franz Pöchhacker and Miriam Shlesinger, 386–97. London and New York: Routledge.

Crossey, Mark. 2005. 'Improving Linguistic Interoperability'. *NATO Review* (Summer). http://www.nato.int/docu/review/2005/issue2/english/art4.html (accessed 12 June 2012).

De Lama, George. 1993. 'Military Language School is Much More Than Talk'. *Chicago Tribune*, 30 May.

Department of Defense. 1995. *Bosnia Country Handbook*. [Washington DC]: Department of Defense.

Development Concepts and Doctrine Centre. 2009. *Joint Doctrine Note 1/09: the Significance of Culture to the Military*. Bicester: DSDA Operations Centre.

Dörnyei, Zoltan (ed.). 2003. *Attitudes, Orientations, and Motivations in Language Learning: Advances in Theory, Research, and Applications*. Oxford: Wiley-Blackwell.

Dragović-Drouet, Mila. 2007. 'The Practice of Translating and Interpreting During the Conflicts in the Former Yugoslavia (1991–1999)'. In *Translating and Interpreting Conflict*, edited by Myriam Salama-Carr, 29–40. Amsterdam and New York: Rodopi.

Duncan, Alastair. 1994. 'Operating in Bosnia'. *International Boundaries Research Unit: Boundary and Security Bulletin* (October): 47–57.

Duncanson, Claire. 2009. 'Forces for Good? Narratives of Military Masculinity in Peacekeeping Operations'. *International Feminist Journal of Politics* 11 (1): 63–80.

Eckert, Penelope. 2000. *Linguistic Variation as Social Practice: the Linguistic Construction of Identity in Belten High*. Oxford: Blackwell.

Fischer, Tim. 1999. 'Bosnian Conducts Language Classes'. *The Talon*, 5 February: 4.

FIT-IFT, AIIC and Red T. 2012. 'Conflict Zone Field Guide for Civilian Translators/Interpreters and Users of Their Services'. Version 3. http://red-t.org/documents/T-I_Field_Guide_2012.pdf (accessed 15 June 2012).

Fitchett, Linda. 2012. 'The AIIC Project to Help Interpreters in Conflict Areas'. In *Languages and the Military: Alliances, Occupation and Peace-Building*, edited by Hilary Footitt and Michael Kelly, 175–85. Basingstoke: Palgrave Macmillan.

Flew, Anthony. 1975. *Thinking about Thinking: or, Do I Sincerely Want to be Right?*. London: Fontana/Collins.

Footitt, Hilary, and Michael Kelly (eds). 2012a. *Languages and the Military: Alliances, Occupation and Peace Building*. Basingstoke: Palgrave Macmillan.

——. 2012b. *Languages at War: Policies and Practices of Language Contacts in Conflict*. Basingstoke: Palgrave Macmillan.
Ford, Curtis. 2002. 'Language Planning in Bosnia and Herzegovina: the 1998 Bihać Symposium'. *Slavic and East European Journal* 46 (2): 349–61.
Frantzen, Henning A. 2005. *NATO and Peace Support Operations, 1991–1999: Policies and Doctrines*. Abingdon: Frank Cass.
Gagnon, V. P., Jr. 2004. *The Myth of Ethnic War: Serbia and Croatia in the 1990s*. Ithaca, NY: Cornell University Press.
Gatalo, Veselin. 2004. *SFOR: siesta, fiesta, orgasmo, riposo*. Sarajevo and Zagreb: Zoro.
Gellner, Ernest. 1983. *Nations and Nationalism*. Oxford: Blackwell.
Ghosh, Amitav. 1994. 'The Global Reservation: Notes Toward an Ethnography of International Peacekeeping'. *Cultural Anthropology* 9 (3): 412–22.
Goldsworthy, Vesna. 1998. *Inventing Ruritania: the Imperialism of the Imagination*. New Haven, CT: Yale University Press.
Gordy, Eric D. 1999. *The Culture of Power in Serbia: Nationalism and the Destruction of Alternatives*. University Park, PA: Pennsylvania State University Press.
Gow, James. 1997. *Triumph of the Lack of Will: International Diplomacy and the Yugoslav War*. London: Hurst.
Greenberg, Robert D. 2000. 'Language Politics in the Federal Republic of Yugoslavia: the Crisis over the Future of Serbian'. *Slavic Review* 59 (3): 625–40.
——. 2005. *Language and Identity in the Balkans: Serbo-Croatian and its Disintegration*. Oxford: Oxford University Press.
Hammond, Andrew. 2007. *The Debated Lands: British and American Representations of the Balkans*. Cardiff: University of Wales Press.
Hawkesworth, Celia. 1986. *Colloquial Serbo-Croat*. London: Routledge and Kegan Paul.
Higate, Paul, and Marsha Henry. 2009. *Insecure Spaces: Peacekeeping, Power and Performance in Haiti, Kosovo and Liberia*. London: Zed.
Hill, Michael. 2009. *The Public Policy Process*. 5th ed. London: Longman.
Hoare, Marko Attila. 2004. *How Bosnia Armed: The Birth and Rise of the Bosnian Army*. London: Saqi.
——. 2007. *A History of Bosnia*. London: Saqi.
Hoyle, David. 2006. *Quality Management Essentials*. London: Butterworth-Heinemann.
Hromadžić, Azra. 2008. 'Discourses of Integration and Practices of Reunification at the Mostar Gymnasium, Bosnia and Herzegovina'. *Comparative Education Review* 52 (4): 541–63.
Jansen, Stef. 2006. 'The Privatisation of Home and Hope: Return, Reforms and the Foreign Intervention in Bosnia-Herzegovina'. *Dialectical Anthropology* 30: 177–99.
Jenkins, Richard. 1997. *Rethinking Ethnicity: Arguments and Explorations*. London: Sage.
Jennings, Kathleen M. 2010. 'Unintended Consequences of Intimacy: Political Economies of Peacekeeping and Sex Tourism'. *International Peacekeeping* 17 (2): 229–43.
Kaldor, Mary. 1999. *New and Old Wars: Organized Violence in a Global Era*. Oxford: Polity.

Kalyvas, Stathis N., and Nicholas Sambanis. 2005. 'Bosnia's Civil War: Origins and Violent Dynamics'. In *Understanding Civil War: Evidence and Analysis*, edited by Paul Collier and Nicholas Sambanis, 191–230. Washington, DC: International Bank for Reconstruction and Development / World Bank.

Karakasidou, Anastasia N. 1997. *Fields of Wheat, Hills of Blood: Passages to Nationhood in Greek Macedonia 1870–1990*. Chicago, IL: University of Chicago Press.

Kelly, Michael. 2012. 'Languages and Peace Operations'. In *Languages at War: Policies and Practices of Language Contacts in Conflict*, edited by Hilary Footitt and Michael Kelly, 89–105. Basingstoke: Palgrave Macmillan.

Kitchen, Veronica M. 2010. *The Globalization of NATO: Intervention, Security and Identity*. London and New York: Routledge.

Kronsell, Annica. 2012. *Gender, Sex, and the Postnational Defense: Militarism and Peacekeeping*. Oxford: Oxford University Press.

Kudesia, Suprita, and Robert Rubinstein. 2009. 'Exchanges of Value in Peace Operations: Complex Meanings of "Private" and "Transnational" Transfers'. *International Studies Review* 11: 430–9.

Kujamäki, Pekka. 2012. 'Mediating for the Third Reich: on Military Translation Cultures in World War II in Northern Finland'. In *Languages and the Military: Alliances, Occupation and Peace-Building*, edited by Hilary Footitt and Michael Kelly, 86–99. Basingstoke: Palgrave Macmillan.

Laušević, Mirjana. 2000. 'Some Aspects of Music and Politics in Bosnia'. In *Neighbors at War: Anthropological Perspectives on Yugoslav Ethnicity, Culture and History*, edited by Joel M. Halpern and David A. Kideckel, 289–302. University Park, PA: Pennsylvania State University Press.

Lewis, Justin. 2012. 'Languages at War: a UK Ministry of Defence Perspective'. In *Languages and the Military: Alliances, Occupation and Peace-Building*, edited by Hilary Footitt and Michael Kelly, 58–69. Basingstoke: Palgrave Macmillan.

Long, Michael H. 2005. *Second Language Needs Analysis*. Cambridge: Cambridge University Press.

Lovrenović, Ivan. 2001. *Bosnia: a Cultural History*. Translated by Sonja W. Bičanić. London: Saqi.

Maček, Ivana. 2009. *Sarajevo Under Siege: Anthropology in Wartime*. Philadelphia, PA: Pennsylvania State University Press.

Malcolm, Noel. 2002. *Bosnia: a Short History*. 3rd ed. London: Pan.

Malkki, Liisa. 1992. 'National Geographic: the Rooting of Peoples and the Territorialization of National Identity among Scholars and Refugees'. *Cultural Anthropology* 7 (1): 24–44.

Markowitz, Fran. 2007. 'Census and Sensibilities in Sarajevo'. *Comparative Studies in Society and History* 49 (1): 40–73.

Martin, Lawrence L. 1993. *Total Quality Management in Human Service Organizations*. Newbury Park: Sage.

McNulty, Mel. 1999. 'Media Ethnicization and the International Response to War and Genocide in Rwanda'. In *The Media of Conflict: War Reporting and Representations of Ethnic Violence*, edited by Tim Allen and Jean Seaton, 268–86. London: Zed.

NATO. 2004. *NATO Training Group Handbook*. Brussels: NATO Training Group Section.

NATO/Russia Joint Editorial Working Group. 2002. 'NATO–Russia Glossary of Contemporary Political and Military Terms'. Brussels and Moscow: NATO Publications. http://www.nato.int/docu/glossary/eng/index.htm (accessed 12 June 2012).

NATO Standardization Agency. 2008. 'NATO Glossary of Terms and Definitions (English and French) / Glossaire OTAN de termes et dèfinitions (anglais et français) AAP-6 (2008)'. Brussels: NATO. http://www.fas.org/irp/doddir/other/nato2008.pdf (accessed 24 April 2012).

Nazemroaya, Mahdi Darius. 2012. *The Globalization of NATO*. Atlanta, GA: Clarity Press.

Norris, David A. 1993. *Teach Yourself Serbo-Croat*. London: Hodder and Stoughton.

O'Neill, Onora. 2002. *A Question of Trust*. Cambridge: Cambridge University Press.

Okey, Robin. 2004. 'Serbian, Croatian, Bosnian?: Language and Nationality in the Lands of Former Yugoslavia'. *East European Quarterly* 38 (4): 419–42.

Paris, Roland. 2002. 'International Peacebuilding and the "Mission Civilisatrice" '. *Review of International Studies* 28 (4): 637–56.

——. 2004. *At War's End: Building Peace after Civil Conflict*. Cambridge: Cambridge University Press.

Passerini, Luisa. 1987. *Fascism in Popular Memory: the Cultural Experience of the Turin Working Class*. Translated by Robert Lumley and Jude Bloomfield. Cambridge: Cambridge University Press.

Pattinson, Juliette. 2007. *Behind Enemy Lines: Gender, Passing and the Special Operations Executive in the Second World War*. Manchester and New York: Manchester University Press.

Pickering, Paula M. 2006. 'Generating Social Capital for Bridging Ethnic Divisions in the Balkans: Case Studies of Two Bosniak Cities'. *Ethnic and Racial Studies* 29 (1): 79–103.

Porch, Douglas. 2010. *The French Foreign Legion: a Complete History of the Legendary Fighting Force*. New York: Skyhorse Publishing.

Pouligny, Béatrice. 2006. *Peace Operations Seen from Below: UN Missions and Local People*. London: Hurst.

Pugh, Michael. 2002. 'Postwar Political Economy in Bosnia and Herzegovina: the Spoils of Peace', *Global Governance* 8: 467–82.

——. 2008. 'Employment, Labour Rights and Social Resistance'. In *Whose Peace?: Critical Perspectives on the Political Economy of Peacebuilding*, edited by Michael Pugh, Neil Cooper and Mandy Turner, 141–58. Basingstoke: Palgrave Macmillan.

Pupavac, Vanessa. 2006. 'Discriminating Language Rights and Politics in the Post-Yugoslav States'. *Patterns of Prejudice* 40 (2): 112–28.

Quinn-Judge, Paul. 1995. 'US Military Steps Up Deployment Effort'. *Boston Globe*, 5 December: 21.

Razack, Sherene H. 2004. *Dark Threats and White Knights: the Somalia Affair, Peacekeeping, and the New Imperialism*. Toronto: University of Toronto Press.

Richards, Jack C., and Theodore S. Rodgers. 2001. *Approaches and Methods in Language Teaching*. Cambridge: Cambridge University Press.

Rovegno, John S., Linda Hajdari, and Drita Perezic. 2003. 'Interpreters in Intelligence Operations'. *Military Intelligence Professional Bulletin* 29 (4): 25–9.

Rubinstein, Robert A. 2008. *Peacekeeping under Fire: Culture and Intervention*. Boulder, CO: Paradigm Press.

——, Diana M. Keller, and Michael E. Scherger. 2008. 'Culture and Interoperability in Integrated Missions'. *International Peacekeeping* 15 (4): 540–55.

Sampson, Steven. 1996. 'The Social Life of Projects: Importing Civil Society to Albania'. In *Civil Society: Challenging Western Models*, edited by Chris Hann and Elizabeth Dunn, 121–42. London and New York: Routledge.

——. 2002. 'Weak States, Uncivil Societies and Thousands of NGOs: Western Democracy Export as Benevolent Colonialism in the Balkans.' In *The Balkans in Focus: Cultural Boundaries in Europe*, edited by Barbara Tørnquist-Plewa and Sanimir Resic. Lund: Nordic Academic Press. http://www.anthrobase.com/Txt/S/Sampson_S_01.htm (accessed 21 December 2010).

Schiffman, Harold F. 1998. *Linguistic Culture and Language Policy*. London and New York: Routledge.

Simms, Brendan. 2002. *Unfinest Hour: Britain and the Destruction of Bosnia*. Harmondsworth: Penguin.

Simons, Marlise. 2005. 'War Crimes Case Revives Passions in a Divided Croatia'. *New York Times International*, 12 December.

Sorabji, Cornelia. 1993. 'Ethnic War in Bosnia?'. *Radical Philosophy* 63: 33–5.

——. 1995. 'A Very Modern War: Terror and Territory in Bosnia-Herzegovina'. In *War: A Cruel Necessity? The Bases of Institutionalized Violence*, edited by Robert A. Hinde and Helen E. Watson, 80–95. London: Tauris.

Stahuljak, Zrinka. 2000. 'Violent Distortions: Bearing Witness to the Task of Wartime Translators'. *TTR: Traduction, terminologie, rédaction* 13 (1): 37–51.

——. 2010. 'War, Translation, Transnationalism: Interpreters in and of the War (Croatia, 1991–1992)'. In *Critical Readings in Translation Studies*, edited by Mona Baker, 391–414. London and New York: Routledge.

Standing, Guy. 2011. *The Precariat: the New Dangerous Class*. London: Bloomsbury Academic.

Stankovic, Milos. 2000. *Trusted Mole: a Soldier's Journey into Bosnia's Heart of Darkness*. London: HarperCollins.

Steger, Manfred. 2009. *Globalization: a Very Short Introduction*. 2nd ed. Oxford: Oxford University Press.

Stewart, Bob. 1993. *Broken Lives: a Personal View of the Bosnian Conflict*. London: HarperCollins.

Suljagić, Emir. 2005. *Postcards from the Grave*. Translated by Lelja Haverić. London: Saqi.

Summerfield, Penny. 1998. *Reconstructing Women's Wartime Lives: Discourse and Subjectivity in Oral Histories of the Second World War*. Manchester and New York: Manchester University Press.

—— and Nicole Crockett. 1992. '"You Weren't Taught That with the Welding": Lessons in Sexuality in the Second World War'. *Women's History Review* 1 (3): 435–54.

Tabeau, Ewa, and Jakub Bijak. 2005. 'War-Related Deaths in the 1992–1995 Armed Conflicts in Bosnia and Herzegovina: a Critique of Previous Estimates and Recent Results'. *European Journal of Population/Revue européenne de démographie* 21 (2–3): 187–215.

Thompson, Paul. 2000. *The Voice of the Past: Oral History*. 3rd ed. Oxford: Oxford University Press.

Thomson, Alistair. 1994. *Anzac Memories: Living with the Legend*. Melbourne: Oxford University Press.
Tobia, Simona, and Catherine Baker. 2012. 'Being an Interpreter in Conflict'. In *Languages at War: Policies and Practices of Language Contacts in Conflict*, edited by Hilary Footitt and Michael Kelly, 201–21. Basingstoke: Palgrave Macmillan.
Torikai, Kumiko. 2009. *Voices of the Invisible Presence: Diplomatic Interpreters in Post-World War II Japan*. Amsterdam: John Benjamins.
Vadász, Istvánné. 2011. 'What's Behind the Test?' *Academic and Applied Research in Military Science* 10 (2): 287–92.
Valenius, Johanna. 2007. 'A Few Kind Women: Gender Essentialism and Nordic Peacekeeping Operations'. *International Peacekeeping* 14 (4): 510–23.
Venuti, Lawrence. 1995. *The Translator's Invisibility: a History of Translation*. London and New York: Routledge.
Viezzi, Maurizio. 2012. 'The SIGTIPS Final Report'. *European Journal of Language Policy* 4 (1): 110–14.
West, Richard. 1994. 'Needs Analysis in Language Teaching'. *Language Teaching* 27: 1–19.
Winslow, Donna. 2004. 'Misplaced Loyalties: the Role of Military Culture in the Breakdown of Discipline in Two Peace Operations'. *Journal of Military and Strategic Studies* 6 (3): 1–19.
Woodward, Rachel, and K. Neil Jenkings. 2011. 'Military Identities in the Situated Accounts of British Military Personnel'. *Sociology* 45 (2): 252–68.
—— and Trish Winter. 2007. *Sexing the Soldier: the Politics of Gender and the Contemporary British Army*. London and New York: Routledge.
Woolley, Monty. 2004. *Cleanse Their Souls: Peace-Keeping in Bosnia's Civil War 1992–1993*. Barnsley: Pen & Sword Military.
Žarkov, Dubravka. 2007. *The Body of War: Media, Ethnicity and Gender in the Break-Up of Yugoslavia*. Durham, NC: Duke University Press.

Index

Jill Mountain

A TEMPLAR BOOK

Published by Orbis Publishing Limited
20-22 Bedfordbury
London WC2N 4BT

ISBN 0-85613-868-1

This book was devised and produced by Templar Publishing Ltd,
Old King's Head Court, Dorking, Surrey

Colour separations by Positive Colour Ltd, Maldon, Essex

Printed by Grijelmo S. A., Bilbao, Spain

Dedicated to Maxine and Sam who were never really afraid

WHO'S AFRAID of the dark?

Written by Richard Carlisle
Illustrated by David Anstey

ORBIS · LONDON

I'm afraid of
things I can't see,
monsters and burglars
hiding from me.

Under the bed
it's darker than night.
I wish, without moving,
I could turn on the light.

I'm afraid when
I'm lying in bed,
just thinking of things
my big brother said.

He told me things crawl,
he told me things creep
over the blankets
when I lie asleep.

Perhaps it's an insect
of extraordinary size.
I wish I could see it
without opening my eyes.

I'm afraid of
the whistling wind.
Someone's outside
and he's trying to get in.

He's riding a horse,
his hair is bright green
and he wants me to go
to visit his queen.

She's the queen of the night
and she wants me to stay,
but I'd really prefer
to go in the day.

I'm afraid of
the sound of my clock.
The tick is so loud
and so is the tock.

It sounds like a monster
who's stuck in a box,
and he's tapping his teeth
while he unpicks the lock.

Perhaps if I lie still
and don't try to peep,
the box will stay locked
and the monster will sleep.

I'm afraid that
the wardrobe is full
of men with long beards
of white cotton wool.

They'll rush out to get me
unless I keep still,
so I won't move a muscle,
I'll pretend I'm a hill.

I'm afraid of
the shapes on the wall.
One looks quite short
but the other one's tall.

I know they're just shadows
but I'm scared that they may
start moving towards me
to melt me away.

I'm afraid of
the toys on my floor.
I think that they're running
to open the door.

And when I'm not looking
they watch me instead,
with eyes that pop out
from the back of their head.

I'm afraid that
the curtains might hide
somebody waiting
to drag me outside.

A bat or a burglar
and an army of spoons,
licking their lips
in the light of the moon.

I'm afraid of
the sound of the rain.
It pitters and patters
and then starts again.

It sounds like a hiss
or the rush in a race
to be the first rain-drop
to fall on my face.

I'm so afraid
that sometimes I'll cry,
and I'll call for my Mum
with a tear in one eye.

Then I show her the wardrobe
and point under the bed,
at the window I tell her
what my big brother said.

But she's quick to remind me
that there's nothing to fear,
the wind has stopped whistling
and the wardrobe is bare.

Under the bed it's
an old friend of mine,
a cuddly old teddy
with a lopsided smile.

And after she's kissed me
and tucked me in bed,
I know all those fears
were just in my head.

I'm not afraid now
so I'll start counting sheep
and I'll think of a dream
where I'm falling asleep.

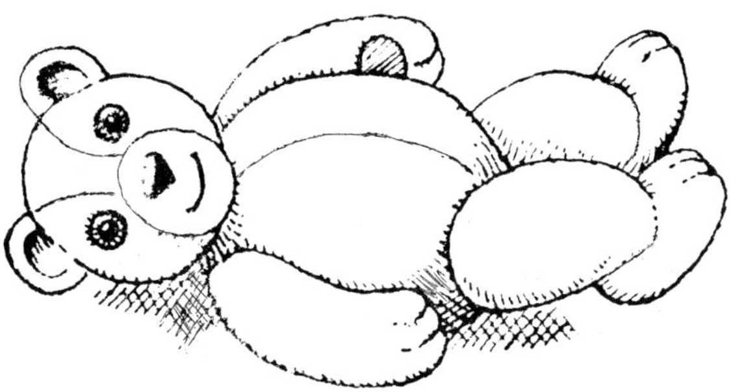